The Social Determinants of Health in India

Devaki Nambiar · Arundati Muralidharan
Editors

The Social Determinants of Health in India

Concepts, Processes, and Indicators

With Forewords by Mirai Chatterjee and Gita Sen

Springer

Editors
Devaki Nambiar
The George Institute for Global Health
New Delhi, Delhi
India

Arundati Muralidharan
WASH in Health and Nutritions,
WASH in Schools
WaterAid India
New Delhi, Delhi
India

ISBN 978-981-10-5998-8 ISBN 978-981-10-5999-5 (eBook)
https://doi.org/10.1007/978-981-10-5999-5

Library of Congress Control Number: 2017947476

Printed on acid-free paper

This Springer imprint is published by Springer Nature
The registered company is Springer Nature Singapore Pte Ltd.
The registered company address is: 152 Beach Road, #21-01/04 Gateway East, Singapore 189721, Singapore

For Kleio and Surya, who joined us on this journey and made us understand more deeply the importance of this work. You inspire us!

Foreword I

Concerns and analyses on the social determinants of health (SDH) are not new in India. The pre-independence, landmark Bhore Committee outlined the 'Causes of the Low Level of Health in India', with whole chapters devoted to nutrition, the 'Health of the Industrial Worker', housing and even on women workers.[1] It is remarkably contemporary in both its analyses and its recommendations. The less widely quoted Sokhey Committee, a subcommittee on health of the National Planning Committee chaired by Jawaharlal Nehru, is equally explicit and incisive about the state of public health. In the introduction of its report, it notes:

'The root cause of disease, debility, low vitality and short span of life is to be found in the poverty, almost destitution, of the people, which prevents them from having sufficient nutrition, clothing and shelter.' It notes that per capita income in India was Rs 80 per annum at that time. It goes on to acknowledge: 'Apart from the root cause, there are several other factors also responsible for this phenomenon.'[2]

However, it does not stop at diagnosis. It goes on to call for a plan of action: 'The maintenance of the public health requires the fulfilment of certain conditions which include the provision of an environment conducive to healthful living, adequate nutrition, the availability of health protection to all members of the community, irrespective of their ability to pay for it, and the active cooperation of the people in the maintenance of their own health.'

It also acknowledges and endorses the Bhore Committee's recommendations, adding that 'popular education' is required. Both of these committees, and the many that followed in independent India, are significant not only for their vision and foresight, but also for their relevance to public health in India today. While neither used the phrase 'social determinants of health', both of these and other committees and declarations, including the Alma Ata declaration to which India was a signatory

[1] Government of India. [Bhore Commission] Report of the Health Survey and Development Committee (4 volumes). New Delhi: Government of India; 1946.

[2] World Health Organisation Commission on Social Determinants of Health. Closing the gap in a generation: health equity through action on the social determinants of health Final Report of the Commission on Social Determinants of Health. Geneva: World Health Organisation; 2008.

several decades ago, in essence advocated for social determinants, noting that without addressing these root causes, the health of the public would not improve much, if at all.

In the Alma Ata period of global public health initiatives, 'intersectoral action' and 'convergence' became common parlance. It would be another decade plus before the 'social determinants of health' entered the public health lexicon.

Meanwhile, our members at SEWA—all workers in the informal economy—understood social determinants of health and intersectoral action very well. They lived it. As a public health worker years ago, I remember Ayeshaben, a home-based garment worker, saying:

'How can we ever be free of TB if we live in such homes, with no ventilation, no water and sanitation, not enough food and little income for medicines?'

Or Sumanben, a street vendor, explaining: 'We need to have four or five children so that two or three survive.' She had lost two of her own.

Lakshmiben, a handcart puller, told us how pulling carts through the dusty streets of Ahmedabad, with the cart's crossbar hitting the lower abdomen, resulted in frequent miscarriages among the workers.

The lives and world of work of informal women workers, and men, are full of stories of how their work and health are linked and interwoven, like the warp and weft of life itself. They also speak about how the lack of basic services and infrastructure—housing, water and sanitation, electricity, fuel, health care, child care, insurance, pension and other financial services, education and food of proper quality and quantity and more—is keeping them in poverty and in poor health.

In addition, over four decades of working with informal women workers, we have understood the importance of organizing them for their rights, and for their voice and representation at every level of our economy and society. They bring this understanding and the skills of organizing to SEWA's health work as well. For them, community action for health is the first and most important building block for improving their health and also obtaining the services and entitlements that are their due, and are the social determinants of health.

Such understanding of health and its determinants are shared by many others in India and across the globe. Hence, in 2005, the World Health Organization (WHO) decided to set up a Commission on the Social Determinants of Health (CSDH) to garner the evidence on how action on social determinants can result in improved health outcomes, and to recommend further action at various levels, from the grassroots to the global level, in every country. As a Commissioner, I had the great privilege and opportunity of learning from countries and organizations on every continent. It was a rich harvest. Perhaps not surprisingly, whether of the North or South, rich or poor, whatever the age, race, ethnicity, gender, language group or religion, the experiences of the human family with regard to the social determinants were remarkably similar. Who knew, until Prof. Michael Marmot, Chairperson of the CSDH, showed the evidence that adult men in Glasgow had lower life expectancies if one moved from middle class to working class neighbourhoods? It seems common sense, but policymakers need the evidence and concrete experiences to show that such a gradient exists and that such inequity that has to be addressed by policies and programs to acknowledge and correct for this.

Another crosscutting finding is the importance of early childhood for improved health. Again, this is not a new discovery, but most countries are yet to incorporate this in appropriate policies for their children, with adequate investments of public funds. Similarly, despite numerous international and national committees recognizing women's work and the need for economic empowerment, still much remains to be done for, with and by women—not only for economic empowerment but gender quality more generally.

This volume, therefore, is a timely and much-needed contribution to the discourse and praxis of the social determinants of health. It is a significant contemporary contribution to the recognition, research and action on the social determinants of health whose journey began long ago, with the Bhore, Sokhey, Alma Ata, CSDH and so many more national and international initiatives for improving the health of all the citizens on our planet.

The volume is divided into sections on conceptualization, operationalization and oversight, with contributions from authors, several of whom I have had the pleasure of working with closely, either in the Public Health Foundation of India like Dr. Gita Sen, Drs. Devaki Nambiar and Arundati Muralidharan, the book's editors, Dr. Abhay Shukla, my colleague in the Advisory Group on Community Action of the National Health Mission (NHM) and Renu Khanna, a long-time friend from the women's and community health movements. It also includes my own SEWA sisters, Dr. Sapna Desai and Sushmita Goswami. I am fortunate to connect with the other authors through their significant contributions to this volume, and I hope we will all collaborate to push forward the agenda outlined in the CSDH report, 'Closing the Gap'.[3]

In fact, the CSDH report's recommendations were the outcome of inputs, experiences, research and policy impact of thousands of health and people's advocates across the globe. This volume both continues the conceptualization and building of evidence through solid research, and also shows how the social determinants can be put into practice at the grassroots, with the poor, and especially women, in the lead. It also tells us what it takes to monitor action on the social determinants, and more broadly, local people's health rights.

During the CSDH, when we met leaders in several countries, including our own, discussions on social determinants evoked a sympathetic but somewhat puzzled response. All agreed on this approach, but were apprehensive about its operationalization and monitoring, as well as the need for more evidence to show that this is a workable way to move forward in public health. As we move in the direction of universal health care or universal health assurance, as enunciated in the National Health Policy of 2017 with its emphasis on social determinants, this volume will no

[3] World Health Organization Commission on Social Determinants of Health. Closing the gap in a generation: health equity through action on the social determinants of health Final Report of the Commission on Social Determinants of Health. Geneva: World Health Organisation; 2008

doubt help to move us steadily in the direction of action and research. It also brings the experiences of Sumanben and Ayeshaben, and millions of other Indians to the fore, acknowledging the importance of action on the social determinants of health on the long road to social justice and equality, and a world that works for the well-being of all.

Mirai Chatterjee
Director
Social Security, Self-Employed Women's Association
India

Foreword II

In 2008, the WHO Commission on the Social Determinants of Health (CSDH) began its final report, *Closing the Gap in a Generation: Health Equity through Action on the Social Determinants of Health,* with a broad and bold statement: 'Social justice is a matter of life and death. It affects the way people live, their consequent chance of illness, and their risk of premature death… (I)nequities in health, avoidable health inequalities, arise because of the circumstances in which people grow, live, work and age, and the systems put in place to deal with illness. The conditions in which people live and die are, in turn, shaped by political, social and economic forces.' Writing its report in the midst of significant changes in health systems and health policies, the CSDH was bucking a global trend towards defining the causes of ill-health in ever narrower terms, and designing health policies in silos of issues and funding. Nonetheless, the work of the CSDH followed distinguished and deeply persuasive lines of health research and action that identified determinants outside the health sector as key to governing not only whether and how people get to be healthy or not, but who draws the short and long straws of illness and health, and why.

In India, the most distinguished proponent of the importance of social determinants of health was Dr. V. Ramalingaswami who consistently used his credibility and professional positions to argue for a broad approach that would push the policy boundaries well beyond narrowly defined health services, placing equity and social justice at the core of research, policies and action. It is fitting, therefore, that this Centre's first major publication should be an edited volume that takes a similarly broad approach.

The book, based on a joint WHO-PHFI consultation held in 2013, brings together the work of researchers and practitioners from public and private not-for-profit sectors, supplemented by short commentaries from reviewers of individual chapters, themselves steeped in health equity work in India. It treats the social determinants of health as a methodological lens through which to focus attention on broad questions of approaches and measurement, big picture challenges such as conflict, urbanization and the informal economy, specific issues such as child nutrition, menstrual hygiene and maternal health, and programmatic concerns including the role of the municipal health officer and of panchayats.

In covering this ambit, a number of themes emerge: the need to take a broader view on what a social determinant is; the idea of convergence that is the Indian neologism for action on social determinants of health; and the key role of civil society in promoting oversight and accountability. The papers use a range of methodologies sensitive to context across India's diversity, and lay critical emphasis on process, rather than outcomes, targets or indicators alone. This volume exemplifies but does not encompass the richness of work on social determinants of health in India. We at the Ramalingaswami Centre of the Public Health Foundation of India are glad to present this book to the larger health community, and look forward to continued engagement and collaboration on these important themes.

Gita Sen
Distinguished Professor & Director
Ramalingaswami Centre on Equity
& Social Determinants of Health
Public Health Foundation of India

Acknowledgements

We are deeply grateful for the determined and detail-oriented coordination assistance of Ms. Shelley Dhar. We also gained from the insights and reviewing assistance provided by Dr. Prathibha Ganesan and Ms. Preety Rajbangshi. We are thankful also for the tenacious help of Ms. Aditi Rao.

The following reviewers are thanked for their critical inputs: Dr. Prabir Chatterjee, Ms. Jashodhara Dasgupta, Dr. Abraham Joseph, Dr. Purnima Menon, Dr. Arima Mishra, Ms. Sulakshana Nandi, Dr. R. Srivatsan, Dr. Padmini Swaminathan, and Dr. Rajani Ved.

Our work was inaugurated by the vision and support of World Health Organization Commissioner for the Social Determinants of Health, Dr. Mirai Chatterjee, who has been a true inspiration. We are deeply grateful for her encouragement and the confidence she reposed in us in carrying out this work.

The idea for this volume emerged as a result of discussions at a workshop the Public Health Foundation of India held in June of 2013 in collaboration with the World Health Organization Country office, with great stewardship from the headquarters and the regional offices. We owe a special debt of thanks to Theadora Koller-Swift, Ahmad Hosseinpoor, and participants at this workshop for motivating this work and setting us on our path. We look forward to continuing to learn from you all.

We are grateful to our colleague Ms. Shinjini Chatterjee and her team at Springer for their enthusiastic and well-coordinated support of this manuscript.

This material has been funded by UK aid from the UK government, however, the views expressed do not necessarily reflect the UK government's official policies.

Contents

Editors and Contributors

About the Editors

Devaki Nambiar is Program Head at the George Institute for Global Health. Formerly a senior research scientist at the Public Health Foundation of India (PHFI), her work employs social science theory and mixed methods to understand and address health inequalities and social exclusion in health systems of resource-poor settings. She concurrently supports postgraduate training and capacity building in health policy and systems research as an associate professor at the Indian Institute of Public Health—Delhi. She is also a Bernard Lown Scholar at the Harvard School of Public Health working with community health workers on improving access to primary health care services related to non-communicable diseases. She has a doctorate in Public Health (Ph.D.) from the Johns Hopkins Bloomberg School of Public Health.

Arundati Muralidharan is Policy Manager for WASH in the Health and Nutrition Schools at WaterAid India. From 2012–2016, she was a senior research fellow at PHFI. As a public health practitioner and qualitative researcher, she is interested in addressing the factors that underlie and influence health and health behaviour, with the aim to identify and promote effective, evidence-based strategies. Her focus is on water, sanitation, and hygiene (WASH) and gender. She has a Masters in Medical and Psychiatric Social Work from the Tata Institute of Social Sciences in Mumbai and a doctorate in Public Health (DrPH) from Boston University, USA.

Contributors

Nandita Bhan works as Research Scientist – India at the Center on Gender Equity and Health at UC San Diego. Her research interests include issues at the intersection of urbanization, gender and equity in science and policy impacting women and girls, with particular focus on methodology and measurement in social and behavioral sciences. Prior to this, Nandita worked at the Public Health Foundation of India, where she was supported by the Wellcome Trust-PHFI Career Development Research Fellowship and Government of India's (Department of Science and Technology) Inspire Faculty Awards. In her research at PHFI, she focused on urbanization, particularly in relation to chronic conditions, equity and ageing. Nandita holds a Ph.D. in Social and Behavioural Sciences from the Harvard School of Public Health, with previous degrees in Social Epidemiology (University College London), Social Work (Delhi University) and Economics (Delhi

University). She has previously worked at the World Bank on the 'Moving out of Poverty' Study, at Cardiff University on a Cochrane-Campbell systematic review on slum upgrading interventions and on environmental determinants of nutrition at the University of Sao Paulo, Brazil.

Indira Chakravarthi is a Delhi-based public health scholar. She works in the area of health systems, and technology-medicine-public health, and has several publications in these areas. She has given lectures at several institutions, including National Institute of Epidemiology, Chennai and Center of Social Medicine and Community Health, Jawaharlal Nehru University, New Delhi.

Rajib Dasgupta is Chairperson at Centre of Social Medicine and Community Health, Jawaharlal Nehru University, New Delhi. He was Fulbright Senior Research Fellow and visiting associate professor at Johns Hopkins Bloomberg School of Public Health during 2010–11 where he worked on social determinants in the context of program implementation, culminating in the book, *Urbanising Cholera: The Social Determinants of its Re-emergence* published by Orient Blackswan. He serves in key national advisory positions including with the Indian Council of Medical Research (ICMR), the National Certification Committee for Polio Eradication (NCCPE) and the National Health Mission.

Sapna Desai is a researcher and public health practitioner based in New Delhi who focuses on women's health, community health workers and impact evaluation. She previously spent close to a decade with SEWA, where she led its national health program, working to scale up community health worker programs across six states of India. She also directed a mixed-methods research study to evaluate the impact of community health worker led education on women's health and treatment-seeking behaviour in Gujarat. She is currently an associate with the Population Council in New Delhi and an associate editor of the journal *Reproductive Health Matters*. Dr. Desai holds a Ph.D. in Epidemiology and Population Health from the London School of Hygiene and Tropical Medicine, an MS in Population and International Health from Harvard University and a BA in International Relations from Brown University.

Prathibha Ganesan is Research Associate at the Public Policy Research Institute, Government of Kerala, Thiruvananthapuram. Her areas of interest are political economy, public policy, urban health and sanitation. From 2013 to 2015, she was a research associate at PHFI specializing in Social Determinants of Health. Prior to this, she worked as a consultant to Technical Resource Group to National Urban Health Mission at National Health Systems Resource Centre, New Delhi. She has a Ph.D. in Science Policy from Centre for Studies in Science Policy, Jawaharlal Nehru University, New Delhi.

Samir Garg is a practitioner involved in the implementation of the Mitanin Program comprising of 70,000 Community Health Workers in Chhattisgarh state. His areas of interest are community participation and public management in program on health, nutrition and food security. He has studied engineering, is a postgraduate in management (Institute of Rural Management Anand) and has 19 years of experience of working with community-based initiatives in tribal regions of India. He is also an honorary advisor to the Commissioners of the Supreme Court on Right to Food.

Sushmita Goswami is a research scholar at Department of Economics, Patna University. She has been associated with SEWA Bharat for more than 3 years and coordinated the research for "Shram Jeevani", Report of the Special Task Force on women in Informal Economy in Bihar. She has authored/co-authored in few research studies for SEWA Bharat. "Voices of Women in Bihar", 2013; "Women in Art and Craft Industry in Bihar", 2013; with Dr. Rita Jalali, "Challenges of Maintaining Hygiene in Rural Bihar", 2014; with Niraj Kumar, "Status of women in informal economy in Jharkhand: An Exploratory Study", 2015. Along with it she has keen interest in caste-class dynamics and its impact on women labourers of rural Bihar.

Renu Khanna is a feminist women's health and rights activist. She is the founder of SAHAJ (Society for Health Alternatives) based in Vadodara. She was an active member of a vibrant interdisciplinary centre called WOHTRAC (Women's Health Training, Research and Advocacy Centre) in the WSRC, MS University, Vadodara which functioned creatively between 1992 and 2008. She has been a part of Shodhini, a feminist women's network that authored *Touch Me Touch Me Not: Women, Plants and Healing* (Kali for Women). Renu co-edited *Towards Comprehensive Women's Health Policies and Programmes*. As an Erasmus Mundus scholar, Renu taught at KIT, Amsterdam and Queen Mary University, Edinburgh in 2008. She continues to be a member of several pro-people's networks like CommonHealth, Jan. Swasthya Abhiyan, PUCL, Medico Friends Circle.

Shweta Marathe is associated with Support for Advocacy and Training to Health Initiatives (SATHI) since 2010. Building upon an academic background of hospital and health care management, in SATHI, she is currently working as a research officer. She has been centrally involved in various research studies on the themes of medicine availability and procurement systems of Maharashtra, expenditure of local level untied funds, utilization of supplementary Nutrition and functioning of the ICDS system, etc. She has acquired popular writing skills and in addition to few academic publications, she has had various newspapers articles published for advocacy purposes. She recently participated in the Inaugural KEYSTONE fellowship course on Health Policy and Systems Research organized by PHFI, Delhi, where she was one of the 20 candidates selected for this national course.

Arima Mishra is an Associate Professor in School of Development at the Azim Premji University, Bangalore. She has been engaged in teaching and research on a range of themes including social determinants of health, health system governance, maternal and child health, health among indigenous communities and medical pluralism. She has earlier taught in University of Delhi and has been an academic visitor to University of Minnesota in USA, University of Edinburgh, University of Bristol and Glasgow Caledonian University in UK, and University of Oslo in Norway. She has published widely in the peer reviewed literature and authored a highly acclaimed book on hunger and famine, followed by an edited volume of ethnographic readings on health and illness. She has also guest-edited special issues of *Indian Anthropologist* (2013) and *Global Public Health* (with Katerini Storeng 2014).

Abhay Shukla is a public health physician and health activist, who initiated the SATHI team (earlier part of CEHAT, Pune) with colleagues in 1998. He was centrally involved in organizing Jan Swasthya Abhiyan's national 'Right to Health Care' campaign (2003–2004), and is a national co-convenor of Jan Swasthya Abhiyan (People's Health Movement—India). Developing accountability of health and social services, with a focus on promotion of health rights in the public and private healthcare sectors are his major areas of work. He has been involved in developing the framework for community-based monitoring and planning (CBMP) of health services at national level, and is coordinating its implementation in Maharashtra along with SATHI team members. He is currently a member of the National Rural Health Mission's Advisory Group for Community Action (AGCA), and is a member of the National Human Rights Commission's (NHRC) Core group on Health.

B. Subha Sri is an obstetrician by training with experience working in tertiary and primary care settings. She was awarded the Health and Population Innovation Fellowship of the Population Council for working on maternal health issues. Since 2006, she has been working with Rural Women's Social Education Centre, a grassroots Dalit women's organization working on reproductive health and rights issues in Tamil Nadu. She is currently the chairperson and steering committee member of CommonHealth, a national level coalition working on maternal and neonatal health issues.

T. Sundararaman is currently Professor & Dean, School of Health Systems Studies, Tata Institute of Social Sciences. Prior to this, he served as Visiting Professor at the Centre for Social Medicine and Community Health at Jawaharlal Nehru University; Founding Executive Director, National Health Systems Resource Center (where he served as Member-Secretary of Technical Resource Group to National Urban Health Mission), Founding Director of the Chhattisgarh State Health Resource Centre and Professor in the Department of Medicine at JIPMER.

He has published widely on a range of health systems and equity related issues, served on a number of Boards, Steering Committees and Resource Groups for the Indian Government, and as advisor on health systems issues to the World Health Organisation.

Veda Yumnam is Assistant Professor at the Department of Social Work, Tezpur University, Assam. She worked as a technical officer (PPTCT) in the National AIDS Control Organization, Ministry of Health and Family Welfare. She has also worked in various positions in both national and international NGOs in many disaster management projects in the states of Orissa, Rajasthan, Himachal Pradesh and Gujarat. She was also involved in many research projects in the public health domain. Her interest is in the area of social determinants of health, nutrition and conflict studies.

Commentary Authors

Prabir Chatterjee
State Health Resource Centre, Raipur, Chhattisgarh

Jashodhara Dasgupta
SAHAYOG, Lucknow

Sulakshana Nandi
Public Health Resource Network, Raipur, Chhattisgarh

R. Srivatsan
Anveshi Research Centre for Women's Studies, Hyderabad

Padmini Swaminathan
Tata Institute of Social Sciences, Mumbai

Rajani Ved
National Health Systems Resource Centre, Delhi

List of Figures

List of Tables

Chapter 1
Palimpsests of 'Social Determinants of Health'—From Historical Conceptions to Contemporary Practice in Global and Indian Public Health

Devaki Nambiar

> Health is a function, not only of medical care, but of the overall integrated development of society – cultural, economic, educational, social and political. ... Health also depends on a number of supportive services – nutrition, improvement in the environment and education; and the influence of these services on health status is far greater than that of medical care. The major programmes which will improve health are thus outside the realm of health care proper. These were comparatively neglected in the last 30 years ...this error should not be repeated [1].

Abstract Policy attention to the Social Determinants of Health (SDH) has waxed and waned over the years, both in the international and national arena. From famine to plagues, malnutrition to outbreaks, food and hygiene are 'determinants' in that they have motivated the very evolution of public health in India and the globe—albeit stochastically. Moving from colonial to nationalist to neoliberal imperatives, a coherent and abiding vision of social determinants, globally or within India for that matter, has neither endured nor arisen. This vacillation reflects the truly political nature of public health, and also of policymaking on SDH. Following deliberations held in 2013 on an Indian "Health Equity Watch" in which academicians, activists and officials participated, it was acknowledged that for India, there is in fact a substantial literature on SDH that does not explicitly reference the term SDH per se. Thus, this volume seeks to explore two interrelated questions: first, how is action around SDH conceptualized by key stakeholders in our country, and second, what are the themes that bring these conceptualizations together? We have compiled the views of academics and practitioners in both public and private not-for-profit settings to expand upon this issue, supplemented by short commentaries from individuals who reviewed individual chapters and who are involved with the project of health equity in India. From these contributions, we note that there are various vocabularies used to talk about SDH, as well as contestations,

D. Nambiar (✉)
The George Institute for Global Health, New Delhi, Delhi, India
e-mail: devaki.nambiar@gmail.com

D. Nambiar and A. Muralidharan (eds.), *The Social Determinants of Health in India*, https://doi.org/10.1007/978-981-10-5999-5_1

various stakeholders, scales and types of activities. Detailing and showcasing this diversity is the contribution of this volume.

Keywords Health equity · Commission on Social Determinants of Health
India · Global health

It has long been recognized that health has to do with far more than medical care. Sadly, the complaint that not enough is done in these other domains outside of health is, similarly, long-standing. The quote above comes from the 1981 *Health for All report*, the culmination of an unprecedented, five-year transdisciplinary collaboration between two premier institutions in India—the Indian Council for Medical Research (ICMR) and the Indian Council for Social Science Research (ICSSR) [1]. This important report was released in India in the wake of the 1978 Alma Ata Declaration, which had invigorated international attention around Primary Health Care, reflecting an ambitious, revolutionary agenda for health until the turn of the century, involving the widespread transformation of society beyond the health sector alone.

The idea that health is determined by factors beyond the health system, in popular and public health parlance today, is encapsulated in the notion of Social Determinants of Health, or SDH. The concept received global traction due to the work between 2003 and 2008 of the World Health Organization's (WHO) Commission on the Social Determinants of Health (CSDH). In its final report, the Commission defined SDH as 'the conditions in which people are born, grow, live, work and age, including the health system' [1, 2]. As we argue in this volume, SDH include interlinkages of ascriptive dimensions of identity (gender, religion, ethnicity, and others), material circumstances that shape our lives and well-being (like housing, sanitation, water supply), and socioeconomic opportunities (education, employment), all shaped by larger concatenations of power and ideology in the functioning of the world. Quite simply, SDH include who we are, where we are, what we do, and how things work in relation to health.

So what was the need to coin this set of ideas, this notion of SDH—at the particular time? And what does it allow us to do? What does it preclude?

Social Determinants of Health: A Palimpsest of History

The seeds for the notion of SDH were sown in the very foundation of modern public health [3–7]. As the Industrial Revolution widened the scale of impact on the health of populations across Europe and the Americas, consideration of the determinants of health grew (motivated by a desire to sustain technological progress and increase productivity). At the turn of the nineteenth century, a bevy of public health and welfarist pioneers including Rudolf Virchow, Robert Koch and Oswaldo Cruz, Louis-Rene Villerme, Edwin Chadwick, John Snow, Thomas McKeown, and

Friedrich Engels sought to broaden understandings around various determinants of health [3, 8]. Far from holding aligned views, these scholars contributed to long-standing debates on the causes of ill health [3]. Of these, 'Virchowian social medicine has long played an important part in international public health efforts and continues to inspire "public health's biggest idea"—its inextricable intertwining with the politics of social justice' [3].

The mid-nineteenth century also saw the genesis of multipartite development cooperation in health via International Sanitary Conferences held between 1851 and 1892 [9]. Staples notes that there was dissent about the nature of epidemic disease, and the creation and evolution of international sanitary codes and regulations had served to resolve these differences. Much of the emphasis at this time was geographically in Europe (through the Office of Public Health in Paris) and the Americas (through the Pan American Sanitary Bureau) and topically on water pollution and purification as determinants, owing to the toll of vector-borne illnesses in these locations. In the early twentieth century, the Rockefeller Foundation also convened regional conferences on hygiene, sanitation education and engineering, and funded a number of field projects in India and China. Social reform movements were at their zenith in both these countries during this period, adding to the ferment of nationalism [10].

Urged by Rockefeller, delegates from erstwhile British India attended meetings hosted by the Office of Public Health, and were tasked with formulating and enforcing sanitary regulations [11]. The colony was also heavily affected by cholera mortality (data on this was only systematically collected after the epidemic of 1865, though cholera is reported as far back as 1817 in what is now Bangladesh) [5]. Motivated by bouts of plague, colonial authorities devolved responsibility for public health and social welfare to 'Improvement Trusts' in cities, which were tasked with reducing overcrowding, removing insanitary dwellings, and improving ventilation [12]. The Bombay Improvement Trust, established two years after the 1896 plague was the first such body established, followed by similar institutions in the ensuing decades.[1] This devolution of power, shared with provincial governments, led to substantial improvements in local sanitation, and also set a precedent for the design and functioning of urban health systems in India.[2]

In the interwar period, from 1919 onwards, when the League of Nations came to be formed, India was still under British colonial domination, but was given membership citing extraordinary circumstances (although the terms of its participation were vexed and contested). The League possessed a Health Organization

[1]The very next Improvement Trust was formed in Mysore (1903), followed by Calcutta (1919), and various other cities under the United Provinces Improvement Act of 1919, which was amended to include Delhi in 1937. Decades later, these trusts were to evolve into Municipal Corporations with dedicated officers overseeing a range of social determinants in urban areas (see Ganesan et al. in this volume, for more). Examining how SDH are viewed in these documents was beyond the scope of our work but remains a key area of further study.

[2]As Amrith points out, this devolution circumscribed the social welfare policymaking abilities of municipal and state governments alike because of their inability to raise resources [10].

under its aegis, which had a narrow, biomedical preoccupation covering epidemic control (more than prevention), medical education, and medical product standard-setting [13]. Further, wider goals were likely subordinated under the circumscribed ambit of the League of Nations—which had limited membership.

Following the Second World War, when the World Health Organization was formed, its core function included that of improving 'nutrition, housing, sanitation, recreation, economic or working conditions and other aspects of environmental hygiene' [14]. Independent India's first major policy exercise—aptly termed the Health Survey and Development (Bhore) Committee, was influenced by these developments in health across the world [15, 16]. The Bhore Committee noted that 'public health requires the fulfilment of certain fundamental conditions, which include the provision of an environment conducive to healthful living, adequate nutrition, the availability of health protection, preventive and curative, to all members of the community irrespective of their ability to pay for it and the active co-operation of the people in [their] own health' [17]. The Committee held the state squarely responsible for providing 'health protection' to its people, reflecting the nationalist imperative that had seen health as part of its agenda for Indian independence and also drew inspiration from welfare states in Europe, the Soviet Union and New Zealand [10].

Under the newly drafted Indian Constitution, the protection and promotion of health and nutrition were placed in the Directive Principles for State Policy. During the 1950s, a number of achievements were made in reducing mortality and morbidity, with an initial emphasis on immunization and then malaria eradication. Though these efforts were described with great fervour and optimism, the responsibility of public health had begun to be placed squarely on the shoulders of the citizen, even as commensurate improvements in health services infrastructure were neglected in relative terms. Meanwhile, starting with India's first Five Year Plan, population control became a major priority, further eclipsing the attention needed for health services and other key determinants. In 1967, in what could be regarded as the apotheosis of Malthusianism in Indian policymaking, a hegemonic paradigm was set in motion for family planning and population control, deflecting attention away from health, particularly among the vulnerable [18]. As Amrith points out, this shift 'was immanent in the political culture of public health; in the sexual, racial and caste-based anxieties underlying the Indian nationalist movement's discussions of health, and in its privileging of the centralised state as the prime instrument of change' [15].

It was around this time that the national trend began to contrast significantly with the deeply politicised, mass-based, and institution-focussed efforts under way in the southern Indian state of Kerala, which would stand out in the coming decades. In states like Kerala, as elsewhere on the globe, following more than a decade of emphasis on vertical disease eradication programmes, the 1960s and early 1970s saw attention begin to re-center on the social, economic and political dimensions of health. Meanwhile, the Indian Planning Commission in 1975 initiated a Minimum Needs Programme which sought to improve the living standards, particularly the underprivileged and underserved Indian masses by catering to the following needs: (a) Rural Heath; (b) Rural Water Supply; (c) Rural Electrification; (d) Elementary

Education; (e) Adult Education; (f) Nutrition; (g) Environmental improvement of Urban Slums; and (h) Houses for landless laborers [19, 20].

At the global level, the WHO, under the leadership of Halfdan Mahler, sought to crystallize developmental experiences and lessons from other nations, which were then put together in the WHO's 1978 Alma Ata Declaration on Primary Health Care. The Declaration states that 'in addition to the health sector, all related sectors and aspects of national and community development, in particular agriculture, animal husbandry, food, industry, education, housing, public works, communication, and other sectors; and demands the coordinated efforts of all these sectors' [21]. Working groups were created in a special bespoke unit on Intersectoral Action for Health at the WHO across many of these categories.[3] Various governments included this feature in their health policies, and systematic research on health inequalities was launched in many countries (the Black report in the UK, and similar efforts in other Western European countries) [4].

In India, the landmark report mentioned at the outset of this chapter tried to set the tone for research on SDH in India. It was authored by two leading Indian Institutions, the Indian Council for Medical Research—with V. Ramalingaswami at its helm—and the Indian Council for Social Science Research—guided by J.P. Naik in a truly unprecedented and heralded collaboration. Building on Alma Ata, Naik and Ramalingaswami proposed an alternative strategy for *Health For All*, which also served as a precursor to the National Health Policy of 1983 [22]. The main SDH identified were: full-scale employment; improvement in the status of women; adult and universal elementary education; welfare of scheduled castes and tribes; creation of a democratic participatory form of government; organization of the poor and underprivileged groups. The report called for '(i) integrated plans for health and development including family planning; (ii) reorientation of existing priorities so that bulk of the funds can be spent on programmes on nutrition, improvement of environment, immunization and education rather than on curative services, and on basic community services at the bottom than super-specialities at the top; and (iii) replacement of the existing model of health care with an alternative model which integrated promotive, preventive and curative services and is community-based, participatory, decentralized, and democratic' [22].

Shaped by the ICMR/ICSSR report, India sought to mirror the WHO's governance arrangement to address health determinants. The 1983 National Health Policy states that 'all health and human development must ultimately constitute an integral component of the overall socioeconomic developmental process in the country. It is thus of vital importance to ensure effective coordination between health and related sectors. This may require setting up standing mechanisms, at the Centre and in the States, for securing inter-sectoral coordination of the various efforts in the fields of health and family planning, medical education and research, drugs and pharmaceuticals, agriculture and food, water supply and drainage, housing, education and

[3]The most crucial areas were adequate food intake/nutrition, and women's education, identified in Rockefeller's famous report on 'Good Health at Low Cost' [45].

social welfare and rural development' [23]. This policy called for the creation of standing mechanisms—and went on to suggest coordination and review committees.

Sadly, however, efforts such as did not prove either consistent or sustained but episodic and short-lived, foreclosed on the one hand by intragovernmental rivalries where health held a relatively weak position across ministries, and on the other hand, by the ever-present challenges posed to intersectoral action of coordination across donors and competition across ministries. An additional critical negative factor was the active promotion of a 'pragmatic, financially palatable and politically unthreatening alternative to comprehensive primary care' propounded by the Rockefeller Foundation, the Ford Foundation, the World Bank, and the US Agency for International Development [4]. Much like the New International Economic Order [24], the movement for comprehensive primary health care including intersectoral action for health was vitiated almost immediately after it was proclaimed. Moreover, India's financial dependence on international donor aid, meant that it was rendered pliable to their preference for vertical, technology-driven disease control programmes [25]. This compartmentalized and fragmented health into packages of care increasingly paid for out of people's pockets.

As Irwin and Scala point out, the resultant compartmentalization and fragmentation were only set to increase [4]. The Washington Consensus, linked to the rise of neoliberal, conservative governments in donor countries including the US, UK, and Germany, and buttressed by the waning of the Cold War led to the ascendance of neoliberal ideology in both national and international development policy [24]. Social sector reform agendas were promoted in the area of health, but also in many of its determinants such as nutrition, housing, water and sanitation, social protection which involved increasing the presence of the private sector, the splitting of financing, purchasing and service provision, unregulated and poorly stewarded decentralization, and the creation of a split between efficiency and equity [4]. As a result, not only did health spending decrease, but also spending on its determinants, leading to soaring out of pocket health payments, with little (or no) long-term gains expected from the reform measures. Around this time, the World Bank began playing more of a role in global health, to some extent displacing the authority of the World Health Organisation [4, 26, 27].

By the late 1990s, the deleterious impact of these approaches began to become clear, and while the World Bank sought to reform its strategies, the WHO—under the leadership of Gro Harlem Brundtland—tried to resurrect the Alma Ata Health for All agenda and intersectoral action for health, linking it to the pragmatics of financing. In 2000, the WHO launched the Global Commission on Macroeconomics and Health, setting a precedent for extensive international research on health inequalities, particularly in relation to income and spending [4].

Overall, while there were extensive research efforts during the early naughties (2000s) in Europe and Oceania, evidence on SDH was scant in most low- and middle-income settings. In India, the Second National Health Policy acknowledged that 'public health indicators/disease-burden statistics are the outcome of several complementary initiatives under the wider umbrella of the developmental sector, covering Rural Development, Agriculture, Food Production, Sanitation, Drinking Water Supply, Education, etc.' [28]. On the other hand, it also took the stand that 'policy aspects relating to inter-connected sectors, which, while crucial, fall outside the domain of the health sector, will not be covered by specific recommendations in this Policy document. Needless to say, the future attainment of the various goals set out in this policy assumes a reasonable complementary performance in these inter-connected sectors' [28]. Later on in the document, the following clarification is given: 'This is not to say that other items contributing to the disease burden of the country will be ignored; but only that the resources, as also the principal focus of the public health administration, will recognize certain relative priorities. It is unnecessary to labor the point that under the umbrella of the macro-policy prescriptions in this document, governments and private sector programme planners will have to design separate schemes, tailor-made to the health needs of women, children, geriatrics, tribal and other socioeconomically under-served sections. An adequately robust disaster management plan has to be in place to effectively cope with situations arising from natural and man-made calamities' [28]. As evident in the lack of policy articulation here in India, it became hard at this point to envision a role for the state in intersectoral action on health. Indeed, from this point onward, there has been a divergence of views on what the breadth and depth of engagement there can be from within the health sector on this issue.

In 2004, upon winning the election, India's United Progressive Alliance resurrected the Common Minimum Programme, committing to an ambitious package of health determinants that would be guaranteed to the population including employment, housing, health, education, sanitation, roads, electricity and water supply [20]. In addition to this, a National Commission on Macroeconomics and Health (NCMH) in 2005 helped reintroduce ideas relating to SDH. This followed on from the global effort, which used the frame of investment and cost-effectiveness, so as to be pragmatic [4]. In India, the NCMH was operating at the time when a number of forces were conspiring in the domain of health in general, and rural health in particular.

A new government was in power, and the People's Health Movement, having declared its Charter in 2000, put pressure on the government to adopt welfarist policies. Jan Swasthya Abhiyan 'reaffirm[ed] our inalienable right to and demand for comprehensive health care that includes food security; sustainable livelihood options including secure employment opportunities; access to housing, drinking water and sanitation; and appropriate medical care for all; in sum—the right to Health For All, Now!' [29]. The People's Health Movement drew attention also to political, financial, agricultural and industrial policies as well as the negative impacts of the processes of economic globalization, liberalization, privatization, and financialization that were creating systemic inequality, foreclosing possibilities for people's participation, and ignoring if not abetting corporate malfeasance on a grand scale. To reverse these processes, the movement demanded greater strengthening of the public sector.

The government itself was comprised of a coalition including Leftist parties that placed greater emphasis on such policies. This resulted in the launching of the

National Rural Health Mission (NRHM). The NRHM Mission Document (2005–2012) states plainly that it 'adopts a synergistic approach by relating health to determinants of good health viz. segments of nutrition, sanitation, hygiene and safe drinking water' [30]. It sees this as being operationalized through district planning, which itself is an 'amalgamation of field responses through Village Health Plans, State and National priorities for Health, Water Supply, Sanitation and Nutrition' governed at the national level by a Mission Steering Group comprising representation from the Health and Family Welfare, Local Self Government (Panchayati Raj), Rural Development and Human Resource Development ministries, as well as the erstwhile Planning Commission [30]. In fact, the term 'social determinants of health' made its first appearance in the 2005 NRHM framework document.

This was, indeed, most fitting, as the coinage of SDH emerged at the turn of the millennium. The WHO Commission on SDH was appointed in 2003 by the newly incumbent Director General, Dr. Lee Jong-Wook. It sought in part to advance and resolve the debates launched from 2000 onwards following the Global Commission on Macroeconomics and Health, which set a precedent for extensive international research on health inequalities, particularly (some would argue narrowly) in relation to income and spending [4]. The CSDH, building upon Chairman Michael Marmot's work in Whitehall, England, highlighted the social gradient in health, emphasizing economic inequalities. In addition, mnemonically and strategically, looking at social determinants afforded an opportunity to think of health in broader terms than merely an economic one. The many knowledge networks created in connection with the CSDH, on gender, globalization, urban health, measurement and evaluation, and others, sought to create a much wider social understanding of the determinants of health and an agenda for action that lay ahead. Finally, the CSDH drew global attention to the 'unequal distribution of power, income, goods, and services, globally and nationally, [and] the consequent unfairness in the immediate, visible circumstances of people's lives' [2].

Meanwhile, in India, the buzzword of choice has been 'convergence' seeking very much to envision responses to the clearly manifest inequalities and hierarchies that are quite blatantly affecting health and well-being. NRHM has been a platform for convergence in health, along with other welfarist measures like the National Rural Employment Guarantee Act, as well as other rights-based campaigns including the Right to Education, the Right to Information and the Right to Food [31, 32]. In 2008, the thirtieth anniversary of Alma Ata was marked by efforts to redraw attention to Primary Health Care—although the vocabulary for reform began to shift to the concept of Universal Health Coverage [33].

In 2010, India's Planning Commission appointed a High Level Expert Group (HLEG) on Universal Health Coverage, chaired by Prof K. Srinath Reddy. Joining him were a number of individuals closely involved with the CSDH process, including Dr. Mirai Chatterjee, a WHO Commissioner on SDH and Dr. Gita Sen, convenor of the Knowledge Network on Women and Gender Equity. Critically, the Expert Group highlighted the SDH as part of its agenda for Universal Health Coverage reform, noting that in India, it was possible to build on the momentum generated and experience amalgamated by civil society groups and academia, as well as government stakeholders, in various contexts and through myriad approaches.

In doing this, the Expert Group proposed no single framework to understand or act upon SDH [34, 35]. Rather, members converged upon illustrative domains of action: Nutrition and Food Security; Water and Sanitation; Social Exclusion (on the basis of gender, caste, religion, tribal status, geography, etc.); and Work (In) Security, Occupational Health and Disasters [34]. They called for greater thought and deliberation upon what India's approach to the social determinants of health ought to be. They also called for the adoption of some kind of monitoring framework on health equity that would link to SDH.

At the global level, a World Conference on Social Determinants of Health was convened by WHO and the Government of Brazil in 2011, resulting in the Rio Political Declaration on Social Determinants of Health, ratified at the 2012 World Health Assembly. This declaration articulated political will to 'improve public health, and reduce health inequities through action on the social determinants of health. The focus is on addressing the challenges of eradicating hunger and poverty; ensuring food security; enabling access to healthcare and affordable medicines; and improving daily living conditions through provision of safe drinking-water and sanitation, employment opportunities and social protection; protecting environments and delivering equitable economic growth' [36]. The Declaration has been critiqued as being depoliticized (unlike the Alma Ata Declaration) [13]—with SDH always manifesting as a familiar (re)listing of determinants in various policy pronouncements.

The National Urban Health Mission Framework document, released in 2013, made a commitment to 'systematically work towards meeting the regulatory, reformatory, and developmental public health priorities of urban local bodies. It will promote convergent and community action in partnership with all other urban area initiatives. Vector control, environmental health, water, sanitation, housing, all require a public health thrust. NUHM will provide resources that enable communitization of such processes. It will provide resources that strengthen the capacity of urban local bodies to meet public health challenges' [37]. The document noted that 'there was a lack of effective coordination among the departments that lead to inadequate focus on critical aspects of public health such as access to clean drinking water, environmental sanitation and nutrition' while adding that community efforts played an important role in improving access to drinking water, sanitation, nutrition services and livelihood. It also talks about convergence with programmes from four other ministries and within its own programmatic areas.[4]

[4]Convergence is proposed in the NUHM framework document with (a) the Ministry of Urban Development and Ministry of Housing and Urban Poverty Alleviation for (i) the Basic Services to the Urban Poor sub-mission of the Jawaharlal Nehru National Urban Renewal Mission of, which has a seven point charter including land tenure, affordable shelter, water, sanitation, education, health, and social security—all coordinated through a City Development Plan; (ii) Rajiv Awas Yojana to integrate slums into the formal system; (iii) the Swarn Jayanti Shahri Rozgar Yojana to federate existing Development of Women and Children in Urban Areas (DWCUA) and

As can be seen in this historical account, policy attention to the determinants of health has waxed and waned repeatedly over the years, both in the international and national arena. What we now have is a palimpsest, where some themes have been recurrent and others have emerged and evolved. From famine to plagues, malnutrition to outbreaks of disease, challenges of food and hygiene are 'determinants' in the sense that they have motivated the very evolution of public health in India and around the globe—albeit stochastically. More broadly, however, the plurality of vocabularies and rationales in the SDH discourse, reflect the highly political and context-sensitive nature of this topic in international and national development.

India's particular history of SDH may be periodized into four major phases. First, we have colonial rationales for Improvement Trusts, which sought to contain disease and control famine, albeit for narrow purposes and exclusive (colonial expatriate) populations. Then, we have nationalist visions of Bhore and the First National Health Policy that were part of the ferment of Alma Ata. Strong attention was paid here to SDH. This was followed in the late 1980s onwards, by neoliberal imperatives represented in the Second National Health Policy, where the state's role in health and its determinants was purposively enfeebled. The policy framework for the National Rural Health Mission inaugurated a fourth phase, encapsulated by an attempt to bridge and reconcile the second and third phases. This is evident in the inclusion of, but also the generality in, pronouncements related to SDH, evident in the High Level Expert Group on Universal Health Coverage [35], the Draft 2015 National Health Policy and the 2017 National Health Policy. The last of these seems to relegate SDH to ecological factors like pollution, as well as risk factors like diet and exercise [38] while according far less attention to the larger political and economic frames and distributions of power that affect health and action on health more broadly. In a sense, the latest National Health Policy makes no major departure from these earlier listings and categorizations, even as it doesn't necessarily reconcile or resolve them.

A Vision for SDH?

Unsurprisingly, a coherent and abiding vision of social determinants, globally or within India for that matter, has not endured or arisen. What we have instead is a palimpsest, where some themes have been recurrent and others have emerged and

---

(Footnote 4 continued)

Neighbourhood Committees groups into Mahila Arogya Samitis; (b) the Ministry of Women and Child Development for local coordination with Anganwadi Centres and Anganwadi Workers for Community Health and Nutrition day and other health promotion activities; and (c) the Ministry of Minority Affairs through convergence with the Multi Sectoral Development Programme underway in 90 minority districts which includes semi-urban areas, by developing district-specific plans for provision of infrastructure for education, sanitation, housing, drinking water, electricity supply, and income generation; (d) within the health ministry, school health programmes as well as adolescent health programmes are also seen as nodal points for convergence, as well as inclusion of specific programming to map, reach, and attend to the special needs of vulnerable groups [37].

evolved, and some have been forgotten altogether. From famine to plagues, malnutrition to outbreaks of disease, challenges of food and hygiene are 'determinants' in the sense that they have motivated the very evolution of public health in India and the globe—albeit stochastically. This reflects the truly political nature of public health, and indeed also of policymaking on its determinants. In addition to this, ascriptive determinants, like gender, ethnicity, caste, and religious affiliation that describe one's position in societal hierarchies and conjugate the determinants of food and hygiene, have also emerged as social determinants. And evocatively and iteratively argued by thinkers on inequality—from Marx to the CSDH—are the socioeconomic determinants of education and class. The palimpsest reflects variegated attention across these categories to these determinants in relation to the health of populations, and indeed of the health systems themselves.

Throughout all this, as scholars have pointed out, overtly political agendas in the international arena have been subject to sabotage, and consensus has usually meant deeply problematic compromise [4, 39]. Further, existing frameworks can at times be challenging for action on SDH—not merely in their profusion (which poses problems of which criteria may be used to choose one thing and reject others), but also their importation or adaptation outside of the contexts in which they were conceived [4]. The actual 'work' of action on SDH can therefore become siloed in academic and conceptual discourses, ripe for analysis, with interpretation prior to adaptation, and yet can be segmented and separated from what already exists on the ground.

For many, this goes against the very idea of the 'social' in SDH. We see a recurrent yearning for popular revolution, an uprising of people's ownership of and demand for improvement in social determinants [40]. In India, this was articulated first by the Bhore Committee: 'No measures designed to improve existing conditions can produce lasting success unless the people are aroused from their apathy to tolerate the insanitary conditions around them and the large amount of sickness that prevails, can be overcome […] In the programme of health development, which we put forward, the need for securing the active co-operation of the people in the day to day functioning of the health organisation should be prominently kept in view' [17]. The most recent (re)iteration of this is India's 2017 National Health Policy, which calls for the 'development of strategies and institutional mechanisms […] popularised as the Swasth Nagrik Abhyan—a social movement for health' [41]. What wasn't to become in Bhore may yet (not) arise six decades on, but clearly there is extensive policy precedent and at least de jure a discourse on SDH in India. Throughout, there has been a persistent suggestion—call it hope—that a people's movement for health and its determinants may help melt the glacial pace of health reform in India.

Policy documents tend to be aspirational and declarative, offering an incomplete picture of what is de facto the reality of SDH in India. Given that health is a state subject while other determinants are often not, and moreover, given the country's profound diversity, what warrants a closer examination is what has been happening at subnational levels in the realms of both thinking and action in this area, that both instantiates and challenges these larger trends. As others have articulated, we have also felt that what is needed is an ‘in depth understanding of the unique interplay between local, national and global SDH in a local setting, gathered by ethnographic research, is needed to be able to address structural SD in the local setting and decrease health inequity’ [4].

In the summer of 2013, we had the opportunity to bring thinking and action perspectives together to participate in a national, WHO-sponsored consultative workshop on health equity. A range of stakeholders from three countries and eight Indian states attended the workshop, including the Central Bureau of Health Intelligence (CBHI), Delhi’s Ministry of Women and Child Development (MWCD), the National Health Systems Resource Centre (NHSRC), civil society and grassroots organisations including the People’s Health Movement/Jan Swasthya Abhiyan (JSA), the Society for Nutrition Education and Health (SNEHA), the Self Employed Women’s Association (SEWA), the Child in Need Institute (CINI), a variety of research institutions including the International Institute of Population Sciences (IIPS), Institute of Public Health (IPH), Anveshi Research Centre for Women’s Studies, and Azim Premji University (APU), as well as senior technical resource persons from Brazil and from the headquarters of the World Health Organization.

Presenters described in enthusiastic detail how action on SDH and health equity was being incorporated in state-wide missions, schemes and programmes, as well as private interventions and mobilizations supporting the poor [42]. In each case, elements converged around a unifying pivot, but across cases, the pivot itself was variable: administrative reform to provide multiple services through one delivery window, deliberation around myriad village development issues on one decision-making platform, legal, police, and medical action around one salient health issue, or fulfilling a charter of residential improvements for one population group [43]. Here again, we did not arrive at a single model or framework for SDH. This got us thinking—do we just not have a unified framework on SDH in India? Do we need one?

It follows that, for India, there is in fact a substantial literature on SDH that does not explicitly reference the term SDH per se (for example, there are many studies from the 1990s onwards on health inequalities [44]). Why is this? As this book argues, there may in fact be historical, contextual, and political reasons why the SDH framework itself may not apply ubiquitously in the Indian context. We explore this complex issue by bringing together multiple understandings and experiences from the Indian context.

About This Volume

This volume seeks to explore two interrelated questions: first, how is action around SDH conceptualized by key stakeholders in our country, and second, what are the themes that bring these conceptualizations together?

We have compiled the views of academics and practitioners in both public and private not-for-profit settings to expand upon this issue, supplemented by short commentaries from individuals who reviewed individual chapters and who are involved with the project of health equity in India. It was not difficult to identify these individuals, but to make demands on their time was difficult indeed. Yet, what we have here is, we hope, a set of provocations that reflect the range and depth of thinking on this issue.

We begin with Dr. Mishra's critical appraisal of the social determinants of health concept, exploring what conceptions and methodologies are assumed (problematically) in its application. Dr. Yumnam and Dr. Dasgupta draw on international literature to propose conflict as a social determinant of health, adding reflections from the impact of continuing insecurity in the north-east Indian state of Manipur. Dr. Chatterjee introduces us to domains and categories of study in India that may be drawn upon to advance this nascent work. Dr. Bhan's piece on the urban transition takes apart the notion of the 'urban,' reflecting on how one may 'measure' such a fluid and dynamic construct. This is paired with Ms. Nandi's reflections on the medicalization of the urban and the challenge that befell the National Urban Health Mission in India. Dr. Chakravarthi reflects on the lack of research on distal SDH, using as examples the conspicuously small canon of conceptual thinking and empirical work on labor conditions as an SDH, as well the varied influences of corporations—factors often ignored in mainstream discourses given their highly political nature and the methodological complexity involved in studying them.

Ms. Goswami describes the process of identifying forms of vulnerability and areas of priority for action as part of a task force on women's labor in the informal economy in Bihar. This is complemented with a historiography of feminist research on labor in India by Dr. Swaminathan. Supplementing an extensive field appraisal as part of the National Urban Health Mission's Technical Resource Group with historiography, Dr. Ganesan, Dr. Nambiar and Dr. Sundararaman describe the institution of the urban Municipal Health Officer, which brought health and its determinants into a unified ambit, albeit enfeebled in various patterns across tiers of Indian cities. Dr. Desai tackles the complex but essential question of scaling up action on SDH, reflecting on efforts of the Self Employed Women's Association to address priority determinants that share informal women workers' health and well-being in different states. The need, on the one hand, for a unified approach, but also for customization and flexibility towards local understandings and idioms of action are underscored by them.

Two chapters describe the use of SDH indicators in particular. Dr. Muralidharan describes a collaborative process of developing intersectoral indicators related to menstrual health and hygiene management at the national scale in India.

Contextualizing and politicizing this domain is Ms. Dasgupta's reflection on the social dynamics and cultural frame in which such a process is nested. Mr. Garg describes the Chhattisgarh Swasthya Panchayat Survey experience, which involved the creation of a registry of indicators to be monitored regularly by village committees, allowing the creation of action plans at the local level to address SDH. Dr. Ved's reflection on this highlights the contributions that this work represents, both in terms of generating priorities for local action at the village level and the possibility of simplifying mortality into a count-based monitoring activity, again with great local relevance and the potential for broader and more complex forms of analysis.

Ms. Marathe and Dr. Shukla reflect on efforts to monitor nutrition and health services in Maharashtra, demonstrating how accountability is a necessary and achievable goal for action on SDH. Ms. Khanna and Dr. Subha sri present a bespoke social autopsy methodology to understand maternal deaths using an SDH lens, taking into account individual attributes, family and peer influences, as well as intermediary determinants (health services, community context), and structural determinants (related to governance and policies, as well as cultural and social values).

As these rich contributions came in, we sought to use them as a springboard for further reflection and debate on the individual topics, and on SDH more generally. Reviewers were chosen for each chapter, based on their prior work in these areas, and subject to their availability. Apart from giving comments and inputs to authors, many reviewers also submitted commentaries of their own, adding richness and depth to the writing exercise, and to our understandings as well. Six such valuable contributions came in from senior academics and practitioners in government and civil society and enrich this volume.

From these contributions, we note that there are various vocabularies used to talk about social determinants. While some talk about human development, others use the notion of convergence. Within topical areas, there are contestations, for instance between 'labor' and 'work' in the context of women in the informal sector, between urbanization and health and urban health. Actors who are implicated in this work also constitute a panoply—from various government departments to non-governmental organizations to local committees, unions, and technical agencies. Sometimes actors are also beneficiary populations/populations of interest—informal workers, adolescent girls, young children, people living in conflict—and sometimes not. Scales of operation have also varied greatly in this volume, ranging from the scale of the village, to that of the urban, national and international. We have great richness and diversity in the areas of focus—in all cases, multiple determinants or axes are considered together, ranging from nutrition to labor, and sanitation to conflict. The types of activities reflected upon are also variable—monitoring, research, practices of inclusion, planning, and policy implementation. All in all, we have far surpassed our goal of rendering the diversity of views and experiences on SDH in these pages, to the extent of challenging the concept itself.

References

1. Study Group Set up by the Indian Council of Social Science Research and the Indian Council of Medical Research. Health for All: An Alternative Strategy New Delhi: Indian Council of Social Science Research and the Indian Council of Medical Research; 1981.
2. World Health Organisation Commission on Social Determinants of Health. Closing the gap in a generation: health equity through action on the social determinants of health Final Report of the Commission on Social Determinants of Health. Geneva; World Health Organisation; 2008.
3. Birn A. Historicising, politicising, and 'futurising' closing the gap in a generation. In: Bhattacharya S, Messenger S, Overy C, editors. Social determinants of health: assessing theory, policy, and practice. 1st ed. Hyderabad: Orient Blackswan; 2010. p. 76–113.
4. Irwin A, Scali E. Action on the social determinants of health: a historical perspective. Glob Public Health Int J Res Policy Pract. 2007;2(3):235–56.
5. Dasgupta R. Urbanising cholera: the social determinants of its re-emergence. New Delhi: Orient Blackswan; 2012.
6. Bhattacharya S, Messenger S, Overy C, editors. Social determinants of health: assessing theory, policy, and practice. Bangalore: Orient Blackswan; 2010.
7. Cook HJ, Bhattacharya S, Hardy A, editors. History of the social determinants of health: global histories, contemporary debates. 1st ed. Hyderabad: Orient Blackswan; 2009.
8. Krech R. Social determinants of health: practical solutions to deal with a well-recognised issue. Bull World Health Organ. 2011;89:703.
9. Staples ALS. Constructing international identity: the World Bank, food and agriculture organisation, and World Health Organisation, 1945–1965. Ph.D. Dissertation. Columbus, OH: Ohio State University; 1998.
10. Amrith SS. Health in India since independence. London: Brooks World Poverty Institute Working Paper 79; 2009.
11. Legg S. An international anomaly? Sovereignty, the League of Nations and India's princely geographies. J Hist Geogr. 2014;1(43):96–110.
12. Singh KN. Urban development in India. New Delhi: Abhinav Publications; 1978.
13. Global Health Watch 3: An alternative world health report. London: Peoples Health Movement; Medact; Medicos International; Health Action International; Third World Network. 2011.
14. United Nations. Constitution of the World Health Organisation. Geneva: United Nations; 1946.
15. Amrith S. Political culture of health in India: a historical perspective. Econ Polit Wkly 2007;42:114–21.
16. Murthy P, Sarin A, Jain S, Jain S. International advisors to the Bhore Committee: perceptions and visions for healthcare. Econ Polit Wkly 2013; XLVIII(10):71–7.
17. Government of India. [Bhore Commission] Report of the health survey and development committee, vol. 4. New Delhi: Government of India; 1946.
18. Rao M. From population control to reproductive health: Malthusian arithmetic. New Delhi: Sage Publications; 2004.
19. Vaz LS, Agrawal S, Dudeja P, Jindal AK. Section 3c—health policy and health care systems—public health administration and community health care in India. In: Bhalwar R, Vaidya R, Tilak R, Gupta R, Kunte R, editors. Text book of public health and community medicine Pune: department of community medicine. Armed Forces Medical College/World Health Organisation; 2009.

20. Qadeer I. Political and economic determinants of health: the case of India. In: Cook HJ, Bhattacharya S, Hardy A, editors. A history of the social determinants of health: global histories, contemporary debates. Hyderabad: Orient BlackSwan; 2009. p. 228–48.
21. Declaration of Alma-Ata. International conference on primary health care (6–12 Sept 1978). Geneva: World Health Organisation; 1978.
22. Nayar KR. Three decades of ICSSR-ICMR Committee Report & the re-assertion of social determinants of health. Indian J Med Res. 2012;136(4):540–3.
23. Government of India. National health policy. New Delhi: Ministry of Health and Family Welfare; 1983.
24. Prashad V. The poorer nations: a possible history of the global south. New York: Verso; 2013.
25. Banerji D. Landmarks in the development of health services in India. In: Qadeer I, Sen K, Nayar KR, editors. Public health and the poverty of reforms: the south Asian predicament. New Delhi: Sage Publications; 2001. p. 37–50.
26. Youde J. The relationships between foreign aid, HIV and government health spending. Health Policy Plann. 2010;25(6):523–8.
27. Nambiar D, Rajbangshi PR, Mayra K. The World Health Organization in the South East Asia region: decision-maker perceptions. London: Royal Institute of International Affairs/Chatham House; 2014;101632714.
28. Government of India. National health policy. New Delhi: Ministry of Health and Family Welfare; 2002.
29. People's Health Movement. People's charter for health. New Delhi: People's Health Movement; 2000.
30. National Rural Health Mission [NRHM]. National Rural Health Mission (2005–2012) mission document. New Delhi: Ministry of Health and Family Welfare; 2005.
31. Prasad AM, Chakraborty G, Yadav SS, Bhatia S. Addressing the social determinants of health through health system strengthening and inter-sectoral convergence: the case of the Indian National Rural Health Mission. Glob Health Action. 2013;1(6):1–11.
32. Sharma AL. Mainstreaming of resource convergence in policymaking, programme design and execution. New Delhi: United Nations Development Programme; 2013.
33. World Health Organisation [WHO]. World health report—primary care, now more than ever. Geneva: World Health Organisation; 2008.
34. High Level Expert Group on Universal Health Coverage. Recommendations of the high level expert group on universal health coverage. New Delhi: Planning Commission; 2011.
35. Nambiar D. India's, "tryst" with universal health coverage: reflections on ethnography in Indian health policymaking. Soc Sci Med. 2013;99:135–42.
36. World Conference on Social Determinants of Health. Rio political declaration on social determinants of health (World Conference on Social Determinants of Health). Rio: World Health Organisation; 2011.
37. Ministry of Health and Family Welfare, Government of India. National Urban Health Mission: framework for implementation. New Delhi: Ministry of Health and Family Welfare; 2013.
38. Government of India. National health policy. New Delhi: Ministry of Health and Family Welfare; 2017.
39. Taylor C, Jolly R. The straw men of primary health care. Soc Sci Med. 1988;26(9):971–7.
40. Dreze J, Sen A. An uncertain glory: India and its contradictions. Princeton, NJ: Princeton University Press; 2013.
41. Government of India. Draft national health policy. New Delhi: Ministry of Health and Family Welfare; 2015.

42. Public Health Foundation of India, World Health Organisation—India Country Office. PHFI/WHO consultative workshop on an Indian 'health equity watch': a report of proceedings. New Delhi: Public Health Foundation of India; 2013.
43. Nambiar D, Muralidharan A, Garg S, Daruwalla N, Ganesan P. Analysing implementer narratives on addressing health inequity through convergent action on the social determinants of health in India. Int J Equity Health 2015;14(1):133-015-0267-7.
44. Bhan N, Rao KD, Kachwaha S. Health inequalities research in India: a review of trends and themes in the literature since the 1990s. Int J Equity Health. 2016;15(1):166.
45. Halstead SB, Walsh JA, Warren KS. Good health at low cost. New York: The Rockefeller Foundation; 1985.

Part I
Conceptualization

Chapter 2
Putting the 'Social' Back in: Social Determinants of Health as a Methodological Lens

Arima Mishra

Abstract The messages of the SDH Commission report are not necessarily novel but they have an additional significance in the current climate of health, which witnesses the failure of the Alma Ata declaration of achieving 'Health for All' with increasing evidence on persistent inequities in different parts of the world. The significance of the report also lies in the fact that it provides an apt forum for a *dialogue* among disciplines (roughly between social science disciplines including humanities and conventional health sciences) and different stakeholders including academics, practitioners and civil society advocacy groups. It signals the 'coming together' of a diverse set of actors/perspectives/methodologies that are, more importantly, liberating the study of health from a narrow lens of biomedicine in the common pursuit of striving towards health equity. The spirit of dialogue is hence critical as several concerns relating to conceptualization (the unpacking of the 'social') and operationalization (identifying actions on the social determinants and developing indicators for monitoring inequalities) emanate from such a conversational space among the different actors and disciplines involved. In the spirit of such a conversation, this chapter talks about what the 'social' in social determinants of health entails and its implications in terms of research and actions. It argues that social determinants of health needs to be seen as a methodological lens than rediscovering a new set of factors or causes leading to inequity.

Keywords Commission on social determinants of health · Methodology
Social sciences · Health equity

A. Mishra (✉)
Azim Premji University, Bangalore, India
e-mail: arima.mishra@apu.edu.in

D. Nambiar and A. Muralidharan (eds.), *The Social Determinants of Health in India*, https://doi.org/10.1007/978-981-10-5999-5_2

Locating the WHO Commission Report

> Social justice is a matter of life and death. [...] The Commission calls on the WHO and all governments to lead global action on the social determinants of health with the aim of achieving health equity. It is essential that governments, civil society, WHO, and other global organizations now come together in taking action to improve the lives of the world's citizens. Achieving health equity within a generation is achievable, it is the right thing to do, and now is the right time to do it [1].

These excerpts from the report of the World Health Organization's (WHO) Commission on the Social Determinants of health (hereafter referred to as CSDH) powerfully sum up its mandate, thrust and key messages. The report offers three messages: the first is a forceful reminder that 'social' determinants matter in addressing health inequity. The second conveys that practices of inequities are unnatural, avoidable and preventable through appropriate actions on SDH and the third is a plea for collective actions on health inequity thus putting equity and social justice at the centre stage of discussions on health policies, programs and practices. The setting up of the commission and its subsequent report have generated a lot of discussions and debates about its mandate and content as much as the viability of its recommendations [2–6]. The messages of the CSDH report are not necessarily novel but they have an additional significance in the current climate of health which is witnessing the failure of the Alma Ata declaration of achieving 'Health for All' with increasing evidence on persistent inequities in different parts of the world. On the other hand, several national governments in different countries are seemingly putting forward the agenda of universal health coverage and revitalization of primary health care. The Commission report comes as a timely reminder to focus on the 'right thing at the right time' as academics and practitioners are increasingly wary of the changing discourse in the clamor for Universal Health Coverage that might entail package of health care services for specific diseases alone than ensuring Health for All [7–12]. The CSDH report reinstates a social perspective of health in the discussion of Health for All/universal health coverage.

The significance of the report also lies in the fact that it provides an apt forum for a *dialogue* among disciplines (roughly between social science disciplines including humanities and conventional health sciences) and different stakeholders including academics, practitioners and civil society advocacy groups. It signals the 'coming together' of a diverse set of actors/perspectives/methodologies that are, more importantly, liberating the study of health from a narrow lens of biomedicine in the common pursuit of striving towards health equity.[1] The report signals the reorientation of the established hierarchy of medical knowledge by pushing 'social knowledge' on health from the 'rear to the fore of health assessment' [13].

---

[1]The social composition of the nine knowledge networks makes it a truly multidisciplinary exercise drawing on disciplines as well as professional backgrounds (academics, researchers, activists and practitioners). The very identification of the knowledge networks including early childhood, gender equity, health systems, social exclusion, urban settings, and employment conditions, demonstrate the inclusive understanding of health.

The spirit of a dialogue is hence critical, as several concerns relating to conceptualization (the unpacking of the 'social') and operationalization (identifying actions on social determinants and developing indicators for monitoring inequalities) emanate from such a conversational space among the different actors and disciplines involved. In the spirit of such a conversation, this chapter talks about what the 'social' in social determinants of health entails and its implications in terms of research and actions. It argues that social determinants of health needs to be seen more as a methodological lens with which to approach health equity than as the rediscovering a new set of causes or factors leading to inequity.

Framing the 'Social' in Social Determinants of Health

An important point of contestation has been to understand the 'social' in social determinants of health, or more simply the question is often asked 'what are the social determinants of health?'. Are x, y, z social determinants? Framing the 'social' in social determinants of health is a methodological question rather than a mere listing of factors affecting health/ill health and bracketing these as social/political/ecological or cultural determinants. Social determinants of health is not a new phrase. For social scientists, this phrase is self-evident as their work necessarily locates health in society—its institutions, norms, social categories and processes. However, this phrase has an added meaning with the works of McKeown [14], Illich [15], the UK Black Report on Inequalities in Health (1980), Marmot [16–18] followed by others that show how social forces matter in explaining systematic differences in health outcomes leading to the popular debate on the role of biomedical/technological *vis-à-vis* social interventions (including education, housing and social welfare in addition to better medical care) in achieving equitable health outcomes [19]. SDH are thus necessarily discussed in relation to health equity. The Commission report furthers this understanding by making a conceptual distinction between SDH and SDH inequities largely to argue that it is not enough to talk about social factors that determine health but rather there is a need to identify the factors/causes that shape and reinforce health inequities thus getting at the 'causes of the causes'. It identifies these structural determinants as 'bad politics, unfair economic arrangements and unhealthy policies'. The conceptual framework (Fig. 2.1) clearly reflects this distinction, where the structural determinants of health inequities are explicitly stated as the socioeconomic and political context that includes governance, macroeconomic policies, social and public policies as well as the cultural and societal values that impact and are impacted by socioeconomic positions such as class, gender and ethnicity. Together, these influence material circumstances and individual/group behavior that may lead to inequitable health outcomes and differential experiences of ill-being/well-being.

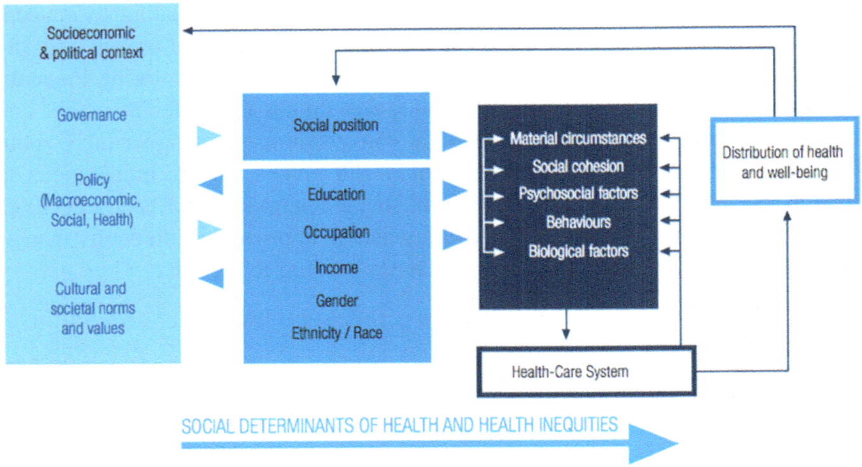

Fig. 2.1 A conceptual framework of social determinants of health (2008). *Source* (1, page 43)

The conceptual framework thus brings home an important realization that poverty by itself is not a cause of inequitable access to health services or maternal mortality, instead the larger public policies, culture of governance (that values health as a public good) and political will to combat poverty are the causes. These structural determinants resonate with the concept of structural violence, which Farmer [20] argues as the 'social arrangements that put individuals and populations in harm's way. The arrangements are *structural* because they are embedded in the political and economic organization of our social world; they are *violent* because they cause injury to people (typically, not those responsible for perpetuating such inequalities') [21: 1686]. The bad politics and unhealthy policies, as Farmer (1999) would argue, are the social fault lines—the way society responds to social locations of inequality that lead to systematic differences in accessing and experiencing health. Such a social lens thus shifts the analysis and understanding of health inequities from the given social categories (caste, class, gender, poverty, education and their associated health outcomes) to structural factors and processes that act on these categories to produce inequitable health outcomes [20].

With such a conceptual framework to locate the 'social', the Commission makes a significant departure from a factorial and/or associational model of approaching social determinants of health that has been widely used in the existing literature.

A factorial model of SDH tends to treat 'social' as one set of factors, the others being cultural, nutritional, environmental, psychological or political. Such an approach is problematic for three reasons. The first, as Parker and Harper [22] argue, it gives rise to a misleading conceptual distinction between science and culture, or science and beliefs. Such an approach 'typically reduces the investigation of social and cultural aspects of disease to discrete, static, quantifiable "beliefs" held by (or sometimes about) the study population. The separation of these beliefs from the ideal medical science and its humanistic outcome has led researchers to investigate the barriers to the uptake of the provision of health services' [22, pp. 1–2]. Social factors (or social knowledge of health) in such a model are considered as a supplement, or an ornament to biomedical knowledge of health and health care [13]. Typically such a model would argue that marriage patterns, local notions of health promotion among the indigenous communities or gendered norms are barriers to the uptake of (bio) medical health services assuming these factors to be static and isolated from the larger political economy in which these operate [23–25].

The second concern emanates from the tendency to assume social categories (caste, gender, ethnic groups, poor and tribal) and phenomena as given. For example, a common explanation I have heard during my research among the indigenous communities in Odisha that 'they are ignorant of scientific medical practices', 'not concerned about the health of their children so do not bring their children for immunization during the Immunization Days', and 'no matter what the state does, they continue to follow their health customs' etc. Such explanations tend to attribute lack of accessing services to typical attributes of the communities while plenty of research evidence shows that community demand/uptake of health services (biomedical or otherwise) is linked to a host of factors including modes of health communications, modes of delivery of health services (through outreach clinics, camps, health centres), social relations with the health workers, previous experiences with state supported medical services, history of overall engagement with the state, and alignment of specific health services with local health priorities etc [26–29]. Attributing the uptake of services to ignorance and typical characteristics of indigenous communities thus impacting on immunization coverage would qualify for what Farmer calls 'immodest claims of causality' [20]. This is immodest because it distracts attention away from social processes and factors that do affect access to health. Further, it tends to blame the communities (projecting them as victims of ignorance or perceptions) thus naturalizing health outcomes. This is misleading as it evades actions that could be taken up to address health inequalities.

The third related discomfort with a factorial model in the study of SDH is that social factors are looked upon as apolitical. For example, gender norms impacting on health access and outcomes are not sui generis. Such norms have political functions serving as a means of social control or disciplining of women's bodies, be it at the household level or state level. It would hence be imperative to understand the everyday practices through which such norms are created, nurtured and reinforced. A factorial model of looking at the 'social' as a distinct, isolated set of factors thus does not help us in addressing questions of inequity.

The CSDH's framing of the 'social' also departs from approaching SDH through the logic of mere associations. There is plenty of sociodemographic and epidemiological research that establishes associations between caste, class, education, age place of residence and ethnicity, with inequitable health access and outcomes. For example, a longitudinal study conducted among a cohort of young adults in the US shows that for individuals born between 1914 and 1939, one additional year of education lowers the probability of dying by 3.6% points. This applies to older adults too where the relationship between educational attainment and health, measured as functional ability among older people in the US showed a positive and significant relationship (0.10 level of significance) [30]. Dahl's study among the Norwegians shows how occupational status is an important predictor of ill health [31]. In India, several studies have utilized the National Family Health Survey (NFHS) data to show associations between socioeconomic variables and health indicators. Dey and Mishra [32] based on an analysis of NFHS–III data show that there is a positive association between age, gender, low income and lack of education with utilization of public health care services private health facilities in India. Other studies, in a similar vein, demonstrate a strong association between mother's education (or parental education) and utilization of maternal and child health services and health outcomes in different parts of India [33–35].

Such evidence is certainly important but it is limiting. While these studies reinforce the point that social factors including gender, caste, class, education, place of residence etc. matter in health, such associations do not explain why and how lower caste groups have inequitable access to health or why they have a higher rate of morbidity than higher castes living in the same area. Or how does mothers' education contribute to better health access and outcomes? Does greater awareness about existing health services or information about causes of a specific disease condition evidently result in better access to services? How do gender norms matter in the utilization of services and health status of women? What are the mechanisms and processes through which such norms are created, practiced and reinforced? Thus, in the language of the CSDH report, evidence on mere associations does not ask fundamental questions about the structures and processes that contribute to and reinforce such inequalities. Additionally, Saikia and Kulkarni [36] in a recent paper argue how the database on the health of the population in India is inadequate to address inequalities in health [36]. This is despite the fact that India draws on more than six different sources for the collection of data on the health status of its population. They argue that many of these surveys are inadequate to reflect on differences in health by socioeconomic groups at district levels and below, and nor do they identify causes of mortality by socioeconomic groups. The framing of the social in the CSDH report is thus beyond identifying 'social factors' (as one set of factors) or associations of social variables with health outcomes. It highlights a social perspective of health whereby the social does not merely add to the predominant form of biomedical knowledge, but shows how health and medicine are socially situated and where the social necessarily includes the political, economic and other factors.

Implications for Research

Social determinants of health as a methodological lens with which to study health equity favours the framing of research questions that demand a deeper investigation of the what, how and why. For example, such a lens, at a broad level, demands interrogation of health inequity by asking: How does one *explain systematic* differences in access, vulnerability and outcomes in health and health care (beyond stating association)? What are the *factors, mechanisms and processes* through which these differences are produced and reinforced (beyond treating health inequity as an individualized, given and natural phenomena)? And what and which levels of *actions* are required to intervene to strive towards health equity (beyond technomanagerial solutions)?[2] Such a line of inquiry, Östlin et al. [37] argue, characterizes a paradigm shift in undertaking health research, demanding the application of a range of methods, perspectives and disciplinary insights largely used in the social sciences and non-biomedical sciences [37]. They explicate this paradigm shift further by identifying four key research priorities. These include the study of (1) global factors and processes that affect health equity; (2) structures and processes that differentially affect people's chances to be healthy within a given society; (3) health system factors that affect health equity; and (4) policies and interventions to reduce health inequity [37].

Such a paradigm shift has several implications in terms of undertaking research through a SDH and health equity lens. We highlight three such implications. The first requires an analysis of factors and processes of inequities at the *intersections* of multiple social locations including caste, class, race, geography etc. Intersectionality as an analytical perspective has been widely used in feminist research to demonstrate how gendered forms of oppression are an outcome of the interactions of different social locations that operate within a connected system of structures and power [38, 39]. Research using an intersectionality framework has shown how inequities never result from individual, isolated and distinct factors (only class, or gender) but are due to the ways that multiple factors intersect with one another. The usefulness of this framework to the study of SDH and health inequity is increasingly being recognized (though often not so explicitly stated as using an intersectionality framework). Samuelsen et al. [40] for example, show how poor, rural, less educated women in Tanzania are subject to systematic processes of exclusion in their efforts to seek care for their sick children. These technologies of exclusion operate in a system of inequitable power relations between health care providers and the women that get reflected in inadequate referral systems, the inefficient organization of health services and the culture of communication [40] explaining how health systems delay the treatment of poor children leading to preventable deaths. Back home, Sébastia [41] shows how patients with severe mental disorders navigate through complex processes of seeking care that are marked by gender, class, place of residence, familial and neighborhood support (and the lack of it) and the responses of the medical institutions. The narratives of these patients defy simple and singular attribution of either gender or class in determining experiences of mental health. Such research, along with many others

[2]IDRC, Canada has begun a Closing the Gap initiative based in the Sree Chitra Tirunal Institute of Medical Science and Technology (SCTIMST), Thiruvanthapuram in order to strengthen the capacity for undertaking health equity research in India. See for details https://www.idrc.ca/en/project/closing-gaps-health-equity-research-initiative-india.

studies in the Indian context and elsewhere, help to explain how multiple locations of disadvantage or multiple axes of discrimination work in ways that lead to inequitable health outcomes [42–46].

Along with intersections, a SDH lens locates research on practices of health inequity at the *interfaces* of different levels and actors—the global/national/subnational and local, the WHO with the national health bureaucracy or the interface of frontline health workers and local communities. Health equity research it requires studying up (Global level initiatives or National Health Mission) as much as studying below (the Village Health and Nutrition Days). Roalkvam et al. [47] expand the usefulness of this concept in a multidisciplinary research on explaining differential immunization coverage in India and Malawi. They seek to demonstrate how 'interfaces' is a useful concept in understanding how global ideas, practices and technologies on health circulate. Interfaces are sites of interactions between different levels and actors which continuously witness processes of translation and the reinterpretation of ideas and practices. Thus ideas/technologies do not flow in a simple, mechanistic way. These sites are on the one hand characterized by relatively established rules and procedures (a Village Health and Nutrition day for example is a not an ad-hoc event but has certain prescribed guidelines that are expected to be followed) and on the other by 'the juxtaposition of distinctive and potentially conflicting sets of values, beliefs, rationalities and intentions' (e.g., notions around institutional delivery or immunization) [44, p. 42] that make translations, reinterpretations and negotiations of policy processes integral to such interfaces. Such a concept enables not merely an examination of the flow and circulation of ideas and technologies across global-local levels but also lends a comparative lens to the understanding of the structural mechanisms at work across different sites. Mishra et al.'s [27] research on Village Health and Nutrition days in the state of Odisha in India and Outreach Vaccination Clinics in districts of Thyolo, Malawi as interfacing sites between the health system and community shows how a focus on such interfaces and observing the interactions that take place between the frontline health workers and mothers offers a granular understanding of the practices and processes that help explain either the increasing rate of immunization coverage or the rate of dropouts from the immunization schedule. As Farmer argues, what happens in Rural Haiti in terms of poor people dying of tuberculosis or HIV/AIDs cannot be comprehended through observing local factors [20]. Thus the tuberculosis deaths in rural Haiti or the local immunization practices in the remote tribal districts in south Odisha or Malawi are manifestations of transnational events/processes. Thus the immunization coverage among the tribal communities in Odisha is as much related to what happens at the sites of the Immunization Day as to the larger global focus on immunization (as part of MDG4 and beyond), the national Government's policies on strengthening of primary health care through the National Rural Health Mission (NRHM) and how these policies unfold through mandatory Immunization Days in each village, incentivizing the health workers and installing stricter monitoring mechanisms. Thus what one witnesses in local sites is a manifestation of global policies as well as a central program like the NRHM unfolding in a specific state and further down the line through a series of translations, interpretations and negotiations [27, 28, 48]. Interfaces like intersections are useful conceptual tools to help understand and map inequitable health practices and the processes that create and sustain them.

A SDH lens distinctly implies that health equity is a political project. It involves the systematic and explicit study of power. The study of power needs methodological sophistication in terms of framing research questions, tools used, sites explored and dissemination of research implications. In an explicit study of power to understand the processes involved in immunization policymaking, McNeill, Andersen and Sandberg examine the different sources of power and authority of a range of actors (including WHO, UNICEF, Bill and Melinda Gates Foundation, International Academic Institutions etc.) [49]. They show how understanding sources of power and how these are played out in concrete situations helps in situating the significance of emerging global alliances, the select verticality of policies and their implementation in national settings, and the continuous changing configurations among different global actors. In an interesting study in Odisha, India, Papp et al discuss how power dynamics in the social accountability process are shaped by providing opportunities and spaces for women to confront those more powerful [50]. Providing these spaces then allows for women to generate the demand for better services and mobilize communities to change the power imbalance. Similarly Sheikh et al.'s [51] examination of the power of different actors unpacks the hidden dynamics shaping the implementation of HIV/AIDS policy guidelines. Recognizing the criticality of addressing power through rigorous research, Erasmus and Gilson [52] draw attention to how power can be methodologically concretized in the study of policy processes in the context of low and middle income countries. While the concept of power is central in social sciences, empirical analyses of power in the emerging field of health policy and system research, and more specifically in addressing health inequity, are few. More research is needed that systematically investigates the role of power in addressing and redressing health inequity.

Implications for Actions

The CSDH Report had a firm message saying that intervening in health inequity is real and actionable, yet this message is marred with ambiguity and contestations. A pertinent tension often expressed by public health practitioners is if research evidence on health equity is so complex that translating it into actions is not feasible, and hence research must be geared towards actionable features. An equally evocative concern shared largely by the academic community is that a focus on 'actions' runs the danger of an inadequate understanding of the 'social' thereby leading to more engineering than systemic solutions. This calls for an ongoing dialogue among several disciplines and stakeholders that demands, in principle, an acknowledgement of such tensions as much as resolving them. Actionable research evidence does not demand compromise on rigor or intellectual blindness but careful translation and dissemination of research findings. Research and practice (focus on actions) are spurious distinctions that will cause harm to the aim of health equity [48]. There is encouraging evidence to show that critical perspectives on SDH are actionable (or are certainly meant to be) and research studies using such perspective do not merely end with messy, thick descriptive data to wonder 'so what?'. If a SDH lens seeks to unpack the understanding of the structural causes of health inequities, it also implies that actions cannot simply be technomanagerial ones. Actions need to have an expanded understanding of unsettling the status quo (where needed), redistribution of power, and knowledge and resources. Such actions qualify for 'system challenging praxis' as much as 'system correcting praxis' [21]. Thus for example, actions need to range from addressing structural features of the health system (the ways in which health systems are governed) to system correcting ones (intersectoral actions, efficient delivery of services etc.) in order to address health. Bhatia and Rifkin [53] argue in this context that a renewed focus on the Alma Ata Declaration in the CSDH demands a *reframing* rather than a mere revitalizing of the principles of primary health care. Research evidence prioritizing a health equity lens shows how actions have included efforts to unsettle gendered norms to prioritize maternal health in a remote community in North Karnataka,[3] ensure equitable health service provision to life threatening illnesses [21], promote equity sensitive primary health care [54], identify and reduce barriers to occupational health [5] and have led to an efficient response by the state to an AIDS epidemic [13]. This volume, in this regard, is an apt and timely exercise to initiate such a dialogue in a meaningful way that showcases several possibilities of combining research with praxis.

Locating the Chapter

This chapter is not necessarily intended to offer anything new. For many social scientists like me, the CSDH report comes as a respite as social science research has been speaking for a long time about why social matters in health are important. The objective of the chapter is not to offer a new set of data, but to reprioritize, revitalize and renew the understanding of SDH in the light of the CSDH report. This is necessary as the collective shouldering of responsibility for actions on health inequity needs a shared understanding of the 'social' conceptually, methodologically and from the point of view of praxis. This chapter has sought to do that by affirming that SDH is indeed a methodological lens with which to approach health inequity, demanding the asking of bold questions and requiring bold solutions to be adopted. Such a framing of the 'social' demands critical and reflective thinking while venturing to crack the complex reality of the conditions which result in health inequities.

[3]The film 'Enough of this silence' (2005), based on research in Koppal district, projects such actions.

References

1. World Health Organisation Commission on Social Determinants of Health. Closing the gap in a generation: health equity through action on the social determinants of health: final report of the commission on social determinants of health. 2008 [cited 2016 Nov 18]; Available from: http://apps.who.int/iris/handle/10665/43943.
2. Bhattacharya S, Messenger S, Overy C, eds. Social determinants of health: assessing theory, policy and practice. Orient Blackswan; 2010.
3. Hunt P. Missed opportunities: human rights and the commission on social determinants of health. Glob Health Promot. 2009;16(1 suppl):36–41.
4. Navarro V. What we mean by social determinants of health. Int J Health Serv. 2009;39 (3):423–41.
5. Schofield T. Health inequity and its social determinants: a sociological commentary. Health Sociol Rev. 2007;16(2):105–14.
6. Irwin A, Valentine N, Brown C, Loewenson R, Solar O, Brown H, et al. The commission on social determinants of health: tackling the social roots of health inequities. PLoS Med. 2006;3 (6):e106.
7. Gwatkin DR, Ergo A. Universal health coverage: friend or foe of health equity? Lancet. 2011;377(9784):2160–1.
8. Latko B, Temporão JG, Frenk J, Evans TG, Chen LC, Pablos-Mendez A, et al. The growing movement for universal health coverage. Lancet. 2011;377(9784):2161–3.
9. Mishra A, Rao SS. Unpacking the discourse on universal health coverage in India. Soc Med. 2016;9(2):86–92.
10. Marmot M. Universal health coverage and social determinants of health. Lancet. 2013;382 (9900):1227–8.
11. Sengupta A, Prasad V. Developing a truly universal Indian health system: the problem of replacing "health for all' with "universal access to health care". Soc Med. 2011;6(2):69–72.
12. Narayan R, Narayan T. Universal health coverage for India. BMJ. 2012;344:e2247.
13. Bastos C. The social determinants of health and the hierarchies of knowledge. Soc Determinants Health Assess Policy Theor Pract. 2010;263–271.
14. McKeown T. The modern rise of population. London: Edward Arnold; 1976.
15. Illich I. Medical nemesis. New York: Pantheon. 1976;30:41.
16. Marmot MG, Rose G, Shipley M, Hamilton PJ. Employment grade and coronary heart disease in British civil servants. J Epidemiol Community Health. 1978;32(4):244–9.
17. Marmot MG, Shipley MJ, Rose G. Inequalities in death—specific explanations of a general pattern? Lancet. 1984;323(8384):1003–6.
18. Marmot MG, Stansfeld S, Patel C, North F, Head J, White I, et al. Health inequalities among British civil servants: the Whitehall II study. Lancet. 1991;337(8754):1387–93.
19. Court SD. Inequalities in health. Report of a research working group. Arch Dis Child. 1981;56(3):161.
20. Farmer P. Infections and inequalities: the modern plagues. University of California Press; 2001.
21. Farmer PE, Nizeye B, Stulac S, Keshavjee S. Structural violence and clinical medicine. PLoS Med. 2006;3(10):e449.
22. Parker M, Harper I. The anthropology of public health. J Biosoc Sci. 2006;38(01):1–5.
23. Narayan T. A violation of citizens' rights: the health sector and tuberculosis. Issues Med Ethics. 1999;7:3.
24. Das V, Das RK. Urban health and pharmaceutical consumption in Delhi, India. J Biosoc Sci. 2006;38(1):69.
25. George A. Persistence of high maternal mortality in Koppal district, Karnataka, India: observed service delivery constraints. Reprod Health Matters. 2007;15(30):91–102.
26. Greenough P. Introduction. Soc Sci Med. 1995;41(5):605–7.

27. Mishra A, Flikke R, Nordfeldt C, Nyirenda L. Immunization is good for your children': local immunization practices in India and Malawi. Prot Worlds' Child Immun Policies Pract. 2013;149–186.
28. Mishra A. "Trust and teamwork matter": community health workers' experiences in integrated service delivery in India. Glob Public Health. 2014;9(8):960–74.
29. Nichter M. Vaccinations in the Third World: a consideration of community demand. Soc Sci Med. 1995;41(5):617–32.
30. Ross CE, Wu C-L. The links between education and health. Am Sociol Rev. 1995;60 (5):719–45.
31. Dahl E. Social inequalities in ill-health: the significance of occupational status, education and income-results from a Norwegian survey. Sociol Health Illn. 1994;16(5):644–67.
32. Dey DK, Mishra V. Determinants of choice of health care services utilization: empirical evidence from India. Indian J Community Health. 2014 Dec 15;26(4):356–63.
33. Mehta S, Parmar GB, Gamit CL, Mansuri BM, Patel PB, Patel SS. Does maternal education affect maternal and child health care utilization? A community based study in a urban slum area of western India. 2014. [cited 2016 Nov 18]; Available from: http://imsear.li.mahidol.ac.th/handle/123456789/176207.
34. Govindasamy P, Ramesh BM. Maternal education and the utilization of maternal and child health services in India. 1997. [cited 2016 Nov 18]; Available from: http://scholarspace.manoa.hawaii.edu/handle/10125/3472.
35. Choudhury PK. Explaining the role of parental education in the regional variations in infant mortality in India. Asia Pac Policy Stud. 2015;2(3):544–72.
36. Saikia, N, Kulkarni P. Data for research into health inequalities in India: Do we have enough? Econ Polit Wkly. 2016;(11):26 & 27.
37. Östlin P, Schrecker T, Sadana R, Bonnefoy J, Gilson L, Hertzman C, et al. Priorities for research on equity and health: towards an equity-focused health research agenda. PLoS Med. 2011;8(11):e1001115.
38. McGibbon E, McPherson C. Applying intersectionality & complexity theory to address the social determinants of women's health. 2011. [cited 2016 Nov 18]; Available from: https://tspace.library.utoronto.ca/handle/1807/27217.
39. Sen G, Iyer A, Mukherjee C. A methodology to analyse the intersections of social inequalities in health. J Hum Dev Capab. 2009;10(3):397–415.
40. Samuelsen H, Tersbøl BP, Mbuyita SS. Do health systems delay the treatment of poor children? A qualitative study of child deaths in rural Tanzania. BMC Health Serv Res. 2013;13(1):1.
41. Sébastia B. The last resort: Why patients with severe mental disorders go to therapeutic shrines in India. Restoring Ment Health India Pluralistic Ther Concepts. 2009;184–209.
42. Roodt D. Yesterday, Film (Language English and Julu). HBO Films: USA; 2004.
43. Sen G, Iyer A, George A. Systematic hierarchies and systemic failures: Gender and health inequities in Koppal District. Econ Polit Wkly. 2007;682–90.
44. Jeffery P, Jeffery R. Only when the boat has started sinking: a maternal death in rural north India. Soc Sci Med. 2010;71(10):1711–8.
45. Holmes SM. An ethnographic study of the social context of migrant health in the United States. PLoS Med. 2006;3(10):e448.
46. Chard SE. Routes to government TB treatment. Med Anthropol Q. 2009;23(3):257–76.
47. Roalkvam S, McNeill D, Blume S. Protecting the world's children: immunisation policies and practices [Internet]. OUP Oxford; 2013.
48. Mishra A. Anthropology and public health. Indian Anthropol. 2013;(special issue):42.
49. McNeill, D, Andersen, S, Sandberg, K. The global politics of health: actors and initiatives. In Roalkvam S, Mcneill D, Blume S, editors. Protecting the world's children: Immunization policies and practices. Oxford University Press.
50. Papp SA, Gogoi A, Campbell C. Improving maternal health through social accountability: a case study from Orissa. India. Glob Public Health. 2013;8(4):449–64.

51. Sheikh K, Porter JD. Disempowered doctors? A relational view of public health policy implementation in urban India. Health Policy Plan. 2010;26:83–92.
52. Erasmus E, Gilson L. How to start thinking about investigating power in the organizational settings of policy implementation. Health Policy Plan. 2008;23(5):361–8.
53. Bhatia M, Rifkin S. A renewed focus on primary health care: revitalize or reframe? Globalisation and Health. 2010;6(13).
54. Wong ST, Browne AJ, Varcoe C, Lavoie J, Smye V, Godwin O, et al. Enhancing measurement of primary health care indicators using an equity lens: an ethnographic study. Int J Equity Health. 2011;10(1):1.

Chapter 3
Conceptual Issues of Conflict as a Social Determinant of Health: Explorations from Manipur

Veda Yumnam and Rajib Dasgupta

Abstract One-sixth of India's population lives in areas of conflict (including the insurgency-riddled states of the North-East, the secessionist violence in Kashmir, and the struggle to capture power by Maoist groups in several regions of the country). Most armed conflicts generate major public health consequences, both in terms of the population's health status and the structure, policies, and financing of the health system (Watts et al. in Social determinants of health in countries in conflict and crises: the eastern mediterranean perspective, [1]; WHO in Regional Office for the Eastern Mediterranean, [2]). Conflict not only has implications for health status, but also has serious consequences for the broad social and economic determinants and conditions that affect people's health crisis settings (Watts et al. in Social determinants of health in countries in conflict and crises: the eastern mediterranean perspective, [1]). The WHO Regional Office for the Eastern Mediterranean [2] identifies conflict as a social determinant of health that bears on health through the loss of human rights, breaches in medical neutrality, and progression from stress to distress and disease that results in constant exposure to life-threatening circumstances. Moreover, conflict reinforces existing SDH: in conflict settings, the marginalized and poverty stricken face a widening of pre-existing inequalities and differentials in health status and consequences. This paper will explore these relationships and their impacts in the Indian context, with a particular emphasis on the state of Manipur, which has been rife with conflict for over four decades.

Keywords Conflict · North-East India · Social and economic determinants Manipur

---

V. Yumnam (✉)
Department of Social Work, Tezpur University, Tezpur, Assam, India
e-mail: veda.yumnam@gmail.com

R. Dasgupta
Centre of Social Medicine and Community Health, Jawaharlal Nehru University, New Delhi, India

D. Nambiar and A. Muralidharan (eds.), *The Social Determinants of Health in India*, https://doi.org/10.1007/978-981-10-5999-5_3

Introduction

The twentieth century has been marked by an unparalleled increase in armed conflicts worldwide [3]. Not only has it affected both the physical and social structures of affected communities [4] but it has also led to enormous destruction of both the human and physical capital that are key to improvements in social and economic development. According to conservative estimates, at least 200,000 people die each year in conflict zones from non-violent causes *besides* direct the immediate fatalities caused by conflicts [5]. Also, ascertaining an estimate of morbidity and mortality data becomes a challenge in most conflict and war-torn areas as the types, length and intensity of conflict differ due to limited data collection and difficulty in recording the data as a large number of indirect deaths and morbidity happen due to collapse or weak health service system [6]. Conflicts are not usually purviewed within the usual framework of social determinants of health (SDH). This review will focus on the emerging concepts that link conflict with the diverse facets of SDH.

Contemporary India is characterized by insurgencies and conflicts rooted in pluralities, hierarchies and socioeconomic inequities [3]. An estimated one-sixth of the country's population lives in areas of conflict that include: (i) insurgency-ridden states of the North-East; (ii) secessionist violence in Kashmir; and, (iii) the struggle to capture power by Maoists in the large 'Red Belt', spread across nearly 200 districts of the country [3, 6]. While the nature, origin and the ideological bases of these conflicts vary, their modes and praxis are shared. In such situations, not only is the harmonious existence of people threatened, but numerous fault lines emerge through diverse forms of newer and intractable inequalities, grievances and recurrences of conflicts [7, 8].

Understanding the Concept

Defining a universally accepted concept of civil war, as well as determining the differences between war, civil war and civil conflict is crucial to developing measures to deal with them at a practical level [9]. The failure to classify these concepts has grave legal and humanitarian consequences as the distinction determines the application of laws under the framework of international humanitarian law (IHL)[1] and its shift to other normative frameworks, if not applicable. Nevertheless, IHL distinguishes between two types of armed conflict: (i) international armed conflicts (IAC) and (ii) non-international armed conflicts (NIAC) [10]. IAC, according to the Geneva Conventions of 1949, common article 2, is defined as '*all cases of declared war or of any armed conflict that may arise between two or more high contracting*

[1]IHL is defined to be the law of war. The laws under it are meant to be active in a situation of armed conflict or during war.

parties, even if the state of war is not recognized…'; NIAC, according to article 3 of the same convention, are '*armed conflicts that are non-international in nature occurring in one of the high contracting parties*' that implies one of the parties involved is non-governmental and does not include other forms of violence like riots or sporadic incidence of violence [11].

It is becoming increasingly difficult to categorise conflicts as either international or non-international in character. Most conflicts are multidimensional, multicausal and involves both inter and intrastate actors.

Understanding Conflict as a Social Determinant of Health (SDH)

Most armed conflicts generate major public health consequences, both in terms of the health status of populations as well as in the structure, policies, and financing of the health system [1, 2]. Conflict, therefore, has implications for health status as well as serious consequences on upstream social and economic determinants that affect people's health in crisis settings [2].

The World Health Organization's (WHO) Regional Office for the Eastern Mediterranean [2] identifies conflict *as* a SDH as well as a factor in reinforcing existing inequities *in* SDH.

(I) **Conflict as a SDH**: Three determinants have a bearing on health in conflict settings: (i) loss of human rights; (ii) breaches in medical neutrality; and, (iii) the progression from stress to distress and disease that results in constant exposure to life-threatening circumstances.

(II) **Conflict reinforces existing SDH**: Conventional SDH are reinforced in conflict settings; inequalities and the differentials in health outcomes widen in marginalized and poverty-stricken communities.

Beyond the immediate increases in mortality and morbidity owing to direct impacts, conflict has a strong bearing on the health of the people as populations are displaced, health and social services collapse, and risk of disease transmission increases [12, 13]. Long-term effects include disabilities and injuries caused by unexploded ordnance and landmines, as well as psychological trauma of survivors and victims.

Recognizing conflict as a determinant has implications for health service delivery in conflict-affected regions of Kashmir, the Maoist insurgencies and other states in the North-East. There is a dearth of documentation of the implications of the conflict on the functioning of the health services. It is an area that has not been well researched and has so far failed to get academic or programmatic (barring limited efforts by the International Committee of the Red Cross in Chhattisgarh) attention in India. Most of the documented work is from war-affected zones in the Western context and some limited work has been carried out in South Asian countries. A lack of a grounded understanding of the implications of conflict in India will have its impact on the health status of the people and the local health services systems. As the states affected by conflict are already marked by a weak health services system (and geographic challenges), it is methodologically difficult to establish a direct causal relationship of the impact of the conflict.

I

Health services systems, as defined by the WHO, are comprised of three crucial components—organizations, institutions and resources—that are involved in actions to improve health [14]. Conflict and political turmoil impact all three of these components [15]. It is imperative to deconstruct the various components and the interfaces that bring about improvement in the health status of the people as either **a** *determinant* and/or a *reinforcer of the existing determinants* [2].

As a Determinant

Caring for the Carer

The Geneva Convention of 1949 and its two protocols of 1977 and 2005 provide protection for health professionals in international and non-international conflicts, mandating adherence from the warring parties. As per the convention, '*medical assistance is viewed as a neutral activity, which should be universally accessible to the wounded, sick and prisoners of war*' (Article 11) and '*impose the duty on warring parties to not interfere with medical care for wounded or sick combatants and civilians, and not attack, threaten, or impede medical functions*' (Article 6). Despite the existence of the normative framework enshrined in the Geneva Convention, providers of health care are under constant threat of impediments to health care delivery. Health care providers face violence and interference from both state and non-state parties in conflict regions while carrying out their responsibilities. They (and not infrequently, family members) face extortion, rape, kidnapping, harassment, brutality and deaths, and may migrate to more peaceful areas [16].

Migration of health care workers to better professional, economic and secured environments is common [17]. The level of security that the place of destination offers plays an important role in decision-making beyond conventional 'pull factors' such as better job prospects and economic incentives [18]. Violence-induced migration not only affects the availability of frontline providers but the absence of teachers in medical colleges and other paramedical institutions hampers the development and rebuilding of the health system in the post-conflict phase [19].

Military expenses may result in cuts in health care expenditure resulting in a decrease of supplies or training, and the transition of the workforce to urban and peaceful areas. The lack of growth and skills development not only causes deterioration of the services but also leads to other adverse outcomes too. Providers working in the public sector may moonlight or practice privately within public facilities and start consultancy, research and teaching activities to compensate for an inadequate salary [20]. The workforce may shift from the public sector to relief and international agencies that provide attractive remuneration and compensation. 'Ghost-workers[2]' may proliferate in conflict settings, continuing to get their salaries despite being absent from duty [21]. Fear of possible abduction and the risk of being exposed to the warring parties makes health care providers hesitant to undertake field visits and consequently monitoring and supervisory visits tend to get severely affected [22].

Health Infrastructure

In conflicts and other situations of violence, health infrastructure can be destroyed by bombing, shelling and shooting [23]. These facilities may be forcibly occupied by militants and security forces alike, entailing the destruction and looting of supplies and equipment, and disruption of basic supplies such as water and electricity [15]. Article 12 of Protocol II of The Geneva Convention sets the legal obligation clearly: '*health infrastructure shall be respected and protected at all times and shall not be the object of attack*'.

Health care facilities may be taken over by security forces for makeshift use or military operations, rendering them unavailable for health care delivery in regions affected by violence and conflict [22]. Entry of the militants and the security forces in search of the enemy or rival groups in the vicinity or inside the facility imposes fear and exposes both the users of these facilities and health care workers to additional risks. Looting of medical supplies and equipment by the warring parties is also reported in conflict areas [24]. Restrictions in the operation of international and relief organizations in civil conflicts and war, and in or other health related projects minimizes the health facilities available to conflict affected regions. To add to the complexity, the economic stresses caused by war/conflict along with the disruption of normal administrative systems, leads to a reduction in the generation of revenues and the failure of the state to impose taxation leading to further declines in the availability of funds for the social sectors [15, 25].

[2]A ghost worker is a person on an organization's payroll, either real or fictitious, who does not actually work for that organization.

II

Reinforcers of Existing Inequities of SDH

A good health service delivery with equitable access is crucial for the health care needs of the people. In conflict settings, service delivery becomes substandard, disrupted and inequitable. Frequent disruption caused by violent activities, strikes, road blockades, restrictions in mobility and threats faced both by the providers and the users render the delivery process compromised, denied or inequitable [1, 2].

Barriers in Services Access and Delivery

In areas with large-scale and prolonged conflicts, access to preventive health care becomes more limited and conditional due to the insecurity exacerbated by the crises. Disruption and hindrance in the implementation of preventive services requiring multiple and sustained activities such as routine immunization, and tuberculosis or leprosy control programmes tend to be the more adversely affected. Average working hours are reduced, thereby impeding the delivery of quality health care amongst the people [26]. The arbitrary denial of services faced by many wounded and sick in conflict-affected regions, and the suboptimal standard of care provided in the public sector generally, lead to the gradual shift to private services [27].

The concentration of more specialists and staff at secondary and tertiary levels and barriers to health care access in remote areas (exacerbated by difficult terrain, lack of road networks and transportation facilities) prevent an equitable delivery of health services. Disruption of preventive services due to a lack of necessary infrastructure such as refrigeration facilities and the proper storage of vaccines and medicines hampers the undisrupted provision of medical supplies and vaccines.

Inequity in Service Provisioning

Conflict itself is the fundamental driver of health inequity in conflict-affected regions. It tends to contribute to the emergence of poverty traps amongst specific vulnerable groups on account of the inequality of opportunities and restricted—or lack of—access to resources [28]. Importantly, availability of resources alone does not ensure accessibility to health care; access is determined by other SDH [2].

Geographic disparities in access to health care are prominent in conflict settings. Moreover, the difficult geographical terrain in conflict-affected regions results in the worst health indicators characterized by high mortality and morbidities due to preventable and treatable conditions. Another aspect that enhances inequities is gender-based violence induced by war and conflict. Gender identity influences the level of exposure to situations that have a bearing on access to health care and the choice and type of services received by them [29].

Service Utilization

Gross underutilization of services and health facilities due to fear of violence, curfews and *bandhs*, and harassment from the security forces lowers access to health services in conflict settings [15, 30]. Under such circumstances, supply side factors such as location and distance that vulnerable communities have to travel, and the level of security both in the area of the health facility and on the way to access the services, determine the likelihood of service utilization [31]. Another important constraint is the delay in receiving health care due to being stopped and questioned at various checkpoints and detours [32].

Conflict situations have considerable impact on the access to and utilization of reproductive and sexual health programs, with morbidities being further escalated [33]. Since information, supplies and access to services are all greatly affected, women may face problems in utilizing family planning services and other obstetric care, resulting in unplanned pregnancies and unsafe abortions, and increased deaths on account of complicated pregnancies [34].

Breaking Down of Social Fabric

Conflict and violence-affected regions are typically marked by disrupted social networks and a lack of trust amongst populations and groups that acts as an adverse determinant of health [15]. Conflicts and fights among different ethnic or social groups can be widespread and protracted. Large displacements due to the conflict destroying the existing social fabric, further act as a significant factor in the increased inequities in health.

Concordance in terms of ethnicity and race has proven to have a strong correlation with patient satisfaction and a higher self-rated quality of health care [35]. It is more visible in protracted conflict where the mobilization of the people is carried out along ethnic and racial lines. Given the situation that providers understand the social and cultural context of the population they serve, the racial/ethnic compositions of the workforce contribute to the availability and accessibility of health care [35]. In situations of sectarian violence, social geography plays a more important role than physical geography [36]. Ethnicity and/or religious affiliation as a contributory factor in determining access to health care and health status in conflict settings is already established. The fear of threats and violence, mutual mistrust and lack of interethnic confidence in the quality of care provided by other communities, may lead to compromises in the quality and access of health care delivered by the other communities.

Identities based on religion, ethnicity, language, livelihood, gender or place of residence may become the core of the conflict and play a strong force in the processes that determine health of diverse populations [2]. Women, children and geriatric populations sufferer the most in conflict and war situations. Gender-based crimes and violence become escalated [6]. Delays in seeking care due to the insecure environment, restricted mobility, unavailability of escorts, and the untimely access of trained birth attendants, have been documented [37]. Childhood morbidity and mortality are exacerbated due to heightened exposure to infectious diseases, living in unsanitary and insecure environments, lack of sufficient food, and access to quality services [6]. A strong influence on health from the changing social behaviour and the erosion of social norms and values system has also been noted. During intense fighting and prolonged war, cases of male migration in search of work or in order to fight, lead to the breaking down of traditional networks that form the foundation of social and family roles [38]. Traditional social networks break down in conflict settings and under such circumstances, cases of women taking up new social and economic roles leads to a change in the social status of the women that may make them more vulnerable and expose them to more risks and pushes them further down the social ladder [1, 2].

Poverty

Pre-existing poverty is exacerbated by long-standing conflict [1]. Landmines, bombing and shelling in conflict and war situations lead to the destruction of livelihoods, agricultural land, crops and livestock, in turn leading to declines in food and grain production. These have a direct bearing on the availability of food and income levels [13]. Poor nutritional intake and the collapse of health care services make people more susceptible to diseases.

III

Explorations from the Manipur Conflict

Manipur is home to more than 36 indigenous tribes groups and has an estimated 30 armed groups representing several ethnicities with multiple and competing demands. The state has witnessed ‘a rise of the culture of assertion or domination of group identity’ [39]. The state has witnessed sustained conflict and its breakdown has been considered as ‘extreme in the media and political circle’ and [40]. The multi-ethnic makeup and the constant power struggle of different ethnic groups for domination of limited resources has made the state an area of protracted conflict. The demands of the various armed groups of the state vary from demands of

Table 3.1 Mapping the causal matrix of Manipur's conflict

Conflict	Causal factors
Naga/Kuki versus Meitei	• Identity • Power struggle • Land/territory preservation
Meitei versus Indian State	• Secessionism • Territory preservation
Naga versus Indian State/Meitei	Sub-nationalism
Meitei versus Meitei-Muslim	Identify and power inequalities

Source Compiled by the authors

autonomy to separation from the Union of India. While most of the valley-based[3] groups seek to restore Manipur's pre-merger status, the hill-based groups want either to carve out an exclusive homeland or to integrate parts of Manipur into the neighbouring state of Nagaland [40–42].

Understanding the nature and typology of conflict in Manipur is complex. It is linked to diverse sociopolitical, economic and historical contexts. Two broad strands emerged while understanding the typology of the situation prevalent in the state: (i) the conflict between the state and the society; and, (ii) the 'internal conflict'—which in the context of Manipur is on the lines of the ethnic identity formation amongst different ethnic communities [43].

Conflicts in Manipur are context-specific, multicausal and multidimensional so underpinning and establishing a direct causal relation of conflict and health outcomes is difficult. Table 3.1 summarizes the diverse discourses of conflict in the state. There are overlaps in the causal factors of the different conflicts.

Frequent *bandhs*, transportation blockades and insurgency have become regular features in the lives of the people in the state; the delivery of public services continues without the consideration to bring any linkages with the prevalent political instability in the state. Despite being in conflict for decades, the implications of the conflict on the health services system of Manipur is grossly under-researched and inadequately understood. Blunted by chronic disruptions to the health services system for decades, consequences that are fallouts of the conflict are instead considered a result of an already weak health services system.

The absence of service providers, lack of drugs and commodities, unequal distribution of health resources, lack of functioning of health infrastructure, and the absence of supervisory visits [44, 45] are under the radar and invisible. Many conditions that threaten or hamper the working of the health services system are not recognized and synced into the larger existing social structure. No literature or government document focuses on the relevant linkages between the two.

[3]Four valley district and five hill districts in Manipur. The valley based groups are Kangleipak Communist Party (KCP), Kanglei Yawol Kanna Lup (KYKL), Manipur People's Liberation Front (MPLF), People's Revolutionary Party of Kangleipak (PREPAK), People's Liberation Army (PLA) and United National Liberation Front (UNLF).

Table 3.2 Incidence of reported violence (media reporting) in Manipur affecting different health services system in Manipur, 2011–2014

Years	Attacks/threats to health care providers*	Bombing/hurling of grenade/planting of IEDs in premises of health care institutions*	Demands of extortion to health care providers*	Arrest of insurgents inside premises of health care institutions*
March 2014	3	Nil	1	Nil
2013	2	7 (4 inside the complex of RIMS)	Nil	2
2012	4	11 (5 inside the complex of RIMS)	Nil	Nil
2011	6	3	Nil	Nil

Source South Asia Terrorism Portal [46]
* Compiled by the author

Health care providers undergo physical and mental violence and the destruction of health facilities has led to the disruption of medical care [45]. The inability to reach health facilities and health campsites—or delays in doing so—were reported by health care providers due to frequent stopping and attendant frisking from both state and non-state conflicting parties and sometimes from civilians supporting the cause. Ambulances are used to provide pick and drop facilities to the doctors and other paramedical staff. Health facilities at the periphery and at district level are provided with security personnel on the premises of the health facilities to allow them to provide the services.

Inequities in the allocation of health infrastructure and human resources *across* hill and plains districts, as well as *within* the conflict-affected districts can be observed. The delivery of public services in Manipur is further hindered by the frequent outbreak of violent conflicts and their impacts, especially in those hill districts and areas which already have the lowest socioeconomic and health indicators. The disruption is felt more in rural areas and hill regions as compared to the plains and the urban areas, and is not merely due to the concentration of health care facilities, but is also due to the presence of better health process determinants like roads and transport. Table 3.2 summarizes media reports to illustrate some of the key findings.

Furthermore, the 'response mechanism' for health services to such a crisis calls forth an increased and sustained action that could be drawn from the learning of other sectors such as disaster risk reduction (DRR) to mitigate the consequences of the crisis. The DRR literature looks at conflict as a hazard that can be mitigated by quick response and relief, and sustained rehabilitative measures. However, in situations of protracted conflict, and in a context like Manipur, with a conflict of multicausal and multidimensional nature, it is crucial for the successful implementation of any programme and service delivery mechanism for humanitarian assistance to respond to a common global agreement on the minimum standards across the humanitarian sector, be it for health or any public service delivery.

International organizations like Médecins Sans Frontières (MSF) and the International Committee of the Red Cross (ICRC) that focus and respond to humanitarian crises are operational in Manipur. The operation of such organizations in itself calls forth for the recognition of the state as a conflict zone (it is currently conveniently described as having a 'law and order' problem) in order to uphold the core humanitarian standards of response to a humanitarian crisis.

Concluding Comments

Conflict areas are an emerging and serious challenge across parts of India. They are characterized by geographical inaccessibility, chronic poverty, tribal and marginal populations, and more than usually weak health (and other public) services. While diverse approaches are underway to strengthen health service systems in India, there is no formal recognition of conflict as a social determinant. While we have reported some of the initial explorations from Manipur, similar experiences abound in other North-Eastern states, and the health consequences of recent ethnic conflicts in Assam are a case in point. Left-wing extremist violence has led to the near collapse of health services in several parts of Central Indian states and districts. That these are considered as war zones in state officialdom has led to the Red Cross being asked to withdraw from some of these areas—where they were the only source of health services. The Chhattisgarh Government has recently taken some out-of-the-box steps to address crises of human resources in selected districts. Formal research is urgently required for a more nuanced understanding of conflict as a SDH in the Indian situation to make meaningful course corrections and interventions. The need for a methodological interface between conflict studies and public health is needed as the understanding of the impact of conflict on health services system still remains weak aside from various fact-finding reports of civil society organizations and various government officials highlighting the impact of conflict on health in India.

Commentary—Violence, Conflict and Health: The Challenges

Prabir Chatterjee
State Health Resource Centre, Raipur, Chhattisgarh, India

Below are some reflections on possible ways to understand how conflicts relate to health. We have different disciplinary areas that have bodies of corresponding research that could help shape our view on this. Equity studies, peace studies and disaster studies are highlighted here.

Equity Studies is the discipline that is well known as addressing the issue of Access in Health. Amartya Sen's book "Equity Re-examined" looked at life expectancy in Dhaka and a slum in New York. Life expectancy was less in the

New York slums. There are also many reports by UNICEF, which take into account access to health services and other social factors.

There are three types of equity that have often been described and have entered recent SDH (Social Determinants of Health) literature;

- Geographic access
- Economic access (poverty, occupation)
- Social access (stigma, gender, class, caste, community and so on).

The authors of the article on Health and Conflict (with examples from Manipur) have rightly pointed to similar categories when describing the social determinants that are affected by conflict.

The reports from Syria recently, of civil war leading to internal displacement; mass exodus to Turkey and Egypt, life in camps, groups falling prey to traffickers, deaths at sea, deaths in trucks, being attacked in Hungary, and crossing to camps in Austria etc. are a common description of the early effects of violence anywhere. Events in India followed a similar pattern in Bangladesh in 1971, or in Jaffna or Punjab or Tibet or Kashmir or Nepal. Even some Afghans, Iranians and Burmese fled to India after conflicts in those regions.

Peace Studies in India (called Conflict Studies in some centres) is still in its infancy. It studies different types of conflict and peace work. 'Riots' are supposedly not wars, yet a riot involving a few armed actors on one side can result in displacement that may resemble the effect of an official war. The effect of riots and long-term displacement may even be more extreme in health terms than that of wars. Wars kill immediately. Displacement kills slowly—sometimes over many years.

This is a report from Bodoland (on the western border of Assam):

> One of the most severe consequences in the camps which is largely being overlooked is the breakdown in the.... care for women experiencing pregnancy... . (and)... for infants.
>
> ...absence of ASHA workers... higher risk of non-detection of medical emergencies ... also... non-distribution of basic supplements such as iron, folic acid, calcium and vitamins...
>
> The... number of ambulances deployed for servicing 19366 displaced persons is 8... a ratio of 242... serviced by 1 ambulance ...
>
> ... There are a number of **camps that are unlisted in the official data that are facing food insecurity and adverse conditions of water, sanitation and hygiene**.
>
> There is also a high presence of risk factors that can lead to waterborne disease ....[4]

While war is a full scale 'epidemic', the conflict/violence in Chirang has persisted for a long time—it is an 'endemic' disaster. In the language of public health,

[4]Sinha S. Field Assessment Report on the ongoing humanitarian crisis in BTAD districts of Assam (post 23 December killings). Chiran District 7–8 January. Centre for Study of Political Violence, OP Jindal Global University; 2014. http://www.jsia.edu.in/cspv/pdf/CPSVHumanitarianAssessmentReportChirangDistrict.pdf.

a riot is an 'outbreak' of violence with immediate casualties. This violence has been studied in the North-East and parts of Central India. The presence of violence is less recognized in the developmental conflicts and displacements such as in Narmada, Kashipur or Kudankulam. And those conflicts are not always counted where caste tensions displace a community to the *cheri* on the edge of a village in South India. Yet this too is endemic violence and has an effect on the health of the displaced persons in the 'colony'. There are also 'outbreaks' of direct violence in places like Karamchedu and Maharashtra, and even 'epidemics' in Kandhmal. Has Kandhmal led to health consequences?

One could also ask questions about much quoted examples from West Bengal in the last decade. Was Amlasole (a tribal village in Midnapore that suffered deaths from starvation) wholly a health/nutrition question, or was it mixed up with violent movements (the 'Lalgarh' movement)?

Is Dheklapara in Jalpaiguri (where the press alleged deaths from starvation) wholly a health/nutrition question, or is it related to colonies of displaced tribals in a tea garden closed for 12 years? Is the displacement of the tea tribes not endemic violence?

Disaster Studies is yet another related area of study. In this field, one category is Man-made Disasters. This term includes disasters due to violent conflicts. Disaster Risk Reduction (DRR) specialists and humanitarian agencies seek to reduce conflicts but also look at health issues that may arise if conflict breaks out. They also prepare for emergencies.

There is a common agreement among humanitarian agencies to follow the Core Humanitarian Standards (www.corehumanitarianstandard.org). In this understanding, humanitarian action is guided by four principles*:

- Humanity: Human suffering must be addressed wherever it is found. The purpose of humanitarian action is to protect life and health and ensure respect for human beings.
- Impartiality: Humanitarian action must be carried out on the basis of need alone, giving priority to the most urgent cases of distress and making no adverse distinction on the basis of nationality, race, gender, religious belief, class or political opinion.
- Independence: Humanitarian action must be autonomous from the political, economic, military or other objectives that any actor may hold with regard to areas where humanitarian action is being implemented.
- Neutrality: Humanitarian actors must not take sides in hostilities or engage in controversies of a political, racial, religious or ideological nature.

In Disaster Studies we find that **R**isk is often dependent on pre-existing inequity/social determinants. A formula that is used is (**R = H** × **V/C**). Here, disaster risk reduction involves describing known **H**azards (like conflict) and identifying **V**ulnerable groups and local **C**apacities to adapt or respond.

By building up community capacities, and by reducing vulnerabilities the community becomes more able to withstand a hazard. This ability of the community to recover after hazards is called Resilience. Increasing resilience means that health risks are less.

Thus malnutrition in children of a middle-class community will be less a month after the riot than the malnutrition among children in a community of poor single parent households. Different social groups have different patterns of malnutrition even during the same conflict. Risk reduction predicts this and tries to ensure services to combat malnutrition even before there is open violence.

Any disaster may change geographic/economic/social access. In which case new 'vulnerable' groups are created. They may be refugees, stay in camps or else stay in areas not currently under the regular administration for either a short period or for years on end (e.g. the Santals displaced in Kokrajhar). And they then need to be responded to in a neutral way by independent agencies. The actors in the conflict are by definition not neutral. So even if a government or an armed actor (e.g. Mukti Bahini in Bangladesh) has a health system, it may be necessary to allow the health department to work independently from the military forces. Otherwise, one could solve this by allowing other neutral agencies to approach groups who are at risk or allow them to coordinate health work until peace is restored.

It would be to our advantage to bring thinking from Equity Studies, studies of the access to health, from Peace Studies, from DRR, from Humanitarian Action, and from Development Studies together in order to promote interdisciplinary and interregional discussions on responses to conflict and health in South Asia.

References

1. Watts S, Siddiqi S, Shukrullah A, Karim K, Serag H. Social determinants of health in countries in conflict and crises: the eastern mediterranean perspective. Health Policy and Planning Unit, Division of Health System Eastern Mediterranean Regional Office, World Health Organization, Cairo; 2007.
2. WHO. Regional Office for the Eastern Mediterranean. Social determinants of health in countries in conflict: a perspective from the Eastern Mediterranean/World Health Organization. Regional Office for the Eastern Mediterranean; 2008.
3. Chenoy AM, Chenoy KM. Maoist and other armed conflicts. New Delhi: Penguin; 2010.
4. Brunborg H, Urdal H. The demography of conflict and violence: an introduction. J Peace Res. 2005;42(4):371–4.
5. Geneva Declaration. Global burden of armed violence report. Geneva: Geneva Declaration Secretariat. 2008. Retrieved from: www.genevadeclaration.org, http://www.genevadeclaration.org/fileadmin/docs/Global-Burden-of-Armed-Violence-full-report.pdf.
6. Siddarth D. et al. Conflict in South Asia and its impact on health. BMJ. 2017; 357:1537.
7. Neogi D. Disparity in socio-economic development and its implications on communal conflicts: a study on India's north-eastern region. Int J Hum Soc Sci. 2010;5:5.
8. Sophie Maier A. Government of India's Northeast policy. India: Heinrich Boll Stiftung; 2009.
9. Andersen D, Barten U, Jensen P. Challenges to civil war research introduction to the special issue on civil war and conflicts. JEMIE. 2009;8:1–9.
10. Chelimo GC. Defining armed conflict in international humanitarian law. Student Pulse. 2011;3(4). Retrieved from http://www.studentpulse.com/a?id=508.

11. Bouvier AA. International humanitarian law and the law of armed conflict. USA: Peace Operations Training Institute; 2012.
12. Iqbal Zaryab. Health and human security: the public health impact of violent conflict. Int Stud Quart. 2006;50(3):631–49.
13. Guha-Sapir D, van Panhuis WG. Armed conflict and public health: A report on knowledge and knowledge gaps. Rockfeller Foundation, New York, USA. Brussels: CRED; 2002.
14. WHO. The world health report 2000: health systems: improving performance. World Health Organization, Switzerland; 2000.
15. Waters H, Garrett B, Burnham G. Rehabilitating health systems in post-conflict situations. Research Paper No. 2007/06. UNU-WIDER; 2007.
16. Seikh M, Gutierrez MI, Bolton P, Thieren M, Burham G. Deaths among humanitarian workers. BMJ. 2000;321(7254):166–8.
17. Pavignani E. The impact of complex emergencies on the health workforce. Health Emergencies. 2003;18. Geneva: World Health Organization.
18. Stilwel B. Migration of healthcare workers from developing countries: strategies approaches to its management. Bull Health Organ. 2004;82:595–600.
19. Burnham GM, Lafta R, Doocy S. Doctors leaving 12 tertiary hospitals in Iraq, 2004–2007. Soc Sci Med. 2009;69:172–7.
20. Van Lerberghe W, Porignon D. Of coping, poaching and the harm they can do. In: Health in emergencies, vol. 18. Geneva: WHO; 2003.
21. Pavvignani E. Mozambique 1990–2002: restructuring the health workforce after the war. In: Health in emergencies, vol. 18. Geneva: WHO; 2003.
22. Devkota MD. An assessment on impact of conflict on delivery of health services. Kathmandu: The World Bank; 2005.
23. ICRC. Health care in danger: A sixteen country study. Geneva: Switzerland; 2011.
24. Rubenstein LS, Bittle MD. Responsibility for protection of medical workers and facilities in armed conflict. Lancet. 2010;375(9711):329–40.
25. Pavignani E, Alessandro Colombo A. Providing health services in countries disrupted by civil wars: a comparative analysis of Mozambique and Angola 1975–2000. World Health Organization, Department of Emergency and Humanitarian Action; 2001.
26. Singh MA. Conflicts in Manipur. National Institute of Advanced Studies. Indian Institute of Science Campus. Bangalore: NIAS Backgounder; 2010.
27. Al Hilfi TK, Lafta R, Burnham G. Health services in Iraq. Lancet. 2013;381(9870):939–48.
28. Ranson K, Poletti T, Bornemisza O, Sondorp E. Promoting health equity in conflict-affected fragile states. London: London School of Hygiene and Tropical Medicine; 2007.
29. Bornemisza O, Ranson MK, Poletti TM, Sondorp E. Promoting health equity in conflict affected fragile states. Soc Sci Med. 2010;70(1):80–8.
30. Kruk ME, Rockers PC, Williams EH, Varpilah ST, Macauley R, Saydee G, Galea S. Availability of essential health services in post conflict Liberia. Bull World Health Organ. 2010;88:527–34.
31. HOPE worldwide Afghanistan. Pilot study on increasing demand for utilization of maternal health and child care services. Ministry of Public Health, Islamic Republic of Afghanistan; 2011.
32. Rytter MJH, Kjældgaard AL, Brønnum-Hansen H. Effects of armed conflict on access to emergency health care in Palestinian West Bank: systematic collection of data in emergency departments. BMJ. 2006; 332(7550):1122–24.
33. WHO. Sexual and reproductive health during protracted crises and recovery. Spain: WHO/HAC/BRO.2011.2; 2011.
34. Foreman M. Improving reproductive health services for forcibly displaced women. 2013. http://www.prb.org/Publications/Articles/2013/refugee-women-reproductive-health.aspx.
35. Betancourt TS, McBain R, Newnham EA, Brennan RT. Trajectories of internalizing problems in war-affected Sierra Leonean youth: examining conflict and post-conflict factors. Child Dev. 2013;84(2):455–70.

36. Mumtaz Z, Salway S, Nykiforuk C, Bhatti A, Ataullahjan A, Ayyalasomayajula, B. The role of social geography on Lady Health Workers' mobility and effectiveness in Pakistan. Soc Sci Med. 2013;91:48–57.
37. Bartlett LA, Mawji S, Whitehead S, Crouse C, Dalil S, Ionete D, Salama P, Afghan Maternal Mortality Study Team. Where giving birth is a forecast of death: maternal mortality in four districts of Afghanistan, 1999–2002. Lancet. 2005;365(9462):864–70.
38. Panhavichetr P. Case studies. The impact of armed conflict on gender relations. Case Study 1: Cambodia. In: El Bushra J, Lopez EP, editors. Development in conflict: the gender dimension. Report of a workshop held in Thailand, February 1993, Oxford Discussion Paper 3; 1993.
39. Singh MA. Backgrounders on conflict resolution. Bangalore: National Institute of Advanced Studies; 2010.
40. Hassan SM. Explaining Manipur's breakdown and Manipur's peace: the state and identities in North East India. Crisis States Programme Working papers series no. 1. Working Paper no 79; 2006.
41. Oinam B. Patterns of ethnic conflict in the north-east: a study on Manipur. Econ Polit Wkly. 2003;38(21):2031–37.
42. Singh MA. Politics of belonging: migrations, citizenships, and conflicts in India. In: Structuring peace: the state and conflict transformation: prospects and challenges in South Asia fourth JTCDM roundtable conference.
43. Singha K. Conflict, state and education in India: a study of Manipur. Am J Educ Res. 2013;1 (6):81–93.
44. MSDR. Manipur State Development Report (Draft), Planning Commission, GoI, Institute for Human Development, New Delhi; 2006.
45. Yumnam V. Unravelling health inequities: a study of the Universal Immunization Programme in two selected districts of Manipur. M.Phil. Dissertation. New Delhi: Jawaharlal Nehru University; 2012.
46. South Asia Terrorism Portal. Retrieved from: http://www.satp.org/satporgtp/countries/india/states/manipur/timeline/index.html.

Chapter 4
Deconstructing the Urban Transition: Conceptualization, Measurement and Mechanisms

Nandita Bhan

> *In this city, there is a strong connection between the seasons and customs, between man and nature, linking the new of the past to the old of the present.*
> —Badrinath in Madras, Chennai and the Self [1]

Abstract Policy discourses on urban health in India have been geared towards addressing the unmet need for health services through the National Urban Health Mission. This approach is limiting and myopic as it ignores urbanization as a determinant of health or the context through which other social determinants of health (SDH) may operate. While it is widely acknowledged that India is rapidly urbanizing, the speed, spread and style of this urbanization exposes several anomalies, relevant to the burden of morbidity and emerging health concerns, particularly chronic diseases and risk factors. This chapter examines some facts of the rural to urban transition in India, the emerging measure of urbanization—'urbanicity', and it simpacts on health conditions. The chapter is divided into three parts. The first part discusses the issues involved in conceptualization what is 'urban' and urbanicity, and the issues involves in this conceptualization. The second part investigates aspects related to the urbanization trajectory in India. Finally, the chapter concludes with some experiences of research and emerging methodologies on urbanization and health in India.

Keywords Urbanization · Urbanicity · Urban health

N. Bhan (✉)
Public Health Foundation of India, Delhi, NCR, India
e-mail: nandita.bhan@phfi.org; nandita.gehindia@gmail.com

D. Nambiar and A. Muralidharan (eds.), *The Social Determinants of Health in India*, https://doi.org/10.1007/978-981-10-5999-5_4

Introduction

Urbanization is a global phenomenon and concern. Estimates from the United Nations show that nearly half of the world's population currently lives in cities and this is expected to grow to two-thirds over the coming decades [2]. This leads us to ask whether urbanization is universal or inevitable. Will everyone live in cities one day, and will villages disappear? [3] Experiences from developed countries show that this may not be so. Despite rapid urbanization, almost 20% (one in five people) of the population in high-income countries continue to live in rural areas. For countries in Asia and Africa, however, most of the future growth in populations will take place in urban centres [3, 4]. Where does India stand in these global demographic and socioeconomic shifts? How will urbanization impact the health and well-being of Indians? There have been several reports on India's rapid and unprecedented rates of urbanization [5–8]. What is the basis of these assessments—are these assessments true?

India's urbanization has been linked to the economic reforms of 1991 and their impacts on institutions, relations and inequality [9, 10]. These reforms exposed India and Indians to global macroeconomic and cultural shifts and world affairs, increasing the aspirations for modernization and wealth, especially among younger populations [11, 12]. Themes macroeconomic and cultural shifts have also impacted on the urban transition in India. The breadth and depth of these issues and their impacts on health have not been mapped systematically by researchers.

Urbanization is complex and multidimensional. In this chapter, I will focus on three aspects of India's urban transition—key concepts related to urbanization, the mechanisms linking urbanization to health and emerging research questions of interest that are related to urbanization. In the discussion on conceptualization, the focus is on defining urban, distinguishing between 'people' and 'place' in the literature on urbanization, and outlining three trends in assessing urbanization in India. In highlighting the mechanisms linking urbanization to health, the chapter will discuss the focus of current research areas such as migration, water sanitation and nutrition. Finally, in outlining emerging research in the area, the chapter will summarize emerging research streams as well as methodologies.

Defining Urban: Origins, Meanings and Challenges

Urbanization versus Urban Health: The term *urban* signifies living arrangements that are based on a non-agrarian way of life, including occupations, lifestyles and values. Health policy in India has related *urban* to *privilege*, and historically, policy documents such as the Bhore Commission report mandated that health care needs were more acute in rural areas, assuming that health systems were developed and available in urban settings. The National Urban health Mission (NUHM) showed that, public health services in urban areas in India were limited and populations relied mainly on private providers [13]. The WHO's Commission on Social Determinants of Health (CSDH) uses the term 'urban health' as a determinant of health and disease [14, 15]. By doing so, the CSDH signified the importance of the term 'urban' as a stratifier to understand inequalities and as a contextual determinant of health and health services. However, the use of the term *urban health* is often limited to the discussions on to the health needs of urban residents and lack of access to health services, and does not extend the boundaries to the findings of the CSDH report.

The terms 'urban health' and 'urbanization' have a substantial overlap. However, health policy often focuses on urban health only. The mandate of the NUHM is on health concerns faced by urban residents, especially the poor, along with residents of slums, migrants and specific vulnerable populations [15, 16]. The program extends the delivery of health services included in rural primary care to vulnerable urban residents, marginalized from health care services in cities and towns. The Urban Health Mission (UHM) was conceptualized using the framework of universal health coverage (UHC) to extend public provisioning of health services [17]. It states that the agenda for urban health is to address the 'unmet need for health services' in urban areas [13]. In urban settings, the development of primary care systems has been slow and has not kept pace with the growth and density of populations. As a result, private providers proliferate, often unregulated, in urban centres and private health services are more likely to be accessed, if affordable. Coverage, cost, quality and access remain issues especially for vulnerable populations and hence have been the focus of new health initiatives [20, 21]. In future, the UHM will also need to include structural dimensions such as regulation of health providers in urban areas, including within its ambit large private health care providers (hospitals and clinics), small private providers (physician clinics and private practice), diagnostic centres and public health services [18, 19].

Urbanization, on the other hand, is considered to be a determinant of health and disease. The current design of the UHM focuses on health services and treatment, and ignores the determinants of health related to urban development and urban social change such as sanitation, substance use and food. In the long term, this approach may be myopic, cost-ineffective and will not lead to development of sustainable solutions to health challenges [20–23]. Urbanization is defined as components or processes that impact transition of a place from rural to urban, determined by aspects of the area or by residents [14]. The SDH perspective considers urbanization as a 'cause', driver, determinant or modifier of health, depending on the mechanism in question. However, focusing on urbanization does not negate the importance of issues of access to health care in urban areas. It only suggests that health begins a long time before the health system comes into play.

Person or Place?

In conceptualizing and measuring urbanization, two 'P's are key—characteristics of '*people*' and characteristics of '*places*' [24–27]. Characteristics of people represent aspects or qualities that can be disaggregated to the individual level, often referred to as compositional characteristics for a geographic unit. Examples include measures of education and occupation of residents, race, class and income of individuals. These measures can be summarized as, say, the percentage of people before poverty line living in census tracts or districts. Characteristics of places represent contextual aspects or qualities that may or may not be reducible to individual aspects for a geographic unit. These may include dimensions of history, political economy and cultural specificities of an area. While researchers often consider characteristics of a place as not being reducible to the sum of individual attributes, this may vary by research question and conceptualization of the problem.

The definition of urbanization in India needs to be considered in the context of both these P's—'people' and 'place'. Statistical definitions of what constitutes *urban* as per census organizations are focused on characteristics of people. These definitions include population size and density, and classifications differentiating agrarian versus non-agrarian occupations [28, 29]. While population is a robust measure for the changing demographics of an area, it does not explain features of the population, especially those relevant to studying the health effects of urbanization.[1] Similarly, occupational classifications of agrarian versus non-agrarian are intuitive and parsimonious. However, these classifications cannot capture the complexities around the transitional or seasonal nature of agriculture or of individuals engaging in multiple occupations in rural and peri-urban areas in India. While the Indian census differentiates urban from rural areas, there is increasing reference to 'peri-urban' as an emerging third classification capturing a spectrum of qualities of an area lying between the rural and urban [30, 31]. Additionally, in India, the metric of density in defining urbanization is based on land use and habitat considerations. Density metrics assume that living in close proximity is a proxy for urbanization processes, but the mechanisms underlying urbanization may remain uninvestigated.

Three Facets of the Urbanization Trajectory in India

Researchers and media often state that India is urbanizing rapidly. This is not backed by systematic and critical assessments on the diverse aspects of the urban transition. Contrary to public perception, cross-national reports show that India's urbanization is slow compared to that of China and Brazil [32, 33]. As per estimates, nearly half of the world's population lives in urban areas; in high-income

[1]The US, similar to India, uses density measures for differentiating rural from urban. However, the industrial nature of the US economy implies that most areas are urban and there is no range of 'peri-urban' areas [41, 42]. Additionally, metropolitan areas are defined by the US census through policies including residential, land-use and zoning policies and are applied to public policies around industrialization and environment regulation. These have been criticized for being heavily skewed in favor of more affluent and white populations, and discriminating against poor and minority populations. The metropolitan classification is now being used in some metro cities to define the greater region around the metropolis and the development of suburban areas as feeders for labor (both white and blue collar).

countries, about 80% of the population lives in urban areas. Urban residents comprise 43% of the population in Asia, 44% on average in African countries and 80% in Latin American countries. In comparison, 30% of the Indian population lives in urban areas [5, 6]. The rate of urbanization in India is expected to be rapid following the structural economic reforms of 1991. However, the rate of increase in urban populations has remained slow. One possible reason for this slow growth may be the focus of economic reforms on trade and markets, without any accompanying improvements in infrastructure development [34, 35]. The inflow of capital from private investment following the economic reforms was concentrated in trade of goods and services, and did not impact on long-term urban development activities such as housing and transport, with influence on the development of urban areas and migration of labor from rural to urban areas. These levels of infrastructure development may be low due to unclear profitability, long gestation period and the view that responsibility for urban infrastructure development belonged to central and state governments. The lopsided and transitory nature of migration may be another influence on the patterns of urbanization. Other factors include the traditional nature of enterprises and the participation of women in the labor force limiting the transformation of rural areas into urban areas [36–38].

Three facets can shed some light on the trajectory of urbanization in India. The first facet of the growth of urbanization is the *speed* of urbanization. Cross-national estimates show that the increases in the number of urban residents has slowed in India compared to several African, Asian and Latin American nations [5, 39]. While the definition of 'urban' itself has not changed over time, agglomeration data adds further complexity. New urban agglomerations in India have grown from 2843 in 1951–5161 in 2001 [5, 6]. The sensitivity of urban transition from rural to peri-urban areas is not captured by measures of urbanization that are solely based on population size and other measures of morphological change are needed. Descriptions of urban often focus on large or small cities and do not include the mechanisms of change underlying these transitions such as the extension of transport networks [39]. The seasonal nature of occupation and mixed land use in agrarian economies implies that measures capturing the speed of urbanization may or may not capture the change in lifestyles as a result of urbanization.

The second facet of measuring urbanization is its *spread*. This captures the degree to which urbanization spreads across areas, patterns of spread and 'domino' effects on connectivity and lifestyles [5, 28]. However, estimating the spread of urbanization is challenging for two reasons. Firstly, urbanization may have multiple components and the spread of urbanization may be sensitive to changes in only a few of these characteristics that comprise a summary measure of urbanization as a whole. Second, understanding the spread of urbanization requires sophisticated methodologies for capturing change similar to those being used in social network analysis. Simple analyses have measured the spread of urbanization by examining change in the characteristics and patterns of migration and movement of populations across area types over time (Fig. 4.1). In the past, ideas around urbanization

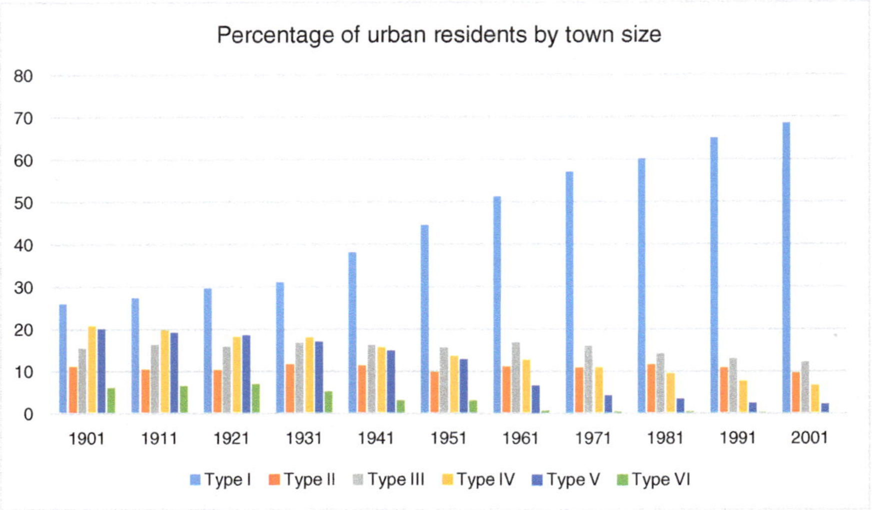

Fig. 4.1 Growth of urban populations by type of urban area. *Source* Data from census of India and Datta [6]

were drawn from migration models such as the Lewis Model[2] that explained the cyclical dynamics of rural to urban change and labor force transitions [40]. These models, based on industrialization, are now considered obsolete as they assume linear-progressive models of labor migration from rural areas to small town to large town and city. In India, urbanization breaks away from these patterns, with direct migrant flow from villages to large cities. This migration is also not attributed to large-scale industrialization except in 'pocket' industrial towns. In many cities, especially in southern India, urbanization may be attributed to high labor needs driven by the services sector [41, 42]. This non-progressive pattern of urbanization from rural areas to metropolitan areas, in fact heightens vulnerability of migrants. Migrants are often economically and socially marginalized and forced to live in poor and hazardous conditions in unequal cities. The influence of urbanization on culture may be positive or negative and may flow both to and from rural areas and cities. The health of migrant populations and the impact of urbanization is a growing area of research and policy.

A third facet relevant in the understanding of the urban transition is the *style* of urbanization. This refers to the components of urbanization and their role in shaping the urban process. The current state of knowledge of urbanization has not examined the origins of urbanization in India, especially if components of the urban transition develop intrinsically within communities (e.g. as different generations are educated) or are introduced in the form of exogenous shocks. The drivers of the urban transition can be investigated by understanding patterns and origins of infrastructure

[2]Lewis received the Nobel Prize in Economics for the model in 1979.

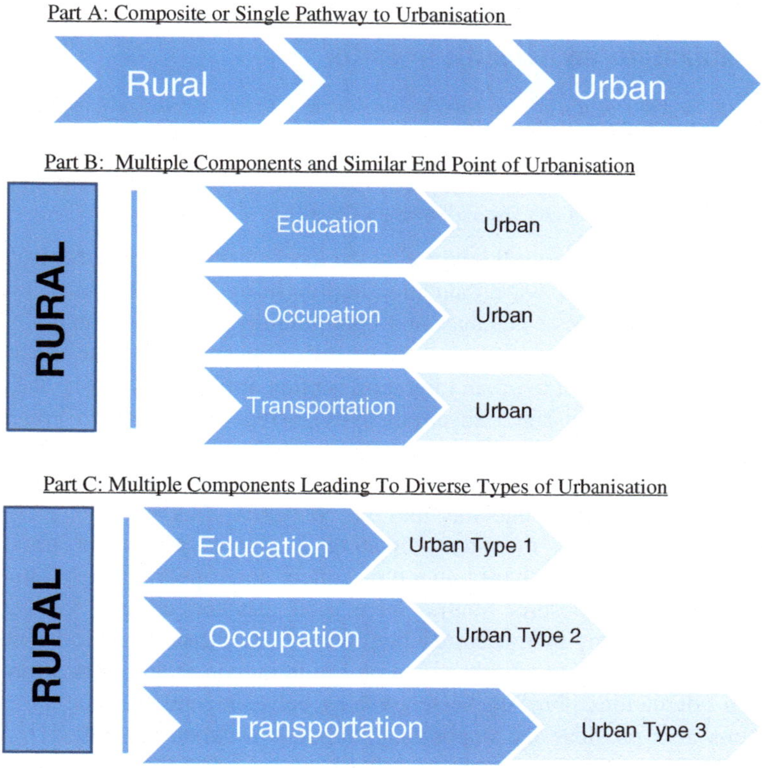

Fig. 4.2 Conceptualizing pathways of the rural to urban transition

changes in the community (e.g. when the first road linking a village to a highway was built and subsequent transport improvements), through individual surveys reporting important community events (e.g. introducing village residents to internet technology for commercial or recreational purposes) or through census or survey-based changes in demographic patterns (e.g. changes in the number of graduates or professionals in the communities over time) [43]. A big (and sometimes misguided) assumption made by research has been to try and identify a unique pathway to urbanization across communities, instead of using empirical community-based research to understand multiple pathways to the urban transition (Fig. 4.2).

Some Experiences and Challenges of Research on Urbanization and Health in India

The basic facilities of a usable school, an accessible hospital, a toilet at home, or two square meals a day, are missing for a huge proportion of the Indian population in a way they are not in, say, China. This makes comparisons of inequality in terms of the aggregate inequality indicators (such as Gini coefficients) of income distributions less relevant and telling. ([44], p. 280, Sen and Dreze, Uncertain Glory)

In this section, some examples highlighting the mechanisms linking urbanization to health, such as migration, water-sanitation and nutrition, are highlighted. In addition, the section identifies challenges and opportunities in these research areas.

Research on urbanization in India often focuses on migration. The urban transition represented by rural to urban migration is often attributed to ‘push’ and ‘pull’ factors such as declining agrarian productivity, rising rural debt and urban economic opportunities [45–47]. Cities offer opportunities for cross-cultural interactions and assimilation [45, 46, 48]. Identities related to religion, caste and region have lower influence, although this may be contested. This leads to temporary, seasonal and permanent migration, creating a unique population group for researchers—migrants. Studying migration offers the opportunity of studying urbanization as an exposure. Studies have used matched designs for studying migration (e.g. a sibling-pair, each residing in rural and urban areas) to understand the influence of moving to an urban area on health outcomes across rural, migrant and urban populations [49, 50]. Distinguishing between rural, migrant and urban populations also provides the opportunity to study acculturation [49–51]. If the influence of urbanization was static or defined by a specific time period of acculturation, then migrants and urban residents will accumulate similar risks. Epidemiological studies, both in India and outside, show that the impact of acculturation varies by time, depending on population and health condition [50, 52, 53]. Protective effects of residing in rural settings are noted for chronic disease risks, but these protective influences may vary by health care access, time spent in different areas and the outcomes considered [50].

The vulnerability of several migrant groups has been explored across a spectrum of health dimensions. Public health studies have examined risk-taking behaviors among migrants, attributed to changing social norms and networks in transitional and urban settings [54, 55]. Poverty also influences accessibility to health services among vulnerable migrant populations. Studies show lower immunization rates, feeding practices of children, and poor nutritional behaviors among poor migrants with lower rates of education [56–59]. Some have argued that compared to rural settings, migration is associated with improved health of populations however, this idea has been contested in Mexico and China [60–63]. Poor migrants to cities often live in slum and resettlement areas without adequate systems and services for water and sanitation [63, 64]. This exposes migrants to a range of exposures leading to diarrheal diseases, malaria, dengue and increases their vulnerability to disasters [63, 64].

Research on water, sanitation and hygiene (WASH) and infrastructure services linked to health have improved our understanding of the challenges faced by urban residents [64, 65]. Other behaviors studied related to urban vulnerability are menstrual hygiene, health behaviors such as tobacco and alcohol use, education of children in slums, crime against women and intimate partner violence [66–73]. However, existing studies among urban residents often focus on proximate factors and ignore contextual determinants such as income inequality and acculturation in urban areas. Research on social networks among migrant communities in urban centres and the role of regional, religion or other community networks that modify health risks remains neglected.

In the future, understanding the influence of urbanization on nutrition and physical activity will be key to developing interventions for the rising burden on chronic diseases in India and other low- and middle-income countries. Nutrition and physical activity are impacted directly by urbanization through patterns of food distribution, systems of transport and sociocultural determinants. Evidence from more urban states such as Gujarat and Maharashtra shows the presence of both under and overnutrition in urban settings [73, 74]. Beyond undernutrition, issues such as hunger and specific nutrient deficiencies are also influenced by the distribution of food resources in urban settings [75]. Inability to afford healthy food, consumption of packaged foods and lack of knowledge about nutrients can influence the health of children and adolescents in urban settings. Transitions within families from urbanization such as smaller, nuclear households, rising labor force participation of women, and lack of alternative arrangements for childcare may need to neglect of children due to reduced time in child care activities in urban areas. Being overweight and obesity are emerging concerns among urban residents [51, 75–77]. Urbanization has been linked to unhealthy diets and food choices through high food inflation [78]. Demands of urban lifestyles lead to a shift from cooked meals to low labor-intensive meals including snacks and junk foods [79–81]. These issues have received much emphasis in developed countries but are only now coming into focus in India.

Apart from nutrition, another key determinant of health influenced by urbanization is physical activity [82]. Physical activity may be related to urbanization in three ways. Firstly, urbanization changes the nature of occupations from agriculture-based to non-agricultural occupations. This is attributed to the transitioning economy (characteristics of the place) as well as to the rising education of the residents (characteristics of the people). Declining agrarian productivity has shifted the nature of work to employment in factories and non-manual work. As education rates rise, younger generations in rural areas no longer want to work in agriculture as lower status is placed on farming and manual occupations. The interaction between urbanization, status and occupational work needs greater examination. Secondly, urbanization influences the changing transport infrastructure in rural settings, particularly the rise of motorized transport [83]. Urbanizing areas witness an increase in two-wheeled vehicles and cars, and in public transport systems. These changes are also accompanied by improvements in road infrastructure and access to rural credit for purchasing motorized transport. Changes in attitudes are demonstrated by population preferences of owning their own transport over public services [84]. Finally, urbanization is also linked with increasing avenues and preferences for recreation, thereby influencing physical activity [82–85]. In rural areas, although playgrounds and recreation services such as gyms may be limited, open spaces for play may be available to children. Recreational activity may vary by gender stereotypes. In cities, while services like gyms and parks may be available (although these may vary with the socioeconomic status of neighbourhood), their use may be limited by price, crime and safety and daily routines. Long working hours and other limitations such as commuting times imply that professionals have limited time for any recreation. Crime and trafficking also restrict outdoor activities for girls, especially in slum settings.

Questions for Future Research

Urbanization is a complex and multidisciplinary area of study involving knowledge from public policy, urban design, nutrition, economics and sociology. Public health research on urbanization is nascent and needs greater focus on the mechanisms linking urbanization to health conditions. Insight from areas like water and sanitation has shown a need for developing metrics for quantifying and studying the impacts of urbanization on households and communities. Metrics developed in select contexts have wider applications for health outcomes across communicable and non-communicable diseases.

Emerging Methodologies

The use of technology in studying urbanization and its mechanisms is new. Two areas may be particularly important as researchers develop interdisciplinary efforts to conceptualize urbanization. Firstly, the use of geospatial technologies is going to be critical in orienting how we view urban space and geographies over time [28]. The use of geospatial maps will improve our understanding of urban change, patterns and key hotspots relevant for health and behaviors [86]. However, these technologies require investments in infrastructure and capacity. These technologies also need conceptualization efforts in order to develop meaningful instruments and tools that can empirically highlight change that goes beyond census-based formulations of urban and rural areas. Similarly, technology has improved the measurement of exposure to air pollution, adding to the evidence on the effects of air pollution on human health [87, 88]. Presently, these technologies are resource intensive and need skill development. Low cost innovations for air pollution monitoring need to be developed along with population-based surveys to assist air pollution assessment.

In addition to the use of technology to measure urbanization, mixed methods research such as integrating qualitative approaches with quantitative surveys is needed to develop context-relevant research questions [89]. Our knowledge in the area of health is presently focused on highlighting the differences in health conditions and service access by rural versus urban residence, and is based on data already collected. However, to undertake innovative new and context-specific research on urbanization, it will be useful to utilize mixed methodologies identifying specific pathways and mechanisms linking urbanization to different health ailments specific to diverse population groups [90]. Research that includes ethnographies and qualitative methods along with quantitative surveys will be effective in investigating the multilayered nature of urbanization and specific microecologies. In India, integrating these questions within varying state contexts will also prove to be crucial.

Emerging Streams of Research

The terms 'urban', urbanicity and urbanization pose challenges for conceptualization and methodology development for researchers. In public health, inferences on urbanization are based on studies comparing health conditions across rural and urban settings. This may not be accurate or comprehensive. An alternative approach to understanding the urban transition involves focusing in-depth on three specific typologies and their relationships to specific health and health access outcomes (Fig. 4.3). The first of these is '*peri-urban*'. A number of recent studies have examined the development trajectory of peri-urban areas [30, 91]. These studies have focused on land use, and on investigating the rise of peri-urban areas as the zone of transition between rural and urban influencing poverty, resources, food, infrastructure and social services. It is quite likely that this will have implications on communicable and non-communicable diseases as well as nutrition. In addition, governance issues in peri-urban contexts highlight the need to develop social support systems and examine the spread of social assistance programs [92, 93]. These will be critical to the health and well-being of vulnerable populations.

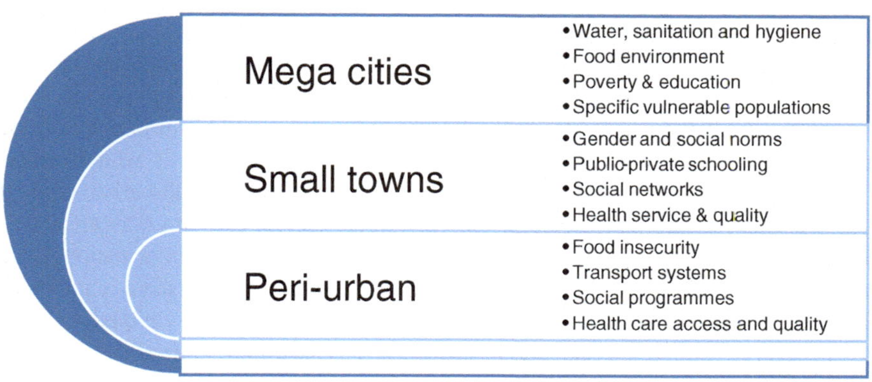

Fig. 4.3 Emerging areas for research

Research on transport in peri-urban areas will have important impacts on health and health access issues, similar to those faced by rural areas. The second urban typology to study is *small towns*. Small towns often represent a sociocultural zone of transition between rural and urban areas. Studying institutions, structures and norms in small towns will be relevant to the understanding of health behaviors and practices [94, 95]. Prominent among these will be changing gender and social norms in these urbanizing settings influenced by transitioning education and employment patterns, with far-reaching effects on families and care-giving especially for children and older people. Recent evidence shows that labor force participation in small towns has stagnated. Patterns of social change may also be more visible in small towns rather than metropolitan areas, where economic rather than sociocultural dimensions play a bigger role. The high burden on the tertiary health care sector in large cities also shows the inability of smaller towns to address the health needs of populations. The mix of private and public services for health care and education will impact on health outcomes in these areas. The study of transitioning social networks in small towns is another key area for study.

The third urban typology to be studied is the health of vulnerable populations in *megacities*. Studies of health systems and services in megacities have focused on specific vulnerable populations such as construction workers, rickshaw pullers, manual laborers, ragpickers, and street children among others [96, 97]. Issues related to their health examine access to health care and the high cost of health services including outpatient consultation fees, costs of medicines and diagnostics, and the opportunity costs arising from loss of labor when sick. In urban areas, public systems for health care have been inadequate and the implementation framework of the National Urban Health Mission (NUHM) advocates addressing these acute health needs of vulnerable urban residents [13]. However, without plans for outreach and implementation the needs of these vulnerable groups in urban areas will remain neglected. The burden of disease from lack of infrastructure systems such as water and sanitation, limited availability of food services and low quality infrastructure such as housing, expose residents of slums and resettlement areas in megacities to acute health challenges [96]. The Technical Resource Group (TRG) made strides in defining the urban advantage versus the ‘penalty’ to the physical and mental well-being of urban residents in India [16].

Equally critical will be integrating research on health outcomes and services with the mandate of the NUHM along with its recommendations for future action. This program is the first systematic attempt to deliver health services in urban areas, and represents an opportunity for assessing what is available and at what quality. The TRG broadened this discussion by defining vulnerabilities in the urban context [16]. Research to strengthen evidence on health and health care in urban areas will need to integrate survey-driven methodologies with geographical information, local area based assessments and qualitative investigations to understand challenges faced by vulnerable populations. Much of this mandate will be defined by how researchers investigate recommendations of the TRG within the emerging research in this area.

Commentary—Urban Areas and Social Determinants of Health

Sulakshana Nandi
Public Health Resource Network, Raipur, Chhattisgarh, India

Urban India encompasses a diverse variety of cities and towns. Some areas have been urban centres for centuries while there are others that have only recently been developed into an urban area. An urban area could be a metropolitan area with a population of a few million or even a block town of 10,000 residents. However, regardless of the kind of urban area, it is the marginalized and impoverished communities and groups, often making up nearly half of the urban population, that are most vulnerable. These groups include the homeless, daily wage laborers, sex workers, transgenders, domestic helpers, ragpickers, manual scavengers, single men, single women, construction workers, street children, rickshaw pullers, old and destitute and many others. Their lives are precarious, marked by uncertainty in employment and insecure habitation rights. There is always a fear of displacement due to urban 'development' projects such as the broadening of roads or building of flyovers. They face extreme helplessness in times of health and other crises. Although in urban areas there is a higher scope for mobility, caste-based occupations like manual scavenging and cleaning toilets still exist. Moreover, urban areas are often distributed spatially, along lines of native region, religion and caste, sometimes taking the form of ghettos. The availability of basic public services like water, sanitation, health, education, and electricity, depends on the income levels, with the poorest having the least access. This has dire implications for their health.

The health sector in urban areas is highly medicalized, while primary essential services such as immunization, are often missing. The private health sector is predominant and the public health system neglected and quite sparse. The private health sector is extremely heterogeneous, ranging from untrained medical practitioners, to large corporate hospitals. The expenditure on treatment for the same condition can range from Rs. 100 to 10,000. The nature of occupation and lack of social security among the poor, along with a non-responsive public health system places the poor at the mercy of the predatory private sector often providing incorrect and irrational treatment at a high price. For instance, for a domestic help or a rickshaw puller, taking a day off from work to undergo a sputum test for TB would mean the loss of that day's wages. Therefore they find it much easier to go to the quack in their slum for a few medicines for their cough. Private hospitals have been known to misuse Government insurance schemes, providing incorrect, irrational and unregulated treatment and refusing to provide free entitled services to people, despite subsidies and reimbursements from the government.

The old health challenges of malnutrition, poor maternal and child health, gastroenteritis, leprosy, and TB etc. remain, along with the new emerging challenges of hepatitis, dengue, road accidents, and vehicular and industrial pollution. The diseases of the poor, like TB and jaundice are neglected while diseases like swine flu are highlighted and acted upon with lots of zeal. The struggle for survival and the increasingly volatile nature of urban areas has exacerbated mental health issues, substance abuse and gender-based violence.

Any attempts to improve health and health services in urban areas have to incorporate all of these dimensions. There are ongoing debates that remain around how the government should go about improving health in urban areas. There are debates with respect to whether the government should provide universal services or target only the poor, and of what should be the extent of private sector involvement and how the various departments and the local governance structures can work in an integrated manner. The National Urban Health Mission (NUHM) had made an attempt to unravel the situation and respond to it. However, in most states the NUHM hasn't taken off due to both a paucity of funds and lack of vision. In places where certain elements like the community-based outreach services have been introduced through Accredited Social Health Activists (ACHAs), Auxiliary Nurse Midwives (ANMs), Women's Health committees, Primary Health Centres and Community clinics, and the results have been positive and the improvements heartening. Through the Women's Health Committees, women have formed collectives around issues of health, nutrition and sanitation, demanding accountability and entitlements. Important work has been done in certain cities by government and civil society, of catering to the homeless. Improving health in urban areas requires equitable and cohesive action around the social determinants of health and public services. A special emphasis on addressing the issues of the most marginalized is crucial.

References

1. Badrinath T. Madras, Chennai and the self: conversations with the city. India: Pan Macmillan; 2015.
2. United Nations. World Urbanization Prospects: The 2003 Revision. United Nations; 2004. http://esa.un.org/unup/. Cited 26 Feb 2007.
3. Satterthwaite D. Will most people live in cities? BMJ. 2000;321(7269):1143–5.
4. Brockerhoff M. An urbanizing world. Popul Bull. 2000;55(3):3–4.
5. Datta P. Urbanization in India. European Population Conference, Bratislava, Slovak Republic. June 2006.
6. Sivaramakrishnan KC, Singh BN. Urbanization. Available Online at the Planning Commission; 2001.
7. Dua R, Mohan V. Rapid urbanization a cause for concern: PM. The Times of India. 15 Sept 2013. http://timesofindia.indiatimes.com/india/Rapid-urbanization-a-cause-for-concern-PM/articleshow/22593196.cms.
8. Menon S. Census shows India urbanizing faster. Business Standard. 20 July 2011. Weblink: http://www.business-standard.com/article/economy-policy/census-shows-india-urbanising-faster-111072000066_1.html.
9. Chadchan J, Shankar R. Emerging urban development issues in the context of globalization. J ITPI (Institute of Town Planners India). 2009;6(2):78–85.

10. Mendez M, Popkin B. Globalization, urbanization and nutritional change in the developing world. Globalization of food systems in developing countries: impact on food security and nutrition 2004:55–80.
11. Glaeser EL. Why has globalization led to bigger cities? The New York Times. Economix. 19 May 2009. http://economix.blogs.nytimes.com/2009/05/19/why-has-globalization-led-to-bigger-cities/?_r=0.
12. Ramakrishnan K. City futures: aspirations and urban imaginaries in Delhi. Kaleidoscope: The Interdisciplinary Postgraduate Journal of Durham University's Institute of Advanced Study 2013. 5.1, ISSN.1756-8137.
13. GOI. National urban health mission. Implementation framework. Ministry of Health & Family Welfare, Government of India; 2013.
14. WHO. Our cities our health our future. Acting on social determinants for health equity in urban settings. Report to the WHO Commission on social determinants of health from the knowledge network on urban settings; 2007.
15. WHO Commission on social determinants of health. Closing the gap in a generation: health equity through action on the social determinants of health: commission on social determinants of health final report. Ed World Health Organization; 2008.
16. GOI. Reaching health care to the unreached: making the urban health mission work for the urban poor. Report of the technical resource group, urban health mission. National Health Systems Resource Center, Ministry of Health and Family welfare.
17. Planning Commission. High level expert group report on universal health coverage for India. No. id: 4646; 2011.
18. Berman PA. Rethinking health care systems: private health care provision in India. World Dev. 1998;26(8):1463–79.
19. Rao M, et al. Human resources for health in India. Lancet. 2011;377(9765):587–98.
20. Balarajan Y, Selvaraj S, Subramanian SV. Health care and equity in India. The Lancet. 2011;377(9764):505–15.
21. Sen G, Iyer A, George A. Class, gender and health equity: lessons from liberalizing India. Engendering international health: the challenge of equity; 2002. p. 281–311.
22. Levesque JF, et al. Outpatient care utilization in urban Kerala, India. Health Policy Plann. 2006;21(4):289–301.
23. Stephens C. Revisiting urban health and social inequalities: the devil is in the detail and the solution is in all of us. Environ Urbanization. 2011;23(1):29–40.
24. Duncan C, Jones K, Moon G. Context, composition and heterogeneity: using multilevel models in health research. Soc Sci Med. 1998;46(1):97–117.
25. O'Campo P. Invited commentary: advancing theory and methods for multilevel models of residential neighborhoods and health. Am J Epidemiol. 2003;157(1):9–13.
26. Merlo J, et al. A brief conceptual tutorial of multilevel analysis in social epidemiology: linking the statistical concept of clustering to the idea of contextual phenomenon. J Epidemiol Commun Health. 2005;59(6):443–9.
27. Diez-Roux AV. Multilevel analysis in public health research. Annu Rev Public Health. 2000;21(1):171–92.
28. Mohan R, Pant C. Morphology of urbanization in India: some results from 1981 census. Econ Polit Wkly; 1982. p. 1579–88.
29. Bhagat RB. Rural-urban classification and municipal governance in India. Singap J Trop Geogr. 2005;26(1):61–73.
30. Narain V. Growing city, shrinking hinterland: land acquisition, transition and conflict in peri-urban Gurgaon, India. Environ Urbanization. 2009;21(2):501–12.
31. Bhagat RB, Mohanty S. Emerging pattern of urbanization and the contribution of migration in urban growth in India. Asian Popul Stud. 2009;5(1):5–20.

32. Rukmini S. India urbanizing, but slowly, UN numbers show. 2014. http://www.thehindu.com/news/national/india-urbanising-but-slowly-un-numbers-show/article6200088.ece.
33. Planning Commission. The Challenges of Urbanization in India. Approach to the 12th Plan. http://12thplan.gov.in/12fyp_docs/17.pdf.
34. Ahluwalia MS. Economic reforms in India since 1991: has gradualism worked? J Econ Perspect. 2002;16(3):67–88.
35. Srinivasan TN. Indian economic reforms: a stocktaking. Stanford Center for International Development, Working Paper 190; 2003.
36. Ganguly-Scrase R, Scrase T. Globalization and the middle classes in India: the social and cultural impact of neoliberal reforms. Routledge; 2008.
37. Kingdon GG, Unni J. Education and women's labour market outcomes in India. Educ Econ. 2001;9(2):173–95.
38. Deshpande S, Deshpande L. Impact of liberalization on labor market in India: What do facts from NSSO's 50th round show? Econ Polit Wkly 1998: L31–39.
39. Calì M. Urbanization, inequality and economic growth: evidence from Indian states and towns. Background note for the World Development Report, London: Overseas Development Institute; 2008.
40. Lewis WA. Economic development with unlimited supplies of labor. Manchester Sch. 1954;22(2):139–91.
41. Todaro MP. A model of labor migration and urban unemployment in less developed countries. Am Econ Rev 1969;138–48.
42. Fay M, Opal C. Urbanization without growth: a not so uncommon phenomenon, vol. 2412. World Bank Publications; 2000.
43. Allender S, et al. Quantification of urbanization in relation to chronic diseases in developing countries: a systematic review. J Urban Health. 2008;85(6):938–51.
44. Drèze J, Sen A. An uncertain glory: India and its contradictions. Princeton University Press; 2013.
45. Qiang L. An analysis of push and pull factors in the migration of rural workers in China. Soc Sci China. 2003;1:125–36.
46. Mitra A, Murayama M. Rural to urban migration: a district-level analysis for India. Int J Migr, Health Soc Care. 2009;5(2):35–52.
47. Cali M, Menon C. Does urbanization affect rural poverty? Evidence from Indian districts. World Bank Econ Rev 2012: lhs019.
48. Hagen-Zanker J. Why do people migrate? A review of the theoretical literature. A review of the theoretical literature. Maastricht Graduate School of Governance Working Paper; 2008.
49. Kinra S, Andersen E, Ben-Shlomo Y, Bowen L, Lyngdoh T, Prabhakaran D, et al. Indian Migration Study Group. Association between urban life-years and cardio metabolic risk: the Indian migration study. Am J Epidemiol. 2011;174(2):154–64. doi:10.1093/aje/kwr053 Epub 2011.
50. Ebrahim S, Kinra S, Bowen L, Andersen E, Ben-Shlomo Y, Lyngdoh T, et al. Indian Migration Study group. The effect of rural-to-urban migration on obesity and diabetes in India: a cross-sectional study. PLoS Med. 2010;7(4):e1000268. doi:10.1371/journal.pmed.1000268.
51. Oyebode O, Pape UJ, Laverty AA, Lee JT, Bhan N, Millett C. Rural, urban and migrant differences in non-communicable disease risk-factors in middle income countries: a cross-sectional study of WHO-SAGE Data. PLoS One 2015;10(4):e0122747. doi:10.1371/journal.pone.0122747. eCollection 2015.
52. Gordon-Larsen P, Harris KM, Ward DS, Popkin BM. Acculturation and overweight-related behaviors among Hispanic immigrants to the US: the National Longitudinal Study of Adolescent Health. Soc Sci Med. 2003;57(11):2023–34.
53. Salant T, Lauderdale DS. Measuring culture: a critical review of acculturation and health in Asian immigrant populations. Soc Sci Med. 2003;57(1):71–90.

54. Ganju D, Mahapatra B, Saggurti N. Male migrants' non-spousal sexual partnerships in the place of origin: an in-depth investigation in two rural settings of India. Cult Health Sex. 2013;15(3):341–57. doi:10.1080/13691058.2012.756932 Epub 16 Jan 2013.
55. Singh YN, Malaviya AN. Long distance truck drivers in India: HIV infection and their possible role in disseminating HIV into rural areas. Int J STD AIDS. 1994;5(2):137–8.
56. Pakhare AP, Pawar R, Lokhande GS, Datta SS. Does seasonal migration for sugarcane harvesting influence routine immunization coverage? A cross-sectional study from rural Maharashtra. Indian J Public Health. 2014;58(2):116–20. doi:10.4103/0019-557X.132288.
57. Kusuma YS, Kumari R, Kaushal S. Migration and access to maternal healthcare: determinants of adequate antenatal care and institutional delivery among socio-economically disadvantaged migrants in Delhi, India. Trop Med Int Health. 2013;18(10):1202–10. doi:10.1111/tmi.12166 Epub 6 Aug 2013.
58. Choudhary N, Parthasarathy D. Is migration status a determinant of urban nutrition insecurity? Empirical evidence from Mumbai city, India. J Biosoc Sci. 2009;41(5):583–605. doi:10.1017/S002193200900340X Epub 10 Jun 2009.
59. Kumar S, Nath LM, Reddaiah VP. Supplementary feeding pattern in children living in a resettlement colony. Indian Pediatr. 1992;29(2):219–22.
60. Hildebrandt N, McKenzie DJ, Esquivel G, Schargrodsky E. The effects of migration on child health in Mexico (with comments). Economia 2005; 257–89.
61. Nandi A, Galea S, Lopez G, Nandi V, Strongarone S and Ompad DC. Access to and use of health services among undocumented Mexican immigrants in a US urban area. Am J Public Health 2008;98(11).
62. Hong Y, Li X, Stanton B, Lin D, Fang X, Rong M, Wang J. Too costly to be ill: health care access and health seeking behaviors among rural-to-urban migrants in China. World health Popul. 2006;8(2):22.
63. Gong P, Liang S, Carlton EJ, Jiang Q, Wu J, Wang L, Remais JV. Urbanization and health in China. Lancet. 2012;379(9818):843–52.
64. Subbaraman R, Nolan L, Shitole T, Sawant K, Shitole S, Sood K, et al. The psychological toll of slum living in Mumbai, India: a mixed methods study. Soc Sci Med. 2014;119:155–69. doi:10.1016/j.socscimed.2014.08.021 Epub 19 Aug 2014.
65. Biran A, Jenkins MW, Dabrase P, Bhagwat I. Patterns and determinants of communal latrine usage in urban poverty pockets in Bhopal, India. Trop Med Int Health. 2011;16(7):854–62. doi:10.1111/j.1365-3156.2011.02764.x Epub 17 Mar 2011.
66. Ray SK, Mishra R, Biswas R, Kumar S, Halder A, Chatterjee T. Nutritional status of pavement dweller children of Calcutta City. Indian J Public Health. 1999;43(1):49–54.
67. Chambers R, Medeazza GV. Sanitation and stunting in India. Econ Polit Wkly. 2013;48 (25):15.
68. Speizer IS, Nanda P, Achyut P, Pillai G, Guilkey DK. Family planning use among urban poor women from six cities of Uttar Pradesh, India. J Urban Health. 2012;89(4):639–58.
69. Gupta V, Yadav K, Anand K. Patterns of tobacco use across rural, urban, and urban-slum populations in a north Indian community. Indian J Community Med: Off Publ Indian Assoc Prev Soc Med. 2010;35(2):245.
70. Bobhate P, Shrivastava S. A cross sectional study of knowledge and practices about reproductive health among female adolescents in an urban slum of Mumbai. J Fam Reprod Health. 2011;5(4):117–24.
71. Garg S, Sharma N, Sahay R. Socio-cultural aspects of menstruation in an urban slum in Delhi, India. Reprod Health Matters. 2001;9(17):16–25.
72. Rocca CH, et al. Challenging assumptions about women's empowerment: social and economic resources and domestic violence among young married women in urban South India. Int J Epidemiol. 2009;38(2):577–85.
73. Subbulakshmi G, Udipi SA. Environmental factors, maternal attributes, and children's age at introduction of supplementary foods in rural and urban Maharashtra and Gujarat. Food Nutr Bull. 1990;12(4):318–22.

74. Harriss J, Kohli N. Notes on the differing 'states' of child undernutrition in rural India. IDS Bull. 2009;40(4):9–15.
75. Panagariya A. Does India really suffer from worse child malnutrition than Sub-Saharan Africa? Econ Polit Wkly. 2013;48(18):98–111.
76. Varadharajan KS, Thomas T, Rajaraman D, Kurpad AV, Vaz M. Overweight and obesity among internal migrants in India. Asia Pac J Clin Nutr. 2013;22(3):416–25. doi:10.6133/apjcn.2013.22.3.14.
77. Raman Kutty V, Joseph A, Soman CR. High prevalence of type 2 diabetes in an urban settlement in Kerala, India. Ethn Health. 1999;4(4):231–9.
78. Ray R. Changes in food consumption and the implications for food security and undernourishment: India in the 1990s. Dev Change. 2007;38(2):321–43.
79. Martin KS, Ferris AM. Food insecurity and gender are risk factors for obesity. J Nutr Educ Behav. 2007;39(1):31–6.
80. Griffiths P, Matthews Z, Hinde A. Gender, family, and the nutritional status of children in three culturally contrasting states of India. Soc Sci Med. 2002;55(5):775–90.
81. Klasen S, Pieters J. What explains the stagnation of female labor force participation in urban India? World Bank Econ Rev; 2015: lhv003.
82. Sullivan R, Kinra S, Ekelund U, Bharathi AV, Vaz M, Kurpad A, et al. Socio-demographic patterning of physical activity across migrant groups in India: results from the Indian Migration Study. PLoS One 2011;6(10):e24898. doi:10.1371/journal.pone.0024898. Epub 14 Oct 2011.
83. Millett C, Agrawal S, Sullivan R, Vaz M, Kurpad A, Bharathi AV. Associations between active travel to work and overweight, hypertension, and diabetes in India: a cross-sectional study. PLoS Med 2013;10(6):e1001459. doi:10.1371/journal.pmed.1001459. Epub 11 Jun 2013.
84. Padam S, Singh SK. Urbanization and urban transport in India: the search for a policy. 2004; SSRN 573181.
85. Yadav K, Krishnan A. Changing patterns of diet, physical activity and obesity among urban, rural and slum populations in North India. Obes Rev. 2008;9(5):400–8.
86. Basawaraja R, Chari KB, Mise SR, Chetti SB. Analysis of the impact of urban sprawl in altering the land-use, land-cover pattern of Raichur City, India, using geospatial technologies. J Geogr Reg Plan. 2011;4(8):455–62.
87. Smith KR, Aggarwal AL, Dave RM. Air pollution and rural biomass fuels in developing countries: a pilot village study in India and implications for research and policy. Atmos Environ. 1967;17(11):2343–62.
88. Smith KR, Samet JM, Romieu I, Bruce N. Indoor air pollution in developing countries and acute lower respiratory infections in children. Thorax. 2000;55(6):518–32.
89. Desai R, Sanyal R. Urbanizing citizenship: contested spaces in Indian cities. SAGE Publications; 2012.
90. Hayter AK, Jeffery R, Sharma C, Prost A, Kinra S. Community perceptions of health and chronic disease in South Indian rural transitional communities: a qualitative study. Glob Health Action. 2015;8.
91. Narain V, Nischal S. The peri-urban interface in Shahpur Khurd and Karnera, India. Environ Urbanization. 2007;19(1):261–73.
92. Khera R. Revival of the public distribution system: evidence and explanations. Econ Polit Wkly. 2011;46(44):36–50.
93. Bloom DE, Mahal A, Rosenberg L, Sevilla J. Economic security arrangements in the context of population ageing in India. Int Soc Secur Rev. 2010;63(3–4):59–89.
94. Hinderink J, Titus M. Small towns and regional development: Major findings and policy implications from comparative research. Urban Stud. 2002;39(3):379–91.

95. Haynes DE. Small Town Capitalism in Western India: Artisans, Merchants and the making of the informal Economy, 1870–1960 (No. 20). Cambridge University Press; 2012.
96. Vlahov D, Freudenberg N, Proietti F, Ompad D, Quinn A, Nandi V, Galea S. Urban as a determinant of health. J Urban Health. 2007;84(1):16–26.
97. Chatterjee M. Slum dwellers response to flooding events in the megacities of India. Mitig Adapt Strat Glob Change. 2010;15(4):337–53.

Chapter 5
Missing the Forest—The Significance of the Distal in Social Determinants of Health

Indira Chakravarthi

> *From time to time since the days of Chadwick and Farr, questions have arisen about how 'social' medicine should be (and equally about what issues and actions a social medicine involves or implies). Throughout this century (twentieth), many public health leaders have urged the importance of social determinants of illness and health. Yet I fear that little of that concern has stuck to become part of the mainstream or core of public health.* [...] *I have trouble shrugging off that dead hand, according to which issues of economic justice or violence (domestic, local, international) belong to one category with one set of institutions, and medical issues belong to another. Perhaps the 'social' is too amorphous, ill-defined or diffuse, but I think we are also trapped by the inertia of a history that informs both professional culture and expectations among the public at large. In that history, the drama of the conquest of epidemic disease has loomed largest. In medical histories (and even in histories of public health), the matter of hunger and overwork as medical problems is often ignored, treated as marginal, or regarded as a recognition of the 20th century.*
>
> *I find a visit to the Sadler witnesses exhilarating because they represent a time when medical professionals did not have to apologize for thinking that social policy affected public health. The split that Chadwick and Farr had effected had not yet taken place.*
>
> *The actions taken at this time had far-reaching implications for public health. A 'political medicine,' with status equal to that of political economy in shaping public policy, failed to develop. The public health field, along with medicine more generally, achieved significant autonomy, yet it did so by sacrificing the claim to speak with authority on many social issues.*
>
> —Christopher Hamlin, in a paper discussing the formative period of modern public health in Great Britain in the 1830s and 1840s (10:863–4).

I. Chakravarthi (✉)
Independent Public Health Researcher, Delhi, India
e-mail: indira.jnu@gmail.com

D. Nambiar and A. Muralidharan (eds.), *The Social Determinants of Health in India*, https://doi.org/10.1007/978-981-10-5999-5_5

Abstract This chapter examines the Social Determinants of Health (SDH) discourse in India and its implications, against the history of SDH and approaches to the issue. This analysis utilizes some of the framework and recommendations of the Commission on Social Determinants of Health (CSDH). However, it also takes the analysis beyond the limitations and deficiencies of the CSDH, and identifies two macro factors not currently considered as SDH in India, namely work and the practices of corporations.

Keywords Commission on Social Determinants of Health · EMCONET
Macrosocial determinants of health · Work · Unemployment · Corporations
Corporate foundations

It is now acknowledged that population health is an outcome of several factors that interact in complex ways to shape health in positive or adverse ways. Since the 1990s, social determinants of health (SDH) has become a convenient term to describe the impact on population health of social factors beyond the conventional biomedical and behavioral risk factor approach to health. This chapter examines the SDH discourse in India and its implications, against the history of SDH and approaches to the issue. This analysis utilizes some of the framework and recommendations of the Commission on Social Determinants of Health (CSDH) [1]. It also takes the analysis beyond the limitations and deficiencies of the CSDH, and identifies two macro factors not currently considered as SDH in India, namely work and the practices of corporations.

I

The Idea and Its Study

The factors shaping health are currently categorized and grouped into five broad categories: genes and associated biology; health behaviors such as dietary habits, tobacco, alcohol and drug use, and physical fitness; medical care and public health services; the ecology of all living things; and social and societal characteristics [2]. Vast amounts of information and evidence are available pointing to the proportionally largest influence of ecological and social/societal factors on population health, exceeding that of the other factors listed above [2–4]. According to Tarlov, 'Efforts to improve population health through policies to modify the other four categories of influence while leaving social/societal characteristics unchanged are unlikely to be successful' (2:283). Tarlov also posits that linear models, multiple independent effects models, and multivariate methods of analysis of these factors have so far not yielded satisfactory explanations of the state of population health. According to him, the interactions of these factors are hugely complex and their study and understanding calls for the application of concepts and methods of complex systems. In parallel, the field of epidemiology also has also been marked for over two decades now by a vigorous debate over the single-cause model, inclining towards recognition of the multicausal nature of production of health. It has been pointed out that the present-day 'pre-occupation with methods and causality at molecular level utilises neither the depth and precision of micro-levels nor the breadth of macro-levels' [3]. Increasingly it is being argued that for scientific reasons we need an epidemiology that moves beyond the dichotomies of biological/social and groups/individuals. The challenge before epidemiology is to put things back together again, to view the biological phenomena within their social contexts, to take account of the role of multiple levels—molecular, individual, social and ecological—and the dynamic interactions within and between the levels in shaping health outcomes. This challenge is being actively worked upon, as evident from the discourse and developments in epidemiology since the 1990s, and the elaboration of ecosocial frameworks and theories of disease causation [4]. Biologists [5, 6] have suggested ways by which it is possible to work out the notion of interpenetration of organism and environment. They argue that all 'causes' of behavior of organisms are simultaneously both biological and social, just as they are simultaneously chemical and physical and are amenable to analysis at many levels. The material universe is organized into structures that are capable of analysis at multiple levels. Within levels, reductionist and holistic descriptions are needed. The problem is of giving primacy to one or the other. What is needed is a unitary view of a material world in which it is impossible to partition out the causes (of an observed phenomenon in an organism) into X% biological and Y% social. The biological and the social are neither separable, nor antithetical, nor alternatives, but are complementary. In health sciences too, the single-discipline approach is seen to be limiting and there are attempts to adopt a framework for interdisciplinary research between social, behavioural and biomedical scientists, addressing multiple levels of analysis. According to Anderson there is a substantial body of research demonstrating connections across 'levels of analysis' in health science. These levels of analysis have been grouped as: social/environmental, psychological/behavioral, organ systems, cellular, and molecular. Each of these levels contains various indices to study health outcomes. For example, the social-environmental level includes economic resources, social support, sociocultural groupings, family environment, and environmental hazards; the behavioural level includes emotion, dietary practices, substance abuse, and tobacco etc., and the molecular level includes genes, DNA, and proteins etc. [7]. Such analysis entails using information, findings and knowledge from one level, to inform research and information at other levels.

Despite the inadequacy of precise quantitative information on the interactions and on the exact causal pathways between social conditions and health, there is still an agreement that existing data is adequate for formulating policies and other actions that could improve population health, and that there is enough information to act [1, 8]. In 2005, the WHO appointed the CSDH to generate evidence on the social causes of poor health and to suggest actions. The CSDH published its report in 2008 [1]. According to the Commission, 'mal-distribution of health care—not delivering care to those who most need it—is one of the social determinants of health. But the high burden of illness responsible for appalling premature loss of life arises in large part because of the conditions in which people are born, grow, live, work, and age. In their turn, poor and unequal living conditions are the consequence of poor social policies and programs, unfair economic arrangements, and bad politics.' The CSDH too holds that, 'There is now a great deal more knowledge, globally circulating, on both the nature of the problem of health inequity and what can be done to address the social determinants of health [...] What is needed now is the political will to implement these difficult but feasible changes' [1].

Thus, it is apparent that in both epidemiology and public health, efforts are on to organize and integrate the vast amounts of information now available at the various identified levels, motivated by concerns to evolve effective interventions and actions to improve health and reduce inequities in health status [4].

The History and Geography

The increased attention in the closing decades of the twentieth century given to the influence of non-medical, social factors on health (expressed often as the social model, as against the dominant biomedical model of health) does not mean that this idea is entirely new. Since the rise of industrial capitalism in Europe from the mid-eighteenth century onwards and the accompanying urbanization and tremendous rise in social and medical problems, there has been a stream in medicine and public health that has pointed to the shaping of health and disease by social factors, including political and economic structures—in general to the structural determinants of health [9]. While Edwin Chadwick is known for his action on implementing urban sanitary measures to improve the health of the laboring populations during the nineteenth century, others such as Rudolf Virchow and Friedrich Engels showed how economic, social and political forces, through their effect on living and working conditions, affected the health of workers and their families in many European cities, and caused disease and early death. Many medical practitioners of that period also wrote about the poor working and living conditions as causing much ill-health and disease [10]. Subsequently, practitioners of Social Medicine (a lesser-known stream of thinking in public health in parts of Latin America), along with sections of sociologists and social epidemiologists working in the historical materialist perspective, showed how the organization of capitalist societies influenced the distribution of economic, social, and political resources within the population, which in turn affected living and working conditions, access to health care, and thereby influenced overall health status. The discourse preceding the 1978 Alma Ata Declaration on Primary Health Care also focused on non-medical factors affecting health and the need to address them, rather than relying on solely medical and technical measures to improve population health. The Alma Ata Declaration not only talked of health systems, but also promotion of food supply and proper nutrition, and the adequate supply of safe water and basic sanitation. Furthermore, it called for action on the political, social, and economic causes of poor health, and placed health within a global context by calling for peace, reduced military expenditure and a 'New International Economic Order' so as to reduce the health status gap between developing and developed countries. Other such analyses of the structural determinants of health in the Indian context [11–14] have been ignored through much of the twentieth century and continue to remain marginalized by the mainstream discourse on determinants of health among policymakers and health researchers, often for reasons such as being ideologically driven and being seen as bringing politics into health. Incidentally, the CSDH attempts to infuse some of these concerns, by referring to 'social injustice killing people on a grand scale' and to the limitations of economic growth to improve—by itself—the health of populations. In her exposition of epidemiologic theory, Krieger [4] provides an absorbing, meticulously-researched account of the historical antecedents and journey of the contemporary idea of SDH: from the mid-nineteenth century emergence of epidemiology bearing the influence of the ideas of Virchow, Villerme and Engels and the structural/societal roots of poverty that gave rise to disease and ill-health; the phases of depoliticization and repoliticization of epidemiologic theory through the twentieth century; the mid-twentieth century idea of social epidemiology as exemplified by Morris's work on uses of epidemiology; the political economy of health and social production of disease frameworks of the late-twentieth century to the present phase of ideas of eco-social epidemiology. While tracing this complex journey of a complex idea, she provides explanations for its periodic eclipse by the dominant mainstream explanations, the conceptual basis of the variants, the similarities and differences between them, their focus and the kind of empirical investigations they generated.

An Attenuated Concept of SDH

While this contemporary interest in SDH in mainstream forums is a welcome counter to the dominant biomedical narrative and interventions to address health problems, SDH is, however, being conceptualized and approached in different ways and the discourse is still not as comprehensive as it could and should be for effective action. For instance, while the CSDH identifies obvious determinants such as living and working conditions, social stratification etc., and recommends actions points on each, it does not attempt to integrate them, or to look into their antecedents and interactions among these determinants. It also adopts a very uncritical, benign view of aid, and of the governments and private sector, and does not address the issue of why they are not accountable and why there is no political will to address the SDH, thereby avoiding larger societal issues of power and politics. Such deficiencies have been raised in other forms—that it does not discuss the actions and influence of the pharmaceutical industry, pharmaceutical policy, the presence of pressure groups that operate upon SDH, and war as an important social determinant that kills, maims and displaces large populations [15]. Yet others have observed that there is limited attention to macrosocial factors, such as the impact of economic priorities and policies, tax regulations, of corporate practices, of gender-race, on factors such as income, which in turn impact health [16]. In other words, the current focus on SDH is more on the proximal, immediately visible determinants, rather than on upstream, distal factors that affect SDH through multiple mechanisms, are not immediately apparent, and are not disease-specific. As rightly pointed out, 'Limited epidemiologic attention to macro-social determinants of health is ironic given that macro-social factors such as the rapid industrialization and urbanization of the nineteenth century contributed to the organization of public health practice and, tangentially, to academic public health research' (16:279).

Overall, the current discourse ends up obfuscating the meaning of social determinants in various ways, emphasizing some proximal social factors, while obscuring and diverting attention away from some other critical factors. Focussing predominantly on proximal factors avoids complexity, directs attention away from features of the social structure and the social and economic policies which give rise to the circumstances in which people are compelled to work, and which determine their incomes, and in turn their living conditions—an important SDH. According to Raphael health, researchers fail to 'acknowledge that the quality of the social determinants of health is influenced by the organization of societies and how these societies distribute material resources among their members'. Furthermore, even fewer bring into their analysis the political, economic, and social forces that shape the organizational and distributional practices of societies [17].

In spite of the global consensus on the relevance and importance of the SDH discourse for global health and on the need to integrate SDH considerations into policies and programs, there are deficiencies in its actual implementation. As the CSDH puts it, there is far too little action on the SDH.

II

SDH in India

In India, food, water, sanitation, housing, health services, education, caste and gender have been identified by and large as SDH. Health policy documents in India refer to these factors and call for intersectoral coordination yet there is little effort to make them available to the entire population and ensure their equitable distribution. Health researchers too pay little attention to the factors/barriers that deprive populations of adequate access to determinants such as nutrition, water, and clean environments—in other words to critical distal determinants such as poverty and its links to work.

What is Addressed

Studies based upon analyses of large-scale surveys, such as the National Family Health Survey (NFHS) data show a social gradient in health from the top to the bottom of the socioeconomic range: the lower a person's socioeconomic status, the worse their health status is such that health status of people second from the bottom was worse than that of people above them, but better than those below [18]. Some other factors identified as major SDH in India and as risk factors contributing to the disease burden are air pollution (both indoor and outdoor), child undernutrition, unimproved sanitation, employment conditions, and gender inequality [19]. Yet another analysis of NFHS 2 and 3 data on women's nutritional status showed that levels of anaemia and chronic energy deficiency among women from disadvantaged social and economic groups was much higher, and within social groups anaemia was highest among women of the lowest wealth quintile, being highest in poor scheduled tribe (ST) women, followed by poor scheduled caste (SC) women [20]. Thus poverty is shown to be an important determinant of malnutrition among women. Some others call for research on understanding health-related behavior among Indians, the social determinants of these behaviours and the social interventions which will work in specific Indian settings [21]. Having identified such determinants, the studies make very generalized recommendations—more data collection to identify other important priorities, studies to understand the failure of interventions and to shape policies to address health inequalities, or recommend that policies should be reconfigured and implemented effectively—'The persistence of these identified challenges in spite of relevant, and in some cases long-term, public policies, indicate that analytical studies are needed to understand the impact of interventions related to a variety of social determinants of health' [19]. There is no attempt to bring in information from other disciplines to understand or ask why existing policies and welfare measures have not been properly implemented by the ruling political classes and the executive, in spite of evidence of effectiveness of certain policies in reducing things such as child mortality and poverty. There are no attempts to raise questions such as what are the reasons for reducing the already meagre social sector expenditures and health budgets, which in turn impacts on the effective implementation of nutrition programmes such as the Integrated Child Development Services (ICDS), and what are the reasons for freezing recruitment of doctors and other health workers in government health centres. In short there is a failure to understand the influence of economic thinking, and of neoliberal thinking on such policies and interventions that shape SDH. In addition, there is a failure to address questions such as why or how do people end up on the lowest rungs of the socioeconomic ladder, why are women and children are undernourished, why are urban slums growing, why do slums lack sanitation and clean drinking water, and why do people migrate from rural to urban areas and live in the urban slums, and so on. Such discourse identifies groups experiencing adverse SDH, takes the situation as given and suggests policy interventions targeted at affected/vulnerable individuals and groups to cope with the adverse SDH that identified groups encounter in their lives, rather than suggesting measures to provide secure/regular employment, raise income levels and reduce poverty, which could improve living conditions. It also does not ask why these are not priority areas for policy and action given their impact upon health.

In other words—the assumption is: having identified adverse SDH and the associated vulnerable populations, the primary means of improving the quality of SDH and promoting their more equitable distribution is through public policy activity or though some behavioral change interventions. Focusing only on policy content and implementation diverts attention from an understanding of the processes which explain why desired policy outcomes fail to emerge, or the reasons behind the genesis of certain policies, and neglects the larger economic and political context within which policies are developed, and the actors involved in policy reform (at the international, national and sub-national levels).

What is not Addressed

Work as SDH

The CSDH established nine knowledge networks in the course of drawing up the report, of which one was on Employment Conditions (EMCONET), in recognition of the fact that the nature of work and good employment conditions can provide financial security, social status, personal development, social relations and self-esteem, as well as protection from physical and psychosocial hazards [22]. There is a significant body of medical, epidemiological and social science work on the impact of unemployment. Unemployment is associated with an increased likelihood of morbidity and mortality. There are clear relationships between unemployment and an increased risk of poor mental health and para suicide, higher rates of all causes and specific causes of mortality, self-reported health and limiting long-term illness and, in some studies, a higher prevalence of risky health behaviors (particularly among young men), including problematic alcohol use and smoking. The negative health experiences of unemployment also extend to families and the wider community, and are not limited to the unemployed [23, 24]. Further, there is a negative relationship between precarious, insecure employment and health [25].

According to the Indian government's own reports, 'We have clearly deviated from the ideal of generating productive employment. The more productive sectors of the economy (manufacturing and services) have not generated enough employment, despite India experiencing the fastest GDP growth ever in its post-independence economic history' [26]. Employment in total and in non-agricultural sectors has not been growing. Further, the growth in unemployment in recent years has been accompanied by a growth in the casualization and informalization of available employment. The share of informal workers in the total Indian workforce is well above that in other emerging market economies—93% of all workers compared to 55% of all workers in Brazil. While the informal nature of employment is predominant in the unorganized sector of the economy, its prevalence is increasing even within the organized sector as well.[1] The National Commission on Enterprises in the Unorganised Sector (NCEUS) [27] created in 2004, highlighted

[1]Informal employment is defined as that form of employment where the employee is not eligible for any kind of social security benefits like provident fund, gratuity, pension, health care, maternity benefit etc. [26].

the low wages/earnings and bargaining power of informal workers, which not only kept them poor but also made them vulnerable. The large overlap between the poor and informal workers was brought into public discourse by one of the NCEUS reports, which came out with the much-cited figure that 77% of the population spent less than Rs. 20 per day in 2004–05. Most of the important recommendations and legislation proposed at the time by the NCEUS have been ignored by successive governments. More than a decade later, there is little change, and much of Indian employment continues to be of an insecure and precarious nature (28:161–2). The minimum wage set by the government is often less than Rs. 15,000 a month,[2] not exactly a decent, living wage that can take care of the minimum needs of a family or even an individual in a city when price inflations, especially of food items are taken into account. Minimum wages, especially for agriculture, are so low that even if workers find employment for every day of the year and are paid the minimum wage, they will not be able to fulfil the basic needs of their family, as specified by various labor committees and courts. In addition, in the vast informal sector, the minimum wage legislation is not applicable [28], while those workers entitled to it have to fight incessant struggles to get the legal minimum wage [29, 30]. The effects of such economic policies, of increasing informalization, and of poor family incomes are visible everywhere around us—in the urban slums and shanties, and in tier II and III cities and towns as well [31–34].

In several other countries, job insecurity and its effect on health is an important area of study in social epidemiology. Continued job insecurity has been shown to be a health risk and secure re-employment to actually improve health. Public health researchers recommend that the reduction of job insecurity should be a part of policy interventions to improve population health [25]. The CSDH also recommends action on employment and the provision of decent work: that national governments should develop and implement economic and social policies that provide secure work and a living wage that takes into account the real and current cost of living for health.

Even with the current estimated labor workforce participation rate of 50.3% [35], the working and living conditions of this vast population should be an important area of study and concern for health, yet we find that work and wages in general, and the increasing informalization of work that affects more than 90% of the working population in India, figure nowhere in the discourse on SDH [36]. Public health researchers do not undertake studies on, or highlight the impact of, such precarious work and employment conditions on income, living standards, and risky health behaviors etc., nor do they make policy recommendations for the payment of decent living wages or for secure employment policies. There is no advocacy or policy recommendation by public health researchers and practitioners that is supportive of workers' rights and their struggles for decent work or which seeks to

---

[2]See: http://www.thehindu.com/opinion/op-ed/Do-we-need-a-minimum-wage-law/article14616002.ece; http://indianexpress.com/article/explained/bharat-bandh-trade-union-strike-minimum-wage-3008835/.

improve employment conditions, prevents the deterioration of employment conditions, reduces contractual, informal and casual work, avoids work insecurity, ensures that minimum wages are a living wage, ensures payment of minimum wages, provides crèche facilities at work, or enforces labor legislation including health and safety legislation at work. In fact, these rights are now being severely eroded, in order to create a more investment-friendly environment etc. Not only does the government not strictly enforce its own labor laws enacted to provide minimum protection to workers, but in practice it also comes down with a heavy hand on workers' struggles for the implementation of their Constitutional rights [28, 29, 37] and is further relaxing labor laws to enable more investment and growth, and is promoting India as a site of cheap labor and lax regulations.

Corporations—Corporate Practices—Private Enterprises as SDH

Another distal, societal factor that does not get the attention it deserves—in public health in general, and much more so in the Indian context—is how corporations, through their practices, activities, power and influence, affect individual and population health. There has been a growth in the power and influence of transnational corporations (TNC) in the twenty-first century, with revenues of several TNCs being larger than those of many national governments, and many exercising increasing social, economic and political influence in the globalized market economy and within individual countries [38–40]. According to the CSDH 'binding trade agreements together with increasing corporate power and capital mobility have diminished individual countries' capacities to ensure that economic activity contributes to health equity, or at least does not undermine it' (1:133). According to The Lancet—University of Oslo Commission on Global Governance for Health 'Private firms have an influential role in contemporary global governance. Large transnational companies wield tremendous economic power, which they can deploy to further their interests in global governance processes and global markets', and that although there were benefits from the operation of TNCs, 'they can also harm health through dangerous working conditions, inadequate pay, environmental pollution, or by producing goods that are a threat to health (e.g., tobacco)' [41]. An increasing amount of research indicates that while there are some positive effects there are significant negative impacts on health from corporate structures, products and practices (Table 1 in 39). So expansive and pervasive is their presence and impact that public health researchers have called attention to the need to systematically study the corporate entity in society and corporate practices as SDH [42, 43].

Corporations impact population health through direct and indirect pathways. Baum et al. [39] have attempted to design a framework for corporate health impact assessment (CHIA) with which to undertake a systematic study of the health impacts of corporations. So far, the following impact areas have been highlighted:

(i) Promotion of highly processed foods, beverages [38] and tobacco, which are risk factors for many non-communicable diseases. According to an ex-Director General of the WHO, 'Today, many of the threats to health that contribute to non-communicable diseases (NCDs) come from corporations that are big, rich and powerful, driven by commercial interests, and far less friendly to health. Today, more than half of the world's population lives in an urban setting. Slums need corner food stores that sell fresh produce, not just packaged junk with a cheap price and a long shelf-life' [44]; and
(ii) Business practices of big pharmaceutical companies that leads to exorbitant pricing of medicines, their control over knowledge through intellectual property rights, patents, data exclusivity, and mechanisms such as World Trade Organisation (WTO) and Trade related Intellectual Property Rights (TRIPS) [45]
(iii) Environmental destruction/pollution by mining and other industries, including release of toxic wastes, and their dumping in third world countries. Apart from these, other areas that are critical and relevant to the Indian context are:
(iv) Production of goods and services that affects labor practices as well as occupational safety and health. 'Manufacturing in the new global economy has shifted from "well regulated," high paying, often unionized plants in the industrial countries to very low wage, unregulated, and non-union production facilities in the developing world, each competing with one another for maximum "competitive advantage"' (40:13). Footloose corporations often move globally, looking for the lowest wages, vulnerable workforces, and lax regulation of labor, environmental and occupational health. These practices affect both developed and developing economies. The CSDH acknowledges the 'increasing power of large transnational corporations and international institutions to determine the labor policy agenda (that) has led to a disempowerment of workers, unions, and those seeking work, and a growth in health-damaging working arrangements and conditions [22]'. Innumerable instances can be cited from across India of exploitative labor practices by both domestic and transnational corporations, such as in the garment, automobile, cement, construction, leather and services sectors etc.[3] [46, 47].
(v) Corporations also influence health services in the following ways:

  (a) Influencing of medical practice, through the pharma industry, and the medical equipment and devices industries.
  (b) Direct provision of health care. The private sector in India is currently undergoing transformation, with the expansion of large and small health care companies, both geographically and in nearly all sectors of medical care [48]. The impact is being felt in terms of unnecessary interventions,

[3]To get an idea of violations in the National Capital Region of Delhi and vicinity, see documentation by the People's Union for Democratic Rights, http://pudr.org.

irrational medical practices, setting of targets for doctors to increase revenues, and corruption [49].

(c) By corporate foundations through their monetary contributions, which are active in shaping health policies and health systems, influencing what is prioritized and what is not in global health, by advocating business models of governance, market mechanisms, and technical solutions, and in diverting attention from SDH itself [50].

The debate on the comparative effectiveness of vertical programmes versus more systemic approaches has emerged periodically since the 1960s, such as in the run up to the 1978 Alma Ata Declaration on primary health care; subsequently as selective primary health care, and later as 'essential packages of care'.[4] The debate is back post-1990s, with growth in funding targeted at specific diseases and services, from sources such as the Global Fund to Fight AIDS, Tuberculosis and Malaria (GFATM) and the WHO's emphasis on health systems strengthening (HSS) and primary care. An ethnographic case study of the GAVI Alliance brings out the role of the Bill and Melinda Gates Foundation (BMGF)—the largest in the world today—in tilting the contested idea of HSS in favour of its disease-specific approach [51]. It locates the policy discourse within a global sphere of expert groups (epistemic communities), comprising transnational expert communities working on research, policy and advocacy within organizations located in centers of global power, although their work is to be implemented in the poorest countries. HSS was a contested issue within the GAVI Board, with very strong 'for' and 'against' camps—Norwegian and British governments and others backing it, while it was 'strongly resisted by many powerful actors in the GAVI Board, including the US Agency for International Development (USAID), senior vaccination experts and the Bill & Melinda Gates Foundation' (51: 868). The Gates Foundation was 'a very loud, vocal voice, saying that we do not believe in the strengthening of health systems', said one of GAVI's strongest health systems proponents, recalling that Bill Gates often told him in private conversations 'that he is vehemently against health systems [...] he basically said it is a complete waste of money, that there is no evidence that it works, so I will not see a dollar or cent of my money go to the strengthening of health systems' (51: 868). The study describes how those who were for HSS got marginalized and the debate was again settled in favour of disease-specific approaches. HSS has become distorted, increasingly meaning little more than the strengthening of the components needed to achieve disease-specific goals or immunization. GAVI—along with other GHIs and the private actors who support them—has embraced rhetoric supportive of 'holistic' health systems and captured the debate on HSS 'in support of its specific ethos and selective approach' (51:872). The board's 'acceptance of the health systems goal was little more than a public relations exercise to temper the emerging criticism of GHIs' negative impact on health systems' (51:870). With many such details, the study

[4]Few issues relating to the organization of health systems and service delivery in developing countries, especially in India, have been discussed so much as the pros and cons of vertical programmes versus comprehensive health systems.

shows how thinking on health systems settled in favour of an ideological convergence around the so-called 'Gates approach' to global health.

Given the importance of BMGF in the health care scenario in India, there is a need for such studies to understand policies and policymaking processes also as macrosocial determinants of health services, to understand the influences on health policymaking in India and its consequences for Indian health systems, where partnership with the private sector is the preferred policy option, not the strengthening of public health systems.

III

'High Quality Policy-Making Demands High-Quality Inputs and High-Quality Debates'[5]

The historic rise and ebb of SDH attests to the reality and the importance to health of distal factors. The contemporary phase provides yet another opportunity for the public health discourse in India to address issues considered to be outside the purview of public health and to take the lead in research, and in formulating and advocating strategies and policies that address issues such as formulating the minimum income needed for healthy living, generating evidence on the impact of casual/insecure employment on income and access to living conditions and on health status, and on the role of various national and international agencies in the making of health policies.

While public health researchers (and policymakers) acknowledge and recognize social conditions as important determinants of health, they tend to take a mechanical and apolitical approach, and end up making generalized policy recommendations that address more proximate or individual level factors such as change in behavior or access to better services. Despite talk of intersectoral measures, even the proximal determinants such as water supply and sanitation in urban slums, incomes, employment conditions, and the working environment are not given as much policy attention, priority and resources as they merit. Health policy researchers fail to point out how government policies negatively impact access to determinants such as income by affecting livelihoods, the environment and nature, and how they affect quality of work, employment and living conditions. They also fail to point out how government's failure to implement many of its existing laws affects workers, their families and where and how they live. Current discourses ignore public policy antecedents and fail to look at or ask why government authorities ignore access to and quality of SDH and their inequitable distribution.

---

[5]Arvind Subramanian Chief Economic Advisor, Government of India, at Dr. V K R V Memorial lecture, 11.5.17. Downloaded from: http://www.thehindu.com/todays-paper/tp-national/high-quality-policy-making-demands-richer-debates/article18431447.ece, 12.5.17.

Studies, for instance, can integrate the poverty factor/income with the nature of work/employment status and caste and gender to help understand their interactions and impact upon health status [46]. Given the nutrition-infection-tuberculosis link, one can systematically study the association of nutrition and food security with incomes, work, the availability of various food items and price of food, and then identify policies that affect these factors, either positively or adversely. While a lot of data seems to get collected, there is still a need to collate them and undertake interdisciplinary analyses, in order to see their relation to population health, and to grasp the respective social, economic, and political determinants, and their impact upon risk factors.

The contemporary interest in SDH is an opportunity to also take note of, and to engage with, the global SDH discourse and developments in epidemiology and health sciences that identify several important macrodeterminants. It is an opportunity to generate locally relevant systems frameworks and methods that can address the upstream and the macrodeterminants, as well as the complexity of the interactions at various levels in the production of health and ill-health. It is yet again a call to take up the challenge of an expanded concept of SDH that makes public health genuinely interdisciplinary, and shows how larger social-economic policy issues affect health, without having to apologize for doing do.

References

1. World Health Organization. Closing the gap in a generation: health equity through action on the social determinants of health. Final Report of the Commission on Social Determinants of Health. Geneva: World Health Organization; 2008.
2. Tarlov AR. Public policy frameworks for improving population health. Ann N Y Acad Sci. 1999;896:281–93.
3. Susser M. Does risk factor epidemiology put epidemiology at risk? Peering into the future. J Epidemiol Community Health. 1998;52(10):608–11.
4. Krieger N. Epidemiology and the people's health (Chapters 6, 7 and 8). Oxford: Oxford University Press; 2011.
5. Lewontin RC, Rose S, Kamin LJ. Chapter 10: new biology versus old ideology. In not in our genes: biology, ideology and human nature. New York: Pantheon Books; 1984. p. 265–90.
6. Levins R, Lewontin R. The dialectical biologist. Massachusetts: Harvard University Press; 1985.
7. Anderson NB. Levels of analysis in health science: a framework for integrating socio-behavioral and biomedical research. Ann N Y Acad Sci. 1998;840:563–76.
8. Bravemann P, Gottlieb L. The social determinants of health: it's time to consider the causes of the causes. Public Health Rep. 2014;129(Suppl 2):19–31.
9. Chakravarthi I. Shifts in processes of diffusion of medical technology in India and implications for public health (Chapter 2). Unpublished doctoral thesis. Delhi: Jawaharlal Nehru University; 2009.
10. Hamlin C. Could you starve to death in England in 1839? The Chadwick-Farr controversy and the loss of the "Social" in public health. Am J Public Health. 1995;85(6):856–66.
11. Qadeer I. Public health in India: critical reflections Part I. Delhi: Danish Books; 2011.
12. Zurbrigg S. Rakku's story. Madras: George Joseph; 1984.

13. Banerji D. Poverty, class and health culture in India, vol. I. New Delhi: Prachi Prakashan; 1981.
14. Indian Council for Medical Research and Indian Council for Social Science Research. Report of the joint committee on health for all by 2000 A.D. New Delhi: ICMR; 1980.
15. Escudero JC. What is said, what is silenced, what is obscured: the report of the commission on the social determinants of health. Soc Med. 2009;4(3):183–5.
16. Putnam S, Galea S. Epidemiology and the macro-social determinants of health. J Pub Health Policy. 2008;29(3):275–89.
17. Raphael D. Social determinants of health: present status, unanswered questions, and future directions. Int J Health Serv. 2006;36(4):651–77.
18. Subramanian SV, Ackerson LK, Subramanyam MA, Sivaramakrishnan K. Health inequalities in India: the axes of stratification. Brown J World Aff. 2008;14(2):127–38.
19. Cowling K, Dandona R, Dandona L. Social determinants of health in India: progress and inequities across states. Int J Equity Health. 2014;13:88.
20. Jose S, Navaneetham K. A fact sheet on women's malnutrition in India. Econ Polit Wkly. 2008;43(33):61–7.
21. Sarkar S. Research on social determinants of health necessary for health equity in India. Int J Med Public Health. 2016;6:1–3.
22. EMCONET. Employment conditions and health inequalities. Final report of the employment conditions knowledge network of the commission on social determinants of health. Geneva: World Health Organization; 2007.
23. Bambra C. Yesterday once more? Unemployment and health in the 21st century. J Epidemiol Community Health. 2010;64(3):213–5.
24. Bambra C, Eikemo T. Welfare state regimes, unemployment and health: a comparative study of the relationship between unemployment and self-reported health in 23 European countries. J Epidemiol Community Health. 2009;63(2):92–8.
25. Bartley M. Job insecurity and its effect on health. J Epidemiol Community Health. 2005;59 (9):718–9.
26. Mehrotra S, Gandhi S, Saha P, Sahoo B. Joblessness and informalization: challenges to inclusive growth in India. Institute of Applied Manpower Research, Planning Commission, Government of India; 2012.
27. National Commission for Enterprises in the Unorganised Sector. Report on conditions of work and promotion of livelihoods in the unorganised sector. Delhi: NCEUS; 2007.
28. Srija A. Implementation of the Minimum Wages Act, 1948—case study of India. Glob J Hum-Soc Sci: F Polit Sci. 2014;14(7).
29. PUDR—People's Union for Democratic Rights. Driving force: labour struggles and violations of rights in Maruti Suzuki India Limited. 2013. Available at http://pudr.org/sections/worker?page=10.
30. Shyam Sundar KR. Industrial violence and labour reforms. Econ Polit Wkly. 2012;47(41): 35–40.
31. Mander H. Twilight children. The Hindu. 2015; December 13. Downloaded from http://www.thehindu.com/opinion/columns/Harsh_Mander/twilight-children/article7980662.ece.
32. Mohanakumar S, Singh S. Impact of the economic crisis on unorganised sector workers in Rajasthan. Econ Polit Wkly. 2011;46(22):66–71.
33. Thomson Reuters Foundation. Deafening power loom muffles desperation in textile hub. The Hindu. 2017 Apr 21.
34. Thomas M. Most gem, textile workers sans provident fund cover. The Times of India; 2017 Jan 21.
35. Government of India. Economic survey 2016–17. Delhi: Ministry of Finance, Department of Economic Affairs, Economic Division; 2017 Jan
36. Chakravarthi I. Work as a social determinant of health: joblessness and informalization in India-implications for health. Samyukta J Women's Stud. 2014;14(2):41–55.
37. Chakravarthi I, Gera S. Repression of workers' struggles in Chhattisgarh. Econ Polit Wkly. 2011;46(18):16–9.

38. Anaf J, Baum FE, Fisher M, Harris E, Friel S. Assessing the health impact of transnational corporations: case of McDonald's Australia. Globalization Health. 2017;13:7.
39. Baum FE, Sanders DM, Fisher M, Anaf J, Freudenberg F, Friel S, et al. Assessing the health impact of transnational corporations: its importance and a framework. Globalization Health. 2016;12:27.
40. Brown GD. The global threats to workers' health and safety on the job. Soc Justice. 2002;29 (3):12–25.
41. Ottersen OP, Dasgupta J, Blouin C, Buss P, Chongsuvivatwong V, Frenk J, et al. The political origins of health inequity: prospects for change. Lancet. 2014;383:630–7.
42. Freudenberg N, Galea S. The impact of corporate practices on health: implications for health policy. J Public Health Policy. 2008;29(1):86–104.
43. Wiist WH. Public health and the anti-corporate movement: rationale and recommendations. Am J Public Health. 2006;96:1370–5.
44. Chan M. The rise of non-communicable diseases: an impending disaster. Opening remarks at the WHO Global Forum: Addressing the Challenge of Non-communicable Diseases Moscow, Russian Federation 27 Apr 2011. Available at http://www.who.int/dg/speeches/2011/global_forum_ncd_20110427/en/, downloaded 1.05.17.
45. Global Health Watch. The Pharmaceutical Industry and Pharmaceutical endeavour. In Global Health Watch: An Alternative World Health Report. 2011; Chapter D4. Available at http://www.ghwatch.org/ghw3.
46. Goyal M. At Alang shipbreaking yard worker safety remains a dusty dream. Economic Times; 2016 Oct 23.
47. Hoefe R. Do leather workers matter? Violating labour rights and environmental norms in India's leather production. Netherlands: India Committee of the Netherlands; 2017 Mar. http://www.indianet.nl/pdf/DoLeatherWorkersMatter.pdf.
48. Chakravarthi I, Roy B, Mukhopadhyaya I, Barria S. "Investing in health": The Healthcare Industry in India. Econ Polit Weekly. 2017.
49. Gadre A, Shukla A. Dissenting diagnosis: voices of conscience from the medical profession. Gurgaon: Random House India; 2016.
50. Stuckler D, Basu S, McKee M. Global health Philanthropy and institutional relationships: how should conflicts of interest be addressed? PLoS Med. 2011;8(4):e1001020. doi:10.1371/journal.pmed.1001020.
51. Storeng KT. The GAVI Alliance and the 'Gates approach' to health system strengthening. Glob Public Health: Int J Res, Policy Pract. 2014;9(8):865–79.

Part II
Operationalization

Chapter 6
Shram Jeevani: Special Task Force Report on Women's Labor in the Informal Economy in Bihar

Sushmita Goswami

Abstract The informal sector in Bihar is comprised of more than 13 million women workers, who have for ages been ignored and denied their due place in the economy and society. This is reflected in their health status as well. We know that more than 65% of the women in Bihar are anaemic and Bihar stands fifth highest in terms of the rate of maternal mortality. However, the health of women is promoted not only by the health care system available to them, but is closely connected to the social determinants of work, infrastructure and physical security, and cannot be looked at in isolation. The 'Shram Jeevani Report' is a joint endeavor of Self Employed Women's Association of Bharat (SEWA) and the Government of Bihar, and it aims to provide a view from the ground up of the economy and society that frame the lives of these informal workers. The study report prepared by a Special Task Force set up in early 2012 uses mixed methods for data collection, including both qualitative and quantitative and combines fieldwork-based insights with official survey data. In its final form, the report acts as a strong advocacy document prioritizing the key concerns of informal women workers and provides a basis for further dialogues concerning policy intervention in distributive justice.

Keywords Informal economy · Women workers · Task force · Bihar
Self Employed Women's Association

Background

In Basant Bagh Nayatola in Purnea district, we met Rajani Chatri, who works in the edible lime factory. She had taken the day off due to ill health. Rajani and her family, like other families in Nayatola have been evicted from the land they had

S. Goswami (✉)
Self Employed Women's Association, Patna, Bihar, India
e-mail: sushmita@sewabharat.org

S. Goswami
Department of Economics, Patna University, Patna, Bihar, India

D. Nambiar and A. Muralidharan (eds.), *The Social Determinants of Health in India*, https://doi.org/10.1007/978-981-10-5999-5_6

been living on for as long as they can remember. Relocation is in process but it has been three years since the eviction and no one has received their relocation papers yet. In this environment of uncertainty, Rajani is struggling to eke out a living. She reaches the factory at 9.00 am and works there until 5.30 pm. She earns Rs. 60 per day to pack edible lime. Her husband, Kali Chatri, makes bamboo houses and earns Rs. 200–250 per day. However, he does not get work regularly.

We saw Rajani's hands, which were scalded and burned due to continuous exposure to lime. The women working in the edible lime packaging unit are not provided gloves. When the burns got worse, the employer told Rajani to come back when she was well enough to pack the lime again. She has a Rashtriya Swasthya Bima Yojana (RSBY) smart card but it did not cover her illness. She had to consult a private doctor. Her bills mounted up to Rs. 1400. Now recovered she still goes to the same factory. 'hum aur kuch kar bhi nahi sakte […] humko damma bhi hai' ('I can't do anything much […] I have asthma as well') [1].

Rajani more or less represents the 13 million informal sector women workers in Bihar. The conditions, in which they are born, live and work, shape their perception about their own health. When asked if they have any health issues, the first response was usually 'naah […] sabtheekhai' (everything is fine). A little more probing yielded 'haandard to hotahai […] par sharer hai to dard to hoga hi' ('yes it aches […] but when you have a body it is bound to ache'). The above two statements given by women in Bihar reflect the attitude towards health of a woman that has been historically shaped by the continued denial of their role as contributors to the economy and society.

The official records show rather dismal numbers for all the indicators of health. Life expectancy for women in Bihar is lower than for all of India. Also Bihar has the eighth highest Infant Mortality Rate (IMR) in the country today, with female IMR higher than male IMR [2]. Gender disaggregated IMR data show that male IMR has always been marginally lower than female IMR. The mean age of marriage for women is 17.6 years and Total Fertility Rate is as high as 3.5 [3]. Until the age of 35 years, maternal deaths are a predominant cause of death among women in Bihar. In the Sample Registration System (SRS) of 2007–09, Bihar had the fifth highest Maternal Mortality Rate after Chhattisgarh, Madhya Pradesh, Rajasthan, Assam and Uttar Pradesh [4].

SEWA's experience in Bihar has made us understand that the women are engaged in a variety of livelihood generating activities which fall into the informal economy. The informal and unorganized nature of their work and their low and uncertain incomes as well as their living and working conditions, which include irregular time intervals between meals, long hours of sitting in the same position, unhygienic working conditions, absence of toilets, and access to safe drinking water etc. are responsible for a number of health issues.

For instance, in a weaver's family (where power looms are used), the women generally assist male weavers in reeling and bobbin filling. For this, the women need to stand close to the front of the machines otherwise the threads are wasted. These women usually suffer from Noise Induced Hearing Loss (NIHL) due to a prolonged exposure to high intensity sound.

The agarbatti rollers whose work is contractual and piece rated, try to complete the work once started. They sit for long hours hardly paying attention to the gap between meals. Their hands are soiled by charcoal and once started the women try to finish the piece in hand irrespective of mealtimes. The frequent washing of hands becomes a luxury given the scarcity of water in some regions and the women show symptoms of gastrointestinal problems.

The women in a bamboo worker's household weave baskets of different sizes and shapes. In the process, small fragments of bamboo enter the nail beds leading to the discoloration and abnormalities of the nail bed causing such deformities as abnormal pigmentation, shape, texture and thickness. The skin also gets thickened due to the constant abrasion from the bamboo. Though there are no actual numbers, the women reported that the wound if not treated in time could well lead to amputation of the affected part. It should be noted here that this work is done by scheduled caste people in Bihar, who also happen to fall into the lowest income group.

Health issues associated with bidi rolling have been widely discussed and debated all over India and as a result special hospitals have been set up exclusively for the bidi workers. However, generally the women are not able to visit the hospital or lack a bidi workers card to avail themselves of the benefit of exclusivity. It is the most poorly paid job with a high incidence of health disorders.

In the first case, NIHL could just have been avoided by using earplugs while working. The second case demanded the adherence to the proper intervals between meals. In the third case, deformities could be avoided by applying antiseptics or a timely visit to the doctor. And in the last case, proper food combined with a mask while working would work wonders. As simple as this sound, it becomes difficult in practice. The main reason being the secondary status given to women which has, as mentioned earlier, historically shaped perceptions about women's health. The notion of women's work being considered as an extension of household duties and their earnings as a supplement of household income has for centuries denied a status of equality.

However, because of various women's movements, women's empowerment has found its way in policymaking, and in recent years empowerment has become both a process and a goal of development. The Bihar government has been taking steps in this regard by promoting girls' education through the provision of cycles and scholarships, reservation in panchayat elections, the promotion of safe motherhood through Janani Suraksha Yojana, and many more schemes. Still, it is more important to establish women as not merely a beneficiary, but as a contributor to the economy and society. The first step in this process is the formation of a Special Task Force—a joint initiative of SEWA Bharat and the Government of Bihar.

Methodology

The Special Task Force (STF) was set up in collaboration with the Government of Bihar and supported by the Packard Foundation with an intention to dig deep into the lives of the women workers and bring out the determinants that frame their living conditions. The objectives of the Task Force report were to provide a 'bottom up' view of the economy and society that frame the work and lives of informal workers, with a special focus on women workers. This needed a concrete analysis of the informal economy of women workers, namely their work, conditions of work, earnings, financial inclusion, infrastructure, physical security, government support and organizational capacity.

The report was prepared under the supervision of STF members who have expertise in different fields including labor issues, women's work and organizing women workers, government administration, and research [1].

Drawing upon suggestions from the members as well as discussions at an initial consultative workshop in May 2012, the decision was taken to use mixed methods for data collection, including both qualitative and quantitative methods and combining fieldwork-based insights with official survey data. By using a range of sources, it was expected that any outliers could be easily spotted and findings from one set of data could be compared with those from other sources.

While considerable official data is available, a gender-disaggregated analysis is not always possible from this. A number of small-scale studies were commissioned on different issues to bring in the views of experts (see Box 6.1). The sections on socioeconomic characteristics (Chap. 2 on women and work in rural Bihar) relied heavily on four quantitative studies undertaken by the Institute of Human development (IHD). These studies analysed the data from a primary rural survey carried out by the IHD in 2009–10 covering 3116 households in 36 villages in Bihar. While this survey used the same definitions as the National Sample Survey Office (NSSO), the surveyors were trained to ensure in-depth probing and in particular were sensitive to issues around women's work.

Box 6.1: Studies Commissioned by SEWA Bharat

Mehta, Balwant Singh (2012). 'Women's Work Participation in Bihar'. Associate Fellow, Institute for Human Development, New Delhi

Mehta, Balwant Singh (2012). 'Women's employment in rural Bihar-Major occupations where women work'. Institute for Human Development, New Delhi

Ray, Sarbani and Sharma, Jayprakash (2012). 'Women's work in the primary sector: in the context of rural Bihar'. Research Associates, Institute for Human Development, New Delhi

Chakravarty, Debabani and Sapra, Samidha (2012). 'Our time, their work: an account of women's time spent on work in rural Bihar'. Fellows, Institute for Human development: New Delhi

Satija, Shivani (2012). 'Violence against women'. Research Associate, Institute for Human development: New Delhi

Sinha, Indu B. (2013). 'Floating Isles in the ocean of Poverty- A Study about Organizing Efforts in Bihar'. Visiting Senior Fellow (IHD), Director, ShodhMadhyam, Patna and Editor Chetanshi

Kumar, Niraj (2013). 'Access to financial services to women in the informal economy'. 'Director Nimbus Consulting Pvt Ltd.', New Delhi

Murugan, Ganpathy and Nandi, Sulakshna (2013). 'Health Status of Women and Girls in Bihar'. On behalf of the National Health Systems Resource Center (NHSRC), New Delhi

SEWA Bharat (2013). 'Issues facing women in the unorganized sector in urban Bihar'

Gupta, Neelam (2013). 'Violence against women in Bihar: An Overview'

Gupta Neelam (2013). 'Gender Based Violence and Media in Bihar'

Singh, Aprajita, (2013). 'Access to toilets and its impact on women's lives and health', Mahila Housing Trust

Singh, Aprajita, (2013). 'Housing the poor-Insights from the "Voices of Women in Bihat" study for Bihar'. Mahila Housing Trust

Goswami, Sushmita, (2013). 'Women workers in arts and crafts industry in Bihar'. Research Coordinator, SEWA Bharat

The study commissioned on health issues used mainly secondary data from a variety of sources such as the National Health System Resource Centre, National Rural Health Mission, National Sample Survey Organization, Office of Registrar General and Census Commissioner, Planning Commission, etc. The commissioned study on Financial Inclusion used mainly secondary sources but also relied on focus group discussions. The study on violence relied mainly on newspaper sources, while those on toilets used both secondary sources and direct data from primary surveys.

However, the major findings of the report relied on a field study that was carried out by SEWA Bharat's in-house research team called the 'Voices of Women' and was conducted using a mix of focus group discussions and a structured questionnaire. The team gathered data from 179 villages of 79 blocks in 13 districts, and six urban areas. The field survey covered 11 districts and collected information from women engaged in approximately 40 distinct types of work. The median age of the women met was a little above 37 years and 80% of the women were illiterate. With a very few exceptions, women workers belonged to the informal economy.

The 'Voices' study had to make a decision as to how it would select the villages and towns to be covered. It was felt that women's work, especially in the informal economy, is not only defined by geography, but by cultural factors as well. Therefore, it was decided to select two or three districts from each of the five linguistic regions of the state, reflecting the sociocultural features of the area. These were:

Bhojpur: *West Champaran, Rohtas-Kaimur (Bhabua)*

Magadh: *Patna and Gaya*

Mithilanchal: *Madhubani, Purnea and Katihar*

Angika: *Bhagalpur, Munger and Jamui*

Bazzika: *Muzaffarpur, Sitamarhi*

The selection of blocks, and of villages within blocks, was based on discussions with key informants in each of the districts. Government offices (labor department, DICs, health department etc.), local NGOs and other knowledgeable persons were of great help in mapping the informal works in some clustered activities in addition to agriculture and animal husbandry, which are spread out.

The information is largely qualitative in nature. The fact that a rigorous process of stratified random sample selection was not possible given the absence of data on the population of informal workers, and limitations of time and cost, may be seen as a limitation. However, once clusters were identified, efforts were made by the team to talk to women from all parts of the identified cluster so as to obtain information that would be reasonably representative of that cluster.

The data and information collected through focus group discussion (FGD) allow a holistic picture to emerge of the situation of women workers, their views and voices. Using it alongside data from other sources enables a deeper understanding of the picture available from state-wide surveys. It also allows us to appreciate the variations across regions, within districts and even within blocks, and to thus be better able to appreciate the need for contextually relevant interventions.

The biggest challenge of the study was conducting the FGDs with women in different parts of the state. Opening up about your life in front of complete strangers was probably too much to ask for. The team had to make friends in every area they visited. At times the women refused to talk and showed their anger when the team inquired about their living conditions. One such incident occurred in Phulwari Sharif Block in Patna district where, following the FGD, a group of about 60 women did not allow the team to leave the premises of the community hall. Tension rose when the women were asked about their hygiene habits. Water is scant, therefore the women are only able to take a bath every 3–4 days. There are no toilets so they defecate in the open, which has its own repercussions in the form of physical security and adverse health conditions. The women demanded water and toilets from the team and held the team back in the community hall for hours. It was very difficult to pacify the women and only then was the team allowed to leave the area.

The STF reviewed the commissioned studies from time to time and presented the findings in wide consultations held with government officials, NGOs, academicians, activists, and people with gender concerns. The workshops proved to be of immense help in pooling together the experiences of grassroots organizations and government agencies, identifying gaps in addressing issues concerning women and providing an insight as to how women are viewed in Bihar.

The report with all the information gathered is divided into nine chapters, each dealing with a specific issue and providing relevant recommendations to address that issue. The report addresses the health question not solely as it relates to the health care system but also in conjunction with its social determinants.

Findings

A. Women and work: visibility, conditions of work and earnings

The first and foremost task of the report was to make visible the contribution of women workers in the economy and society. Official figures show that the work-force participation rate of women in rural Bihar is only 11%. This seems to be ridiculously low, and certainly contradicts the evidence of our own eyes. The study shows a WPR of 56%, which is five times higher than the numbers given by the NSSO. We see that almost all women in rural areas in Bihar seem to be working either on their own fields or on other's fields, or looking after cattle or other animals. In urban areas they undertake a large variety of work too. However, greater probing in smaller, more sensitive surveys reveals much higher work participation than that found in official national surveys (Fig. 6.1).

According to the official surveys (NSSO) 80% of women workers in Bihar are engaged only in 'domestic activities' [6]. In Bihar, as in the rest of India, much of the household work involves subsistence activities, which are in fact economic activities. Therefore, although women may be spending significant amounts of time in economic activities, they often perceive their own economic role as non-existent, supplementary, or temporary. Consequently, women's responses to labor force surveys or to the question of what work they do, is often inaccurate. The official investigators have their own biases and due to the patriarchal nature of society, it is usually the man who is considered to be the worker in the family enterprise. The study found that the proportion of women in animal husbandry is close to 80%. In agriculture, half the workforce was found to be women. In addition, women constitute a large percentage of workers in other growing sectors. Nearly 52% of health workers are women, 30% of lower administrative workers are women, and 24% of teachers are women.

When it comes to wages, we find huge interdistrict as well as intradistrict variations. Male and female wages also differ distinctly. Based on the findings of the 2011 IHD household and village survey, women's wages are found to vary

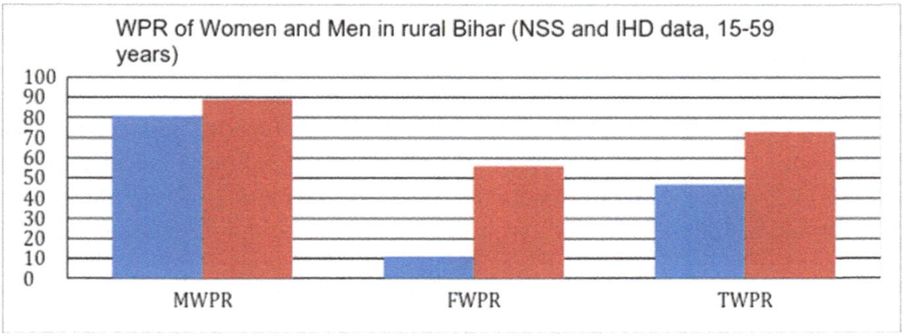

Fig. 6.1 Workforce participation rate of women and men in rural Bihar. *Source* [6, 7]

between Rs. 47 and Rs. 60 per day in 12 villages spread across six districts in Bihar, while men's wages ranged much higher at between Rs. 80 and 117[1] [7].

Apart from the agricultural and animal husbandry work, which are quite widespread across the districts, the SEWA in-house team also came across a variety of home-based work, which provides women with some flexibility to simultaneously look after the house (as caring work is not currently shared by men). The employer is also saved from investing in worksheds and easily avoids the payment of benefits which otherwise would have been mandatory. This home-based work includes bidi rolling, agarbatti rolling, papad making and various craft-based work in rural areas while in urban areas domestic work, casual labor, street vending and waste collection occur. The field study found a variation in wages of the bidi workers of from Rs. 30 per thousand to Rs. 60 per thousand, which is way below the minimum wage set by the Bihar Government for this work, which was Rs. 151. for one thousand bidis in 2012. For agarbatti rolling the women from Pashchim Champaran reported getting Rs. 16 per Kg for 9" of fine agarbatti. The minimum wage set for agarbatti rolling is again Rs. 151 for one kilogram. Their per day earnings were between Rs. 30 and Rs. 35. The median earnings for various craft-based work in Bihar were found to be Rs. 2000 per month.

In the urban areas, as well as the low wages, the women were found to be living in conditions which are a breeding ground for diseases. The informal settlements lacked sewerage, drainage, and adequate drinking water, while due to the inadequate number of toilets open defecation has become more a norm. Here it should be noted that the dwellings for poor people play a central role in their economic activities. In addition to being workplaces, homes are also workshops, warehouses, stores and sites for inputs such as water and electricity into production processes.

Box 6.2: The Desperation of Slums

Ganga Devi lives in a slum in Katihar. She says, 'My children are often ill. I think it must be because the open drain near my house is always overflowing. There are piles of rubbish also and no one collects them, so the flies are always there. Sometimes children get fever and often they get diarrhoea, since there are no toilets here, they go to the drains or sit on the road, I feel sad but what to do?'

Source: [1]

Bihar has seen an overall double-digit growth rate largely due to huge investment in transport and communication, trade and construction. Women in construction are seen to be mainly involved in stone crushing, brick kilns or carrying loads on their heads on construction sites. The crushers and kilns are not gender sensitive and lack basic amenities such as toilets and safe drinking water.

[1]This estimate includes payments in kind, which are commonly made in addition to or in lieu of cash.

The work site is dusty and affects both breathing and eyesight. At all the kilns visited, women complained of sunstroke and gastrointestinal problems. Bricklayers are exposed to extremes in weather and require much physical strength, nevertheless their economic status forces them to face such hardships.

Box 6.3: Destiny Hard as Stone

Meena Devi, a skinny woman in her forties is laboring hard in a brick kiln to eke out living. Her husband had a paralytic attack four years ago and since then is unable to do any work. Meenadevi belongs to Jaikhut village, but has lived for eight months in a brick kiln in Pakki Sarai, Kahalgaon, with her husband Uday Tanti. She lays up to 600–700 bricks a day and is paid Rs. 230 for every 1000 bricks.

When we asked why she had come so far from her village to work in the brick factory, she replied, 'Gaon mein koi kaam nahi hai [...] kabhi kabhi khet mein kaam milta hai par mazdoori bahut kam hai.' ('There is no work in the village. Sometimes there is work during the agricultural season, but the payment is too low'). The brick kiln she works in is devoid of any facilities except for drinking water.

'kamjori to lagta hai didi....par kya karen?' ('I do feel weak sister. But what can one do?'). She has mouths to feed and has to get treatment for her husband. Her own treatment is a distant thought.

Source: [1]

Although women do many jobs, they are still seen as non-workers, giving them a secondary status in society. This also means their hunger is secondary, their comfort is secondary, their pain is secondary, and so is their health.

B. **Physical security**

Another barrier on the way to the well-being of women is gender-based violence. In Bihar according to the National Crime Records Bureau (NCRB), gender-based violence has been on the rise for the last ten decades. Cases of kidnapping and abduction of women in particular have registered a six-fold increase. Cases of sexual violence have seen an increase of approximately 18%. There has been a record 66% increase in cases related to violence inside the house, either by the husband or other relatives, and in cases that have led to the death of the woman [1].

It was found during the group discussions that violence in public spaces largely restricts women's mobility and adversely affects their development through limiting their access to education if the institution is a long way from home. They are confined to home-based work with meagre pay, prevented from participating in social activities or organizing activities and have to silently endure domestic violence.

A study conducted by the National Alliance of Street Vendors in Patna found that the proportion of female vendors has been decreasing over the past decade or so, with main reason giving being harassment from different quarters—from males, the police and the municipal authorities. A lack of protection was reported by 96% of the respondents to be the main problem they faced [8]. A *datwan*-seller[2] complained of harassment by rail officials. She said, '*humse paisa maangta hai […] nahi dene par datwan chheen ke phenk deta hai*'. ('He demands money from us […] if we don't give it, he snatches our *datwan* and throws them away').

According to the World Bank's annual World Development Report, which in 1993 focused on health, gender-based victimization accounts for one in five healthy years of life lost to women aged 15–44 [9].

Box 6.4: The Nightmare of Alcohol
Pramila Devi is an agricultural laborer in Kakda chak village, Muzaffarpur. Her husband is a truck driver and comes home twice a month. His homecoming is more like a nightmare for Pramila as he beats her black and blue when drunk. He snatches away her hard-earned money and inflicts such violence that she is not able to go to work for days. Intermittent fever and time off work is a constant feature. Once she had to take leave off work for a full month. The children also were badly neglected during this period. Once, when very drunk, he threw her out of the house. It was a severely cold winter night in January. She got pneumonia. However, after a month, she started to go at work but it took her almost three years to recover fully. Expenditure on treatment is another burden on her budget.
Source: [1]

The poor health conditions of these women could be correlated to their economic subservience, their social disempowerment and the violence they suffered. Improving health conditions requires an all-round improvement in their economic and social conditions and above all empowerment through organizing.

Empowering Women Through Social Determinants of Health

The findings of the study necessitated steps, which included both short-term corrective measures and measures for long-term impact. As a first step, it was recommended that the proper counting of women in the workforce should take place so that women get their due place in both the statistics and policy. In addition, a tripartite committee should be constituted for the fixation and implementation of minimum wages. The local health infrastructure needs to be strengthened in terms of facilities as well as service delivery. To meet the needs and hours of work of local people, public health facilities should be open to providing services

[2]*Datwan* is a medicinal twig used to clean one's teeth.

accordingly, and district authorities should be given the flexibility to make such changes, especially in the peak agricultural season and at harvest time, etc. Accredited Social Health Activist (ASHA) training needs to be reviewed and strengthened to include occupational health and safety, and mental health, along with non-communicable diseases.

The Sexual Harassment of Women at Workplace (Prevention, Prohibition and Redressal) Act, 2013 needs to be strictly enforced in the informal sector. Short stay homes for the survivors of violence (with counselling) should be present in every district. On preventive notes, awareness programs for adolescent boys need to be undertaken, as a campaign. Panchayat members especially women should be trained to take actions in their local areas to curb gender-based violence. In the long term, the realization of these goals can only be achieved by organizing women and by including women's organizations in decision-making forums and making them part of government programs.

It has been three years since the release of the report and many issues mentioned in it have gained wider acceptance in civil society and government offices. The labor department in Bihar has regularized the registration of workers under the Building and Construction Labor Welfare Board and reorganized the minimum wages fixation committee including in it labor representatives and NGOs working in the field of labor rights. In addition, an Act is under process to secure the welfare of unorganized and migrant laborers.

Since the report came out, there has been a pressure on the government to form state rules under the Unorganised Sector Social Security Act 2008. In 2015, the government brought out the state rules and established an Unorganised Sector Workers Welfare Board. It is a big achievement for the workers—and all the informal workers—who are scheduled under the minimum wages area covered under this Act. The board at present is non-functional, but the women workers are organizing themselves under SEWA and have started a signature campaign across six districts of the state.

In addition, progress has been made in the health sector where, as per the recommendations, the Primary Health Centres are now open for 24 h. Contraceptive supply is regular and available in the sub-centres as well. The sub-centres are active and are equipped with medicines for first line of treatment. The Village Health Sanitation and Nutrition Committees were revived and SEWA was also invited to assist in facilitating the committees. As per the recommendations, the incentives for ASHA have been revised and designed more scientifically.

The progress made is attributed to the efforts of many civil society organizations and workers' organizations that have pushed the recommendations of Shram Jeevani to achieve these results. But, as for the attitudinal changes regarding women, far more has to done—both by civil society and the government.

Commentary—Shram Jeevani Bihar

Padmini Swaminathan
Tata Institute of Social Sciences, Mumbai, India

Prescriptions for poverty reduction and for the empowerment of women in development discourse in general, and in poverty and gender debates in particular, often propel the issues of labor-intensive growth and greater labor force participation by women to centre stage. There is very little useful literature on the character and complexities of 'work' as far as the poor (and women among the poor) are concerned. Even less light is shed on the intensity of and/or gender-specific work intensities. On the contrary, the development objective of increasing female employment has more often than not meant further additions to women's existing work burdens. In a context where investments in basic infrastructure are abysmally low, the combination of household responsibilities and work towards augmenting the household's income results in long working days contributing to what feminists term as a 'time famine' with deleterious effects on women's health and well-being.

Increasingly and in different ways, research by feminists has stressed the significance and necessity of examining the linkages between women, work and health if we are to move towards an understanding of what accounts not only for the persistence of certain forms of disadvantages that confront women, but also the possibilities of seeking resolution to some, if not all of these disadvantages. In this context, feminists have felt the need to legitimize 'work' and not just 'labor' so that the different forms of unpaid work which women are overwhelmingly called upon to perform, are accounted for. Moreover, the emphasis on 'work' rather than 'labor' will also help highlight the fact that 'welfare' in our country is very often linked to 'labor' and since we hardly have any citizenship-based welfare, 'work' is not recognized, resulting in the invisibility of a great deal of women's work.

Research in several developing countries, aimed at capturing women's own perceptions of their main health problems, documents that 'tiredness' and 'not being able to sleep' figured more prominently than reproductive health issues among the problems described by women. The current preoccupation with increasing efficiency and productivity narrowly defined and measured in terms of the output per unit of capital/per unit of labor, etc., cannot accommodate concerns such as reducing work intensity and raising the capacity for work. On the contrary, what one routinely encounters through field level studies is the continued and pervasive exploitation of the laboring poor (men and women) through limitless extension of the working day, through the practice of forced overwork for which the worker receives very little compensation, and through the linking of wages to impossible targets such that workers always receive less pay as a result of those targets not being met, etc. In their constant struggle to reach these targets, workers force themselves to stay put in their workplaces, avoid going to the toilet and even skip meals. Thus, the disadvantages and disabilities under which the poor (and poor women, in particular) labor are several, multidimensional and spread over multiple spaces.

The challenges before us are many, not least among them being the need, at one level, to go back to some of the fundamental tenets that informed the founding of institutions like trade unions, workers' councils, and bodies like the ILO—such as the need to reduce worker exploitation, oppression and insecurity. Over the years, the nature of industrial development and the pattern of employment that it has generated have heightened the sense of insecurity among laborers, both at an individual level and also collectively. Furthermore, the need to meet global standards of efficiency and to contain costs have been used as arguments either for dismantling long-established social protections, or for not raising standards in accordance with the overall economic gains, or for not instituting any standards at all.

In terms of the drafting and implementation of policies for action, there is, however, no substitute for the State. There is official recognition of not just the failure of the State in the operationalization of its own laws and welfare measures towards labor in particular, and citizens in general, but also of the official acknowledgement of the fact that the bulk of laborers in this country work in abysmal conditions, in tasks that impair their health and yet they remain invisible in the official statistics, which denies them their basic rights as workers. After being brought to the fore, some of these issues are being addressed by these same Commissions. There are suggestions, for example, to institute social security measures covering all unorganized labor. While such measures are welcome, they need to be backed by credible administrative structures. What has received some attention in the Report of the Second National Commission on Labor is the theme of Labor Administration. Submissions made to this Report however make it clear that the theme of Occupational Safety and Health of Labor has never been a priority item on the agenda of any government, even going by simple indicators such as the number of posts of safety inspectors created, the number of vacancies left unfilled in these posts despite the growth of industries that mandatorily require monitoring, the number of cases of violations filed, and the numbers disposed of etc. In such a context, any redress sought for women's failing health due to the overburdened nature of their 'work' needs to contend, not just with inimical patriarchal forces, but, also non-transparent and unaccountable State structures.

References

1. SEWA Bharat. SHRAM JEEVANI Report of the special task force on women in the informal economy in Bihar (Internet). India; 2014. http://sewabharat.org/wp-content/uploads/2014/08/Shram-Jeevani_The-Report.pdf. Accessed 23 Oct 2015.
2. Office of Registrar General. SRS Bulletin, vol. 47(2) (Internet). Vital Statistics Division. http://censusindia.gov.in/vital_statistics/SRS_Bulletins/SRS_Bulletin-October_2012.pdf. Accessed 23 Oct 2015.
3. International Institute for Population Sciences. District level household and facility survey 2007–08: Bihar. Mumbai: IIPS; 2010. http://rchiips.org/pdf/rch3/report/bh.pdf. Accessed 23 Oct 2015.

4. Office of Registrar General. Special bulletin on maternal mortality in India 2007–09. Vital Statistics Division; 2011. http://www.censusindia.gov.in/vital_statistics/SRS_Bulletins/Final-MMR%20Bulletin-2007-09_070711.pdf. Accessed 23 Oct 2015.
5. Singh MB. Women's work participation in Bihar. New Delhi: Institute for Human Development (commissioned by SEWA); 2012.
6. National Sample Survey Office. Employment and unemployment survey: NSS 66th round: July 2009–June 2010, Eighth quinquennial survey; 2013.
7. Institute of applied manpower research. India human development report 2011: towards social inclusion (Internet). 2011. http://www.iamrindia.gov.in/ihdr_book.pdf. Accessed 23 Oct 2015.
8. NIDAN. Study on street vendors at Patna (Bihar). http://nidan.in/nidanwp/Documents/Study%20on%20Street%20Vendors%20at%20Patna.pdf. Accessed 23 Oct 2015.
9. Lori H, Pitanguy J, Germain A. Violence against women: the hidden burden. The World Bank; 1994. Report No.: 255. http://www.wds.worldbank.org/external/default/WDSContentServer/WDSP/IB/1999/04/28/000009265_3970716144635/Rendered/PDF/multi0page.pdf. Accessed 23 Oct 2015.

Chapter 7
Who's in Charge of Social Determinants of Health? Understanding the Office of the Municipal Health Officer in Urban Areas

Prathibha Ganesan, Devaki Nambiar and T. Sundararaman

Abstract The need to address Social Determinants of Health (SDH) for a healthy society is uncontested, even though we have less of a sense of how to operationalize this action, or of what institutional structures exist and may be needed for this purpose. We undertook to describe one institutional structure required for action on SDH in urban areas as part of a 31-city appraisal carried out by the Technical Resource Group (TRG) of the National Urban Health Mission (NUHM), supplemented with a purposive review of the literature. We identified the institution of the Municipal Health Officer (MHO), which was particularly designed in the colonial period to address health and its determinants. Limited finances and privatization have led to a non-uniform decline in the powers of the MHO across cities. In metropolitan areas with substantial municipal financial capacity, the office of the MHO has survived along with both clinical and SDH functions. In second tier cities with a lack of financial capacity, State Health Departments have taken over health and clinical services, resulting in an overemphasis on these services and a shift away from SDH. In third tier cities, the office of the MHO was under threat due to the takeover of health facilities by State Health Department along with heavy financial and technical capacity constraints. Notwithstanding this, we conclude that the office of the MHO is an existing and important institutional structure through which to address SDH in an integrated fashion. We argue that this office must be sustained, and efforts redoubled to augment necessary technical support, infrastructure and finance, particularly in second and third tier cities.

P. Ganesan (✉)
Public Policy Research Institute, Thiruvananthapuram, India
e-mail: prathibha.ganesan@gmail.com

D. Nambiar
The George Institute for Global Health, New Delhi, Delhi, India

T. Sundararaman
School of Health Systems Studies, Tata Institute of Social Sciences, Mumbai, India

D. Nambiar and A. Muralidharan (eds.), *The Social Determinants of Health in India*, https://doi.org/10.1007/978-981-10-5999-5_7

Keywords Urban health · National urban health mission technical resource group Municipal health officer

Introduction

The health of urban populations is primarily determined by the physical and social environment of cities and towns. Disease outbreaks are common and are characterized by the interplay of myriad factors including high population density, contamination of drinking water sources, breeding of insect and animal carriers of disease, solid waste management, relative inattention and structural barriers to the maintenance of hygiene and sanitation [1]. Non-communicable diseases are common due to high levels of exposure to air pollution, excessive stress, and the sedentary nature of work [2, 3]. Injuries from road traffic accidents, industrial accidents, domestic accidents, accidents in construction sites, and violence are also much higher in urban areas than in rural areas [4]. The social environment—by way of urban poverty, migration and its attendant problems of illegal status and denial of entitlements, group norms, customs and peer pressures,—also play a major role in impacting health [5]. Broadly, all these factors fall under the umbrella of Social Determinants of Health (SDH). Drawing from 2008 Commission on Social Determinants of Health (CSDH), SDH in this paper refers to the structural, social and environmental factors that determine the overall well-being of a population, including the health system [6]. The thrust of the paper is on the functions typically outside the purview of clinical or medical aspects of the health system in urban areas.

Historically, the science of public health has grown around establishing the interconnections between epidemic disease and its determinants in the urban context. The development of public health systems in the colonial period in India was focused on keeping cities and barracks, where the elite and military lived respectively, safe from raging contagions [7]. This meant that the development of urban health institutions was geared to epidemic prevention. The key institutional structure was the office of the Municipal Health Officer (MHO). Post-independence, these institutions were retained across Indian cities and replicated for new cities. However, Gupta argues that the 'capacity to prevent outbreaks from occurring has atrophied' over the years [8].

A recent appraisal of these institutions was undertaken in 2013, by the Ministry of Health and Family Welfare and the Technical Resource Group (TRG) of the National Urban Health Mission.[1] The TRG was charged with examining the health problems of the urban poor and their match with the design of urban health systems and then with recommending the institutional reforms needed to address these

[1]This TRG was chaired by Mr. Harsh Mander, a former civil servant, known for his work amongst the urban poor.

health needs. The TRG commissioned teams of public health experts to visit a sample of 30 towns and cities to study both the conditions of health and the design and functioning of institutions. One subcommittee of the TRG focused its attention primarily on SDH and the structure and functioning of institutions addressing these issues. In large cities—notably Chennai, Kolkata and Mumbai—the office of the city health officer has retained considerable powers with respect to SDH. This is closely related to the fact that these cities are governed by autonomous corporations which are relatively better financed. Furthermore, insulated as they are from the mainstream state health sector reform processes, there have been relatively few efforts to restructure institutions.

Drawing from the experiences of the TRG as well as the existing secondary literature on urbanism and public health, this paper attempts to understand the institutional structures responsible for the social determinants of urban health. We take a historical view, attempting to chart the history of public health administration in urban areas, tracing how these features serve as a kind of colonial footprint over which subsequent post-independence institutions have been established. Following this, we describe what our latest appraisal under NUHM-TRG revealed to us about these institutions.

The History of Institutions Addressing Social Determinants of Health in India

In India, municipal administration and public health began developing in the colonial era and were, in fact, inseparable. As Table 7.1 shows, public health related developments were either formulated and implemented by the British government, or were developed in the provinces and then expanded.

Table 7.1 shows the nature of colonial public health interventions. Major interventions were in the form of legislation/acts or by instituting public health departments and structures like the establishment of a Justice of the Peace and a MHO etc. The 1857 revolt was a turning point in the history of public health administration and SDH in India. The Royal Commission of 1859 observed a link between epidemics and the sanitation of the city and recommended improvements in sanitation. The colonial administration responded by 'physically separating the army and the British officials from the indigenous city by building new cantonments and civil lines (residential enclaves). The army was provided with new well ventilated barracks while officials built spacious bungalows on wide streets that were serviced by piped water and underground sewers' [7].

In fact, early urban planning in colonial India was premised mostly on keeping cities and barracks (where the elite lived) a safe distance from the raging contagions that periodically affected the rest of the urban denizens—often indicated by a 'cordon sanitaire'. This affected the urbanization process in India spatially by

Table 7.1 Timeline of the history of public health administration

Year	Public health interventions	Description
1764	First Medical Department by English East India Company in Bengal [9]	The medical department was introduced to provide medical services to army troops and civil servants
–	Appointment of Justice of Peace (JP) [10]	JP was entrusted with addressing public concerns by providing local amenities through imposition of taxes on urban dwellers
1842	Bengal Act X	Under this act residents of Bengal if required could approach the government for public services like repairing, cleaning, draining and watching public streets, roads, and drains etc. The services would be provided through appointment of a committee which oversees the functions and assesses tax [11]
1848	General Board of Health (GBH) by British Government	GBH oversees the local boards of provinces and looks after water and sanitation either on demand or when death rate exceeds 23/1000 persons [9]
1859	Royal Commission on the Sanitary State of the Army	This was formed after the 1857 revolt to look into the epidemics and health of army troops [12]
1864	Military Cantonment Act	Under the Military Cantonment Act, Sanitary Police were formed to improve hygiene in the Cantonment area [12]
1868	Civil Medical Department	This department was formed as a result of growing discontent from the general public due to spreading diseases and neglect of commons by the empire [9]
1869	Appointment of Public Health Commissioner (PHC), Statistician, Sanitary Commissioners	PHC was responsible for the Report on Health for the Government of India and consolidation of vital statistical information collected by the Statistician. Sanitary commissioners were responsible for the overall sanitation of districts and control of epidemics, inspection of dispensaries and hospitals etc. [13]
1880	Deployment of Sanitary engineers [9]	Sanitary engineers were entrusted with the disposal of human waste and the supply of potable drinking water
1897	The Epidemic Act [14].	This act conferred special powers upon ULBs to implement necessary measures for control of epidemics
1919	Montague Chelmsford Act	Under this act transfer of Local Government and public services to Indian control was ensured [7]
1920–21	District Municipality Act, Local Boards Act	Local bodies were conferred with legal provisions for advancement of public health
1939	Madras Public Health Act [15]	Addresses various aspects of public health in urban areas

Sources Various; indicated above

creating a divided city. The remnants of this spatial division are still observed in Indian cities in terms of uneven development [16].

After a century of neglect, in the year 1868 a Civil Medical Department was formed in Bengal Province motivated by expressions of widespread discontent among the indigenous population. Changes in municipal administration and services with greater attention to public health services in cities also emerged. Over time, the colonial authorities came to terms with the fact that some diseases were endemic and programmes of research began to be pursued on 'tropical diseases' followed by the formation of various commissions on plague, cholera, and others to look into the causation of epidemics. In most cases, these commissions suggested improvements to hygiene and sanitation. Improvement Trusts were formed in the cities under the United Provinces Improvement Act of 1919 to address the epidemic situation. Some of these Improvement Trusts evolved into Municipal Corporations over time, while others became Development Authorities. This was followed by the Epidemic Act of 1887, whereby urban local governments were conferred special powers to implement the necessary measures for the control of epidemics. These measures included 'forceful segregation of the infected persons, disinfection, evacuation and even demolition of infected places' [9].

A key example of this is the Madras Public Health Act (MPHA), a 1939 piece of legislation that supported the municipal administration and services with a focus on various SDH functions. As per the Act, a Public Health Board, Director of Health Services and a Health Officer were given powers to perform and discharge various public health activities. The Act entrusted local government institutions with the management of health. Provincial medical departments came under the control of local government. Likewise, district-level rural, medical, and sanitary arrangements were carried out under the charge of a medical officer called the Civil Surgeon, who was to superintend district medical institutions as well.

Although such changes were meant to happen in both rural and urban areas, cities had the institutional capacity to address the SDH through the dedicated office of the MHO. The MPHA, for instance, stipulates that

> […] the Health Officer of a local authority shall perform such of the functions and discharge such of the duties, of its executive authority in regard to public health matters […] [15].

This office had the powers of imposing quarantine if need be, forcibly disposing of bodies, ensuring sewers were cleaned, waste collected and disposed, and of whatever additional measures it took to avert or abort an epidemic. These powers were so rigorously invoked that they could lead to considerable public resistance—in one case the Plague Commissioner of Pune, W.C. Rand, was assassinated in 1897 allegedly because he ordered highly intrusive sanitary surveillance and oversight of native neighborhoods and private residences [17].

The institutional structures for public health and sanitation were retained across urban centres post-Independence. However, immediately after Independence, there was a popular demand to reverse the British policy of an almost exclusive focus on urban elites, and the government began an ambitious scheme of developing a network of public health facilities across rural India. In urban areas, a large number of public hospitals mostly attached to medical colleges sprang up, but with little public investment in primary health care [18]. This gap in urban primary health care services was largely closed by a growing private sector, which unlike public facilities, focused exclusively on curative services [19, 20].

Starting in the nineties, a process of neoliberal institutional reform with respect to urban public services across cities began, and this has accelerated in the last decade. This included the *Nagar Palika Act* 1993, a constitutional amendment mandating local governance for urban areas. Strapped for resources, reluctant to raise funds from the rich and allocate them to the health of the poor, urban bodies reduced their spending on health with an expectation that State Departments of Health would take up the slack. Reduced spending on health coupled with the declining role of local governments lead to State line Departments taking over many urban public health institutions. However, in the nineties, State Departments were themselves facing financial constraints. As a result, urban areas, with a thriving private sector, could hardly be seen as a priority for investment in health, especially with so many rural health care demands calling for attention. Though the office of the health officer survived, it lost importance relative to other dimensions of health governance (which was focused on large hospitals and rural primary care) and of urban governance. The powers of MHO were limited to the provision of public services and supervising reforms therein, rather than taking into account determinants.

The two-pronged strategy undergirding neoliberal reforms was to first make public services operate in a more market-driven mode and second, to shift provisioning to corporate entities. The trend therefore began of running these services on commercial lines as cost recovery propositions and increasingly outsourcing them where suitable contracting arrangements were possible [21]. In particular, this approach has been used for the provision of drinking water and water for domestic use, solid waste management, sewage disposal, sanitation facilities, parks, and recreation sites [21].

At this time, institutional arrangements for outsourcing were again subject to civil servant-led initiatives and few efforts therefore emerged to develop the knowledge resources needed within urban bodies. Contracting arrangements have been weak. The community has seldom been consulted, nor has there been much space for participation or contribution in such contracting arrangements [22]. This has resulted in the emergence of a new set of tensions between service providers and the public, and between the employees and the management of these service providers.[2]

The legacy of economic liberalization has been the privatization of many social determinants such that, across cities, the burden of cost recovery through user fees falls disproportionately on the poor [19–21]. Focus group discussions (FGDs)

---

[2]The information is compiled from interviews conducted with Municipal Health officers from Chennai, Viluppuram, for the Technical Resource Group, and Health of Thrissur Corporation in 2011 in the aftermath of resistance from the people of Lalur where the municipal waste was dumped.

conducted among the vulnerable groups during the TRG process confirm this. Social sector reforms are usually guided by technical assistance from international donor agencies, which hire commercial corporate consultancy agencies to do the task, and many of these consultancies also have potential vendors of these services as clients. In such a context, the challenge is often seen as designing viable business models that can provide these services, rather than approaches that ensure equity in access and affordability for the poor. With regard to the urban institutions addressing the social determinants of health and the organization of primary health services, in the years after independence we see the following trends:

(a) Declining finance, weak governance of urban local bodies and weaker institutional capacity to deliver services across urban local bodies.
(b) An increasing separation of management of curative care services and even public health care facilities away from the office/purview of the MHO.
(c) Declining prestige, powers and scope of the health officer and lack of technical support to address the challenges of SDH.

This decline is far from uniform and in our work we have seen wide variations in the role and responsibilities of the health officer which seemed largely related to the size of the urban unit. But this variation also acts as evidence and illustration of the potential of this office and the determinants of its effectiveness, as we discuss in the following section.

Contemporary Urban Health Administration: Lessons from the National Urban Health Mission Policy Recommendation Process (2000–2014)

Through the course of our 30 city visits, we found that neither the extent of urban growth nor the institutional structures for urban health were similar everywhere. The cities could be classified into a triptych typology based roughly on size: Tier 1 cities like Mumbai, Delhi, Chennai, Kolkata etc.; Tier 2 cities like Pune, Kochi, Ambala, Bhopal, and Bhubaneswar etc. with populations over a million, and Tier 3 cities with a population between 100,000 and one million like Villupuram, Tumkur, Gangtok etc.

Almost all the large cities with active and effective public health systems had a long history of urban administration, including an office of the MHO or Commissioner. The office of the Health Officer or Commissioner was in charge of the primary and secondary public health institutions, supported by Sanitary Officers and Inspectors working in areas like vector control, food safety, waste collection, transportation coordination, and so on.

Take, for example, the case of Chennai. The Chennai Municipal Corporation has a 360-year history with specific emphasis on public health management. Even now, the legal framework is of pre-independence vintage—the Madras Public Health

Table 7.2 Roles of the municipal health officer in Chennai

Retained from colonial period	Diverted to other authorities (authority now responsible)	Added to the purview of the municipal health officer
Cleaning, protection and examination of water supply Construction and maintenance of public sanitary conveniences Regulation of 'offensive trades'—industrial waste, sewage, air pollution etc. 'Abatement of nuisance' carcass disposal, accumulation of refuse, chimney smoke monitoring, water (sewage) pollution monitoring Disease prevention, surveillance, notification and treatment Food safety regulation including inspection and licensing of slaughterhouses Sanitary arrangements for public gatherings or festivals, including removal and disposal of garbage Mosquito and disease vector control Upkeep and maintenance of lodging houses Management of public health staff (*N* = 4746, comprising 200 sanitary Inspectors and 300 basic health workers, 4200 mosquito control workers and 46 sanitary officers)	Solid waste management (Engineering Department) Drainage construction (Chennai Metro Water Supply and Sewerage Board) Monitoring air pollution (State Pollution Control Board)	Immunization School health Programme (for municipal government schools) Management of sheltered homes

Source Compiled from the Madras Public Health Act 1939 [15], Report of the Technical Resource Group to National Urban Health Mission, 2014, Interview with Chief Health Officer (CHO), Chennai Municipal Commissioner (CMC)

(MPH) Act of 1939. The public health department under the MHO has a number of functions, which include environmental sanitation and regulation of what are called 'offensive trades'.[3] It was observed that most of the activities stipulated in the 1939 Act remain under the purview of the MHO (see Table 7.2). The exceptions are solid waste management, water supply, and air pollution monitoring. In 1978 the first two of these were shifted to the Engineering Department and Chennai Metro Water Supply and Sewerage Board (CMWSSB), respectively. In 1981, air pollution monitoring in the city was entrusted to the State Pollution Control Board. Notwithstanding this, the scope of the activities was subject to the purse of the city

[3]According to the Madras Public Health Act 1939, Offensive trade means 'trade in which substances dealt with are or are likely to become, a nuisance'. Examples include industries that cause land, water, and air pollution that is physically manifest.

and municipal authorities. Under the 'abatement of nuisance' provision, the MHO also monitors chimney smoke levels, pollution levels in cinemas as well as sewage effluent. The degree of coordination and triangulation across linked roles and activities was indeterminate in the course of our TRG work. We noted further that other major functions of this office include immunization (done every Wednesday through Health Posts), the school health programme and management of sheltered homes for the destitute.

Various configurations and collaborations marked the actual dispensation of these roles and duties. In larger cities, ways have been developed to address epidemics through collaboration between local bodies and health departments and usage of Information and Communication Technologies (ICT). For example, in Chennai, the notification of 22 diseases and action response to the diseases was carried out by all government facilities, and also 650 private nursing homes across the state. This also included the network of facilities under the supervision of the Chennai Municipal Commissioner. Information received was transmitted to the local health post and Urban Health Centre, alerting them to the possibility of more cases. Further, an SMS would also go to the sanitary inspector for necessary action of a preventive nature, and to the MHO to assess the need for additional action/monitoring. Since the city health office was also in charge of vector control and of sanitation, there was the possibility of a wide sense of ownership and accountability.

Kolkata and Mumbai also had similar practices to what was observed in Chennai. Kolkata in fact had an even more robust disease surveillance-notification-response system in place. The Kolkata Municipal Corporation had set up laboratories to test for Dengue and Malaria in the city and each time positive cases were found, SMS alerts were sent to all health officials. The alerts help in identification of the locality for mosquito control activities [20]. Furthermore, one of its abattoirs (located in Tangra) has been modernized using technology and is arguably one of the most modern, safe and hygienic in the country. These are large corporations, which have strong precedents of action on SDH, which in turn has resulted in the existence of dedicated public health cadres, relatively large funding allocations, and ready access to technical know-how in the diverse disciplines required to carry out roles effectively.

Latter day corporations like Bangalore, Hyderabad and Ahmedabad had some components—but not all of these. Their spending on health as a proportion of corporation funds was much lower and there was a greater expectation that the state government would take the lead financially and programmatically in addressing health and its determinants in these cities.

The situation in second tier cities, however, varies. In many cities—Bhubaneswar was an example—the office of the MHO was exclusively for addressing social and environmental determinants, and it remains important. There was usually a separate officer who looked at the clinical services. However, there was no exclusive corporation service nor a public health cadre and the officer in charge—usually a clinician—seldom had the training, interest, or incentive to take the SDH functions seriously. Even where such an officer was conscientious, s/he would seldom have adequate knowledge of the modern technologies now available for the monitoring and management of air pollution, ensuring food safety, organizing efficient solid waste management and carcass disposal, scientific abattoir management, reducing road traffic accidents, and the like.

Worse, as many interviews across cities show, awareness was often lacking that these were areas requiring technical know-how. For example, solid waste management is an obligatory function of local government. Over time, the composition of waste has changed such that its management requires segregation and differential treatment, employing myriad technologies. However, technical expertise is required to determine what technology is suited for which kinds of waste and in which context or scale. Often the health officers in the second and third tier cities lacked of expertise, their action further exacerbated by underfunding. Thrissur Municipal Corporation (TMC) in Kerala demonstrated this problem. TMC was in the limelight for ineffective waste management—a matter raised by the citizenry. And yet, there was no-one answerable to these complaints. At the time of the TRG visit to TMC, the MHO post lay vacant and was unlikely to be filled given this running controversy. In the interim, a Sanitary Officer had charge of solid waste management, a role that was both misallocated and underperformed.

In smaller cities like Gangtok and Raipur, the post of MHO was an entry level posting into government services. It therefore tended to be relatively less sought after or respected. Unsurprisingly, in many cities, this post was found to be lying vacant. To boot, there was contestation between departments of health and municipalities regarding who should govern this office, which in turn led to neglect of the actual duties supposed to be discharged by it.

Findings and Way Forward

The above sections reveal the historical centrality of the determinants of health in the evolution of urban public health services. The office of MHO was a colonial, convergent effort where SDH were linked to health services in urban areas. Various legislations historically have entrusted Urban Local Bodies (ULBs) with the implementation of many key SDH functions. This includes public services such as the provision of safe drinking water, sanitation, sewage and solid waste management, nutrition, management of homelessness, support of vulnerable sections, occupational safety, and epidemic prevention. This office survived into the post-independence period, though with a considerable loss of its role in health care service provisioning —the latter largely due to the gross neglect of the urban primary health sector.

The neoliberal era saw a further sharp but non-uniform decline of the powers of office of the MHO across different cities—this time affecting both clinical and SDH functions. The TRG study brought out other determinants of this decline in the role, such as the type of cities, the financial status of the cities, the privatization of other public Health Officer services, and lack of technical know-how on addressing various SDH.

Despite these overall trends, in large metropolitan areas and second tier cities with substantial municipal financial capacity, the office of MHO survived with both clinical and SDH functions. Even privatization of some of the SDH services has not impaired the importance of the office of MHO. In second tier cities with a lack of financial capacity, a clear separation of the clinical and SDH functions could be observed, where health departments took over the clinical functions. Added to this was the lack of technical know-how, the controversial nature and diminished stature of the office of MHO leading to a situation where there are no takers for the post of MHO. Particularly in third tier cities, the office of MHO was under threat of extinction due to (1) the takeover of clinical functions by the health department and (2) neglect of SDH functions due to severe financial constraints of the ULBs or privatization of the services.

Often when state departments took over the urban health functions, given their vertical disease-specific orientation, attention was given mainly—but not only—to universalizing the subcenter functions of immunization, antenatal care, and some national disease control programmes. The attention shifted away from SDH functions. This is a major challenge to urban health because there is no institutional structure in place other than the office of the MHO that currently incorporates SDH into public health in urban areas. This is substantiated by the findings of the TRG that wherever the office of the health officer was active, innovative steps for addressing the social determinants of health have been initiated, while in others the SDH functions are falling apart.

An immediate after effect of such development is that the urban poor with less purchasing power were found to be disproportionately affected in accessing public service delivery—even essentials such as the daily toilet and bathing [20]. The complexities in service delivery further increased where compartmentalization of service delivery in the institutional design was prominent. For instance, in Ambala, some SDH functions were vested with the Public Health Engineering Department and the office of the MHO was absent. Factors like the illegality of slums have added to the woes of the urban poor as the existing SDH services not only fail to reach these urban spaces, but are also legitimized in their failure to provide these services [23]. Where popular pressures are unable to force a legal status, administration finds it advantageous to maintain the status quo.

Our analysis suggests that the existing institutional design for SDH in the form of the office of the MHO has shown value and needs to be sustained and provided with the necessary technical support, infrastructure and finance. Our analysis also emphasizes the urgency of providing technical guidance for managing SDH-related functions such as scientific management of solid waste, hazardous bio-medical waste, abattoirs, services like a crematorium or a cinema theatre, air pollution, and approaches to managing and considering the needs of vulnerable groups. All these place demands for technological, technical, and domain-specific knowledge that are greater than those possessed by an entry level or medical officer. Some cities have built up such skills in an urban public health cadre, but these are the exceptions. It is conceivable that in each city, functions could be managed through collaboration, common sense and the occasional consultancy.

Our reiteration of the importance of the MHO implies not a mere resurrection of the past, but also a reimagination and restructuring of this office, and an understanding of the potential and the challenges of playing this role in modern times. It includes the creation of technical assistance institutions to play a supportive role. Particular regard in supporting the institution should be given to the second and third tier cities where the fiscal powers of ULBs are not favorable and where all the necessary technical requirements may never be possible as an in-house arrangement. The mechanics of this will have to be carefully determined in each urban context, mindful of the precedents, constraints, opportunities and variations that exist, and the range of stakeholders that must be engaged with.

References

1. Alirol E, Getaz L, Chappuis F, Loutan L. Urbanisation and infectious diseases in a globalised world. Lancet Infect Dis. 2011;11(2):131–41.
2. Moore M, Gould P, Keary S. Global Urbanisation and Impact on Health. Int J Hyg Environ Health. 2003;206:269–78.
3. Kandlikar M, Ramachandran G. The causes and consequences of particulate air pollution in urban India: a synthesis of the science. Ann Rev Energy Environ. 2000;25:629–84.
4. Veron R. Remaking urban environments: the political ecology of air pollution in Delhi. Environ Plan. 2006;38:2093–109.
5. Krumeich MA. Health in global context: beyond the social determinants of health? Glob Health Action. 2014;7:1–8.
6. Commission on Social Determinants of Health. Closing the Gap in a Generation: Health Equity through Action on the Social Determinants of Health. World Health Organisation; 2008. http://apps.who.int/iris/bitstream/10665/69832/1/WHO_IER_CSDH_08.1_eng.pdf. Accessed 21 Sept 2015.
7. Chaplin SE. Indian cities, sanitation and the state: the politics of failure to provide. Environ Urban. 2011;23(1):57–70.
8. Dasgupta M. Public health in India: An overview. https://openknowledge.worldbank.org/bitstream/handle/10986/8541/wps3787.txt?sequence=2. Accessed 24 May 2015.
9. Mushtaq MU. Public health in British India: A brief account of the history of medical services and disease prevention in colonial India. Indian J Community Med. 2009;34(1):6–14.
10. Kaur H. Urban local government and its status under the constitution of India: a study of municipal corporation of Patiala. Chandigarh: Punjab University; 2010.
11. Singh AK. Municipal Government as socio-political entity: a case study. In: City planning: administration and participation, 1st ed. New Delhi: Concept Publishing Company; 1986. p. 124.
12. Harrison M. Public health in British India: Anglo-Indian preventive medicine 1859–1914. 1st ed. New York: Cambridge University Press; 1994. p. 49.
13. Parveen F. Poverty and health in colonial India (1808–1914). Aligarh: Aligarh Muslim University; 2012. http://shodhganga.inflibnet.ac.in:8080/jspui/bitstream/10603/13539/11/11_chapter%205.pdf. Accessed 12 May 2015.
14. Patro BK, Tripathy JP, Kashyap R. Epidemic diseases act 1897, India: whether sufficient to address current challenges? J Mahatma Gandhi Inst Med Sci. 2013;18(2):109–11.
15. St. George Gazette Extraordinary. Madras Public Health Act, 1939. 1938. http://www.sanchitha.ikm.in/sites/default/files/MadrasPublicHealth_%20Act1939.pdf. Accessed 12 May 2015.

16. Morenas LA. Planning the city of Djinns: exorcizing the ghosts in Delhi's post-colonial development machine. Rensselaer Polytechnic Institute; 2010. http://gradworks.umi.com/34/20/3420927.html. Accessed 15 Jan 2015.
17. Chatterjee P. Bombs and nationalism in Bengal. New York: Columbia University; 2004. http://sarr.emory.edu/subalterndocs/Chatterjee.pdf. Accessed 21 Sept 2015.
18. Bajpai V. The challenges confronting public hospital in India, their origins, and possible solutions. Adv Public Health. http://www.hindawi.com/journals/aph/2014/898502/. Accessed 21 Sept 2015.
19. Duggal R. The retreat of the state in health care policy and the right to the city. In: Urban policies and right to the City in India, 1st ed. New Delhi: UNESCO and CSH; p. 133–42.
20. Ministry of Health and Family Welfare. Making the urban health mission work for the urban poor: report of the technical resource group, National Urban Health Mission. National Health Systems Resource Centre; 2014.
21. Kennedy L. New patterns of participation shaping urban governance. In: Governing India's metropolises: case studies of four cities. 1st ed. New Delhi: Routledge; 2009. p. 73.
22. Coelho K, Kamath L, Vijayabhaskar M. Participolis: consent and contention in Neoliberal urban India. 1st ed. New Delhi: Routledge; 2013.
23. Agarwal S, Taneja S. All slums are not equal: child health conditions among the urban poor. Indian Pediatr. 2005;42:233–44.

Chapter 8
Scaling-Up a Community-Based Approach to SDH: Reflections on the SEWA Experience

Sapna Desai

Abstract The Self Employed Women's Association (SEWA), an organization of women workers across India, addresses the social determinants of health (SDH) in practice, through a community-based approach led by health workers. Initially based in Gujarat, SEWA expanded its health program across five additional states through training and collaboration. Committed to addressing social determinants of health, particularly women's working conditions, SEWA learned to adapt its approach in each new setting. Its focus on maternal and child health was changed to a focus on water and sanitation, or to eye health for example, depending on women's needs and gaps in services. Differences in health services in settings such as Bihar, West Bengal and Delhi led to changed roles for health workers as well. Thus, rather than spread a uniform model, SEWA scaled-up a philosophy—and consequently retained a social determinants approach—implemented by health workers. Dynamic, needs-based and community-based programs are required to address social determinants in practice, which in turn calls for changes in approaches to health worker roles and training.

Keywords Scale · Social determinants · Women workers
Community health worker

Introduction

The social determinants of health (SDH) has gained considerable currency as an approach and guiding principle for strategies to improve health outcomes. From an international commission to national initiatives, SDH has entered the consciousness of both policymakers and researchers as a means to recognize the social, economic and political conditions that influence health status. Less discussed, however, is how to incorporate SDH in practice. There is limited discourse—and this is

S. Desai (✉)
Independent Researcher, New Delhi, India
e-mail: sapna.i.desai@gmail.com

D. Nambiar and A. Muralidharan (eds.), *The Social Determinants of Health in India*, https://doi.org/10.1007/978-981-10-5999-5_8

typically not initiated by implementers—on whether and how these principles can be translated into programs. Given the wide range of potential ways to operationalize SDH, there is a clear need for both policymakers and researchers to experiment further with the 'how' of approaches grounded in SDH. Indeed, since SDH does not lend itself to fixed strategies or uniform models, sharing grassroots experiences will be critical to sustaining a movement for its implementation.

In this piece, I reflect on the experience of the Self Employed Women's Association (SEWA) in scaling-up a program approach that seeks to address the underlying determinants of health. A national trade union of over 1.5 million women workers in India's informal economy, SEWA was founded in Gujarat in 1972 in order to organize poor women workers towards self-reliance in areas such as microfinance, livelihoods, social security and capacity building. In 1984, SEWA established a women-led health initiative, implemented by a cadre of health workers who serve their communities. It operates in a decentralized manner, through a system of local leadership and integration of health into a broader agenda for women's empowerment. SEWA's model has been showcased as an example of addressing SDH in practice, wherein women's health is entrenched in a holistic approach to economic and social security [1].

Over the past 15 years, SEWA has expanded its health program from Gujarat into several states of India. Working in partnership with newer, mostly smaller SEWAs, scaling-up has been an experiment in replication, adaption and expansion of the health program in Gujarat. Context, necessarily, has determined the contours of each new initiative. The objective of this essay is two-fold: (i) to document SEWA's experience of scaling-up an SDH approach in practice, as a contribution of experiential evidence to the knowledge base and (ii) to identify factors that promote and impede a community-based SDH approach 'at scale'. This essay is based on a combination of personal implementation experience and external documentation conducted between 2005 and 2013 [2] to reflect on how a SDH-driven grassroots program can be implemented at scale.

SEWA Health: Foundations

SEWA's work in the state of Gujarat has promoted integrated, holistic programs that address employment, work conditions, income, housing, and sanitation as well as access to social security and health services. Well documented elsewhere, the organization provides one example of how to build a health program that addresses both proximate risk and distal determinants [3–5]. Its experience is testament to cross-sectoral work to improve health: a family of SEWA institutions works together to improve individual lives. For example, Mahila SEWA Housing Trust works in partnership with the SEWA Bank to finance safer, cleaner living conditions, while livelihoods cooperatives support women's incomes and union organizers advocate for policies to secure social security for workers in the informal economy.

SEWA's health program is driven by a core philosophy to empower women to improve their own health. Its principles are: (i) Integration of health, financial and employment services for women's well-being (ii) Women-led and women-centered health care (iii) Health care delivered to women's doorsteps and (iv) Financial sustainability [6]. One community health worker (CHW) recruited by SEWA serves the village or urban slum population where she lives. She is recruited from the community based on potential leadership, community rapport, and commitment to service. SEWA builds their capacity to provide health education and support women in accessing low-cost public or private services, with a focus on primary, maternal, and child health. They also serve as local advocates, organizing women to demand quality public health care. CHWs are paid a monthly stipend, which is supplemented by commissions from the sale of medicine and insurance products.

Importantly, even without the inputs of organizations in sectors not working directly on health, SEWA's health program has been entrenched in understanding and addressing social determinants. For example, community health workers integrate women's labor into their operational approach: health education is tailored to working hours and health services extend to specific occupational hazards. Furthermore, health workers address underlying determinants such as clean water and sanitation through education, service linkages and advocacy. Over the course of three decades, the program also established a women-owned cooperative of health workers that engages in income-generating activities to improve health, such as the sale of medicines and the development of *ayurvedic* products.

Scaling-Up

SEWA expanded in the 1980s and 1990s to reach women workers in several states of India, primarily through trade union and microfinance activities. By 2000, the organization operated in nine states through 11 independent SEWAs, bound together by a national federation and shared mission. Limited human and financial resources initially delayed the recruitment of CHWs as newer SEWAs focused on developing microfinance activities. By 2005, however, SEWA had the financial and human resources to scale-up the 400 strong CHW program model in Gujarat into other states. Although across the states SEWA members work in similar occupations—home-based work, agriculture and street vending—the socioeconomic, political and health system environments differ vastly.

The initial approach to scaling-up entailed recruiting and expanding the CHW team, while establishing collaboration and facilitating training between states. SEWA Gujarat had learned through experience that external training agencies, most of whom do not engage in direct program implementation, could provide technical knowledge, but not practical skills. Thus Gujarat's experienced CHWs, supervisors and trainers were chosen to lead the scaling-up process. Individual SEWAs recruited new CHWs, who were trained through a combination of classroom and practical training by SEWA Gujarat. Over seven years, new CHW teams were trained in five states where the organization had already established trade union, microfinance and livelihoods activities. India's National Rural Health Mission was introduced in 2005, and most states had a village health worker, the Accredited Social Health Activist (ASHA), by the time SEWA initiated its own community health programs [7]. An early learning of the scaling-up process was that initial community health strategies employed in Gujarat would need to adapt to each new context, as not just health determinants but also health service delivery structures varied considerably.

Shifting Strategies

The process of scaling-up was initiated in two districts of Bihar, where SEWA Munger and SEWA Bhagalpur organized women workers in agriculture, bidi rolling, weaving and other home-based activities. Self-help groups provided savings and credit, some of which was linked to government schemes. Women's health needs, like those in Gujarat, centered around primary health care and maternal/reproductive health issues. However, women workers in Bihar faced different challenges related to the underlying determinants of health status as compared to their sisters in Gujarat. Work was considerably more tenuous, incomes lower and family sizes larger. In some areas, violence was an everyday threat to life; rifles were commonplace and women's mobility was restricted both due to security and cultural norms. Government health services were also weaker than those in Gujarat, particularly at the primary level.

Nascent programs were tailored accordingly. From an education standpoint, CHWs were trained to focus on home-based sanitation and hygiene and treatment for common illnesses that would normally be provided by primary health centers in other states. In Gujarat, CHWs sold medicines to provide doorstep access while supplementing their own incomes. Given women's lower incomes in Bihar, however, we focused on the sale of low-cost *ayurvedic* medicines and created linkages to local medicine shops. Difficulty in attaining diversity in nutritious food, largely due to poverty, required SEWA health workers to focus on diet and cultural norms in education programs, while promoting greater use of local grains. Facilitated by the local Bihar School of Yoga, we introduced yoga to address occupational health issues for home-based workers such as back pain and eye strain. Family planning and reproductive health formed a larger part of both education and service linkages, as women had limited access to associated options at the village level.

Violence presented a unique issue related to community health workers. ASHA workers had started working in the area around the same time SEWA Munger had introduced village-based CHWs. Yet much of their work overlapped, particularly regarding record-keeping. SEWA had initially maintained parallel records to inform advocacy, a strategy that worked with great success in Gujarat. One evening, we received a frightening phone call: the husband of an ASHA, wielding a rifle, had accosted a SEWA CHW in her home—demanding her immunization records! She initially did not want to relent as she felt the records reflected her hard labor from going house to house to track children's health. The threat of violence forced her to reconsider, and jolted us into changing our program approach. As a result, SEWA began to work to support ASHAs at the village level, and reorganised its staffing such that CHWs worked across three to five villages to prevent overlaps with government services.

As the Bihar program developed, CHWs shifted delivery approach in line with the government and private services available. Whereas Mahila SEWA Housing Trust promoted building individual toilets, in Bihar we were limited to linking with local government schemes to facilitate access to community and individual toilets. Health insurance had played an important role in the development of SEWA Gujarat's program, in partnership with both public and private hospitals. Yet in Munger and Bhagalpur, women's access to limited household income and a surfeit of small private providers demanded that the initial focus remain on helping women use government services. The program in Bihar initiated a tuberculosis DOTS (Directly Observed Treatment, Short Course) partnership with the government, based on experience in Gujarat, but focused on village-level camps with private gynaecologists to address gaps in available services for reproductive health.

We experienced similar shifts in approach driven by varying needs in sites such as Murshidabad, West Bengal, Bareilly, Uttar Pradesh and Delhi. In West Bengal, the chief concerns of women bidi workers were related to tuberculosis and back/eye strain. Environmentally, arsenic levels in the water emerged as the most pressing agenda for advocacy. Rather than focus on maternal health as in Gujarat and Bihar, we linked with local water purification organizations, conducted research on water and educated women about the use of filters. Similarly, the microfinance program provided basic financial services, with a majority of loans related to illness expenditure. Women bidi workers in the area did not have regular, steady incomes: their earnings varied by season and market demand. Accordingly, we decided to link health activities much more closely with microfinance, using SEWA's self-help groups as a base. Health education focused on the illnesses on which women articulated the need for more information, with a focus on how to benefit from existing government schemes.

In Bareilly, women workers in embroidery and fabric embellishment demanded much more of a focus on eye health, resulting in SEWA-run eye camps and linkages with local eyeglass providers—along with working with employers/ middlemen to provide improved tools and workshops. Many women in Bareilly were restricted to the home; CHWs did not feel referral linkages to block-level health providers would be helpful. Instead, we convinced the local clinics to bring services to women's villages through mobile gynaecological clinics and camps. Workers in Delhi, primarily street vendors and daily wage laborers, were well aware of basic illnesses and the government services available. However, their cramped living conditions and sanitation issues were similar to issues faced in Ahmedabad. Working from a model initiated in Gujarat, Mahila Housing expanded its work to building toilets in Delhi's slums. Health workers chose to focus their efforts on tertiary-level illnesses for which treatment in Delhi was prohibitively expensive. A similar pattern emerged in each new location for SEWA's health programs (Table 8.1): social determinants of health, particularly women's working conditions, defined what CHWs addressed, both in content and how they delivered services.

Reflections

For community-based organizations, particularly in recent years, achieving 'scale' has become somewhat of an imperative: donors, policymakers and organizations hold themselves accountable to changes in outcomes at a broader population level [8]. Given that SEWA is a national movement of women workers with a common philosophy, it was assumed that health programs—like microfinance—could be replicated across states to reach more women. Yet SEWA's focus on addressing the social determinants of health such as work, sanitation and external mobility redefined how we approached scale. SEWA's definition of CHW—a community-based worker who responds to local need—ensured it could maintain a dynamic approach to scaling-up where context defined content. By retaining a women-centered approach integrated with microfinance and livelihoods, SEWA created a network of CHWs with a common philosophy, rather than a uniform model across states. This differs from most large scaled-up models of CHW programs, such as the ASHA program or Bangladesh Rural Advancement Committee (BRAC) in Bangladesh, where CHWs provide a similar set of services across a varying context.

In hindsight, shifts in strategy when scaling up by state seem natural for an organization that implements women-led, needs-based health services. Yet changes from the Gujarat model initially presented challenges for the CHW trainers accustomed to prioritizing maternal and child health and sanitation—as well as for donors keen to support the initial 'SEWA model' as defined in Gujarat. In the short term, experienced CHW trainers quickly realized that their role could not be to provide technical knowledge in a fixed modular or classroom approach. Instead, they were required to transfer a 'know-how', an approach to defining health strategy that is dynamic and responsive to local needs. Rather than pre-determining knowledge modules, trainers approached capacity building as a hands-on exercise that combined exchange visits, classroom training and immersion by trainers into a new context. In effect, scaling-up SEWA's SDH approach required trainers to learn how to transfer a longer-term approach to health, one that addressed issues likely to change both over time and across setting.

The decision to spread a philosophy rather than a model, while incorporating local issues, resulted in the growth of community-based health programs that

Table 8.1 SEWA's health program

State	IMR 2005 [13]	Primary occupations of members	CHW program	CHW focus	Current implementation approach
Gujarat	49.7	Agricultural and home-based work, street vendors, construction workers and service providers	1984	Maternal and child health, non-communicable disease and linkages to SEWA health insurance. TB and infectious diseases. Low-cost medicines	1. 1 CHW per village/slum 2. Supervisor for 3–5 CHWs 3. Health education through groups 4. Linkages to public and private referral services 5. Partnership with government programs to facilitate access to services
Bihar	61.7	Home-based incense rollers, agricultural and daily wage laborers.	2006	Infectious disease, occupational health, reproductive and sexual health and promotion of government health insurance	1. 1 CHW per 3–5 villages 2. Health education through groups 3. Linkages to public hospitals 4. Train local ASHAs 5. Advocacy with district health services
West Bengal	48.0	Home-based *bidi* workers	2007	Water and sanitation, arsenic contamination, infectious disease	1. 1 CHW per 3–5 villages 2. Health education with self-help groups 3. Linkages to primary health centers

(continued)

Table 8.1 (continued)

State	IMR 2005 [13]	Primary occupations of members	CHW program	CHW focus	Current implementation approach
					4. Advocacy at village and block level
Delhi	39.8	Vendors, construction workers and home-based workers	2008	Women's reproductive health, non-communicable disease and linkages to affordable care	1. 1 CHW per large slum area 2. Health education through groups 3. Linkages to private and public hospitals 4. Advocacy with municipal government
Rajasthan	65.3	Home-based *papad* rollers	2009	Basic health awareness and occupational health	1. Microfinance and union trained in health 2. Occupational health education 3. Linkages to government hospital
Uttrakahand	41.9	Agricultural and allied workers, home-based workers	2009	Basic health awareness and promotion of traditional medicines	1. Community leaders trained in health 2. Integration of health education into microfinance groups 3. Linkages with affordable local care

addressed SDH and health service delivery. A challenge to wider implementation and scale will be developing a larger training team that is both experienced in grassroots implementation and able to transfer a philosophy. Further, the primary change brought about by the SEWA health movement, the empowerment of women to control their health, requires innovative research, rather than standard monitoring indicators, to track progress and the impact on women's health. Although recent research in South Asia indicates that evaluation of participatory methods is possible [1, 9], evaluating SEWA's program poses an additional challenge as each state focuses on different health issues rather than a common set of health outcomes. The evaluation of the scale-up thus far has been process-driven, rather than through health outcomes research.

SEWA's experience offers lessons for community-based CHW programs, donors and researchers interested in scaling-up an approach grounded in SDH, particularly across diverse settings. The situation was unique in that health was integrated into existing microfinance and livelihoods activities. Also, CHWs were being introduced into organizations that share a similar philosophy towards women's empowerment and mobilizing. A generalizable lesson, however, is that scaling-up programs to address SDH requires, by definition, spreading an approach rather than a model. This method requires hands-on, continuous capacity building with CHWs in *how*, rather than *what*, to implement. SEWA's experience also indicates that community responsiveness can indeed be taught, through a combination of theoretical and skills-based training, ideally by other CHWs.

SEWA's experience also suggests that CHW-led programs that address SDH reconsider how scale and impact are defined. In public health, the potential of CHWs to improve health outcomes has been well established [10]. In developing countries, large government-run CHW programs such as the ASHA in India or the Brazilian Family Health Programme provide health services and linkages to public health systems. In parallel, community-based organizations have also trained and supported CHWs historically as activists or change agents [11], often experimenting with community-driven approaches and participatory methods, some of which have improved health outcomes [9, 12]. These latter, community-based, adaptable programs like SEWA can define scale in two ways. They can attempt to replicate a uniform service package, achieving breadth but risking the very foundation of a CHW's community responsiveness. Or, they can diffuse a philosophy, nurturing CHWs to be change agents who respond to local determinants and mobilize their communities. In this case, as SEWA's experience suggests, expansion is difficult to measure, since scaling up spread an implementation model with necessarily different service targets in each location. Accordingly, both the process and evaluation of scaling-up CHW models must expand to encapsulate a range of results, including the growth of a movement.

Conclusion

As SEWA learned, CHWs can indeed be equipped to address the SDH and health services. Although partnerships are required to improve sanitation, housing and livelihood security, a health program can also expand and adapt to non-health-related determinants. In this way, scaling-up our program did not meet traditional replication or expansion-based definitions of scale: SEWA promoted a philosophy towards health and its varying social determinants. Needs-based, dynamic programming is required if SDH are to be identified and addressed at the community level, particularly across different settings. Yet to promote such an approach, definitions of the role of CHWs, their training and measurement require transformation. Current models mostly limit CHWs to service delivery roles, their training to fixed curricula and evaluation to quantitative targets. While the importance of these features in large, government-led programs cannot be underestimated, it is also critical to recognize that CHWs can lead an SDH approach from the bottom up, if equipped with the appropriate skills.

Acknowledgements I am grateful to Mirai Chatterjee for inputs on this essay, and to her and the SEWA Health team for our learning journey together through the scaling-up process. We also are thankful for collaborations with Shalini Sinha and Rajani Ved which enhanced our understanding.

References

1. Marmot M. Achieving health equity: from root causes to fair outcomes. Lancet. 370 (9593):1153–63.
2. Sinha S. Learning to grow: upscaling the SEWA health program Ahmedabad. Gujarat: SEWA—Lok Swasthya Mandali; 2013.
3. Commission on Social Determinants of Helath. Closing the gap in a generation: health equity through action on the social determinants of health: final report of the commission on social determinants of health. World Health Organization; 2008.
4. Dayal M. Towards securer lives: SEWA's social-security programme. Orient Blackswan; 2001.
5. Ranson MK, Joshi P, Shah M, Shaikh Y. India: assessing the reach of three SEWA health services among the poor. In: Reaching the Poor with Health, Nutrition, and Population Services; 2005. p. 163–87.
6. Sinha S. Organising for health Ahmedabad. Gujarat: SEWA Health; 2006.
7. Ministry of Health and Family Welfare GoI. National rural health mission. New Delhi: Mission Document; 2005.
8. Uvin P, Jain PK, Brown L. Think large and act small: toward a new paradigm for NGO SCALING Up. World Dev. 2000;28(8).
9. Manandhar DS, Osrin D, Shrestha BP, Mesko N, Morrison J, Tumbahangphe KM, et al. Effect of a participatory intervention with women's groups on birth outcomes in Nepal: cluster-randomised controlled trial. Lancet. 2004;364(9438):970–9 PubMed PMID: 20043157516.

10. Lewin S, Munabi-Babigumira S, Glenton C, Daniels K, Bosch-Capblanch X, van Wyk BE, et al. Lay health workers in primary and community health care for maternal and child health and the management of infectious diseases. Cochrane Database Syst Rev. 2010;(3).
11. Lehmann U, Sanders D. Community health workers: what do we know about them?. Geneva: World Health Organization; 2007.
12. Tripathy P, Nair N, Barnett S, Mahapatra R, Borghi J, Rath S, et al. Effect of a participatory intervention with women's groups on birth outcomes and maternal depression in Jharkhand and Orissa, India: a cluster-randomised controlled trial. Lancet. 2010;375(9721):1182–92.
13. IIPS. National Family Health Survey-3. Indian Institute of Population Sciences; 2006.

Part III
Oversight

Chapter 9
Promoting Intersectoral Action on Menstrual Health and Hygiene Management: Arriving at a Framework and Indicators to Inform Policy and Programs

Arundati Muralidharan

Abstract Menstrual health and hygiene management (MHHM) is increasingly recognized as a critical issue facing adolescent girls, affecting their health and well-being, limiting opportunities to pursue education and employment opportunities, and has adverse implications for the environment. Given the range of factors that influence girls'/women's ability to manage their menses, action to improve MHHM calls for an intersectoral approach. While tools to address MHHM exist, a comprehensive framework that facilitates mapping all program components is not easily available. Relatedly, a set of relevant, easy to use program indicators specific to MHHM are not widely accessible. A comprehensive framework can potentially facilitate the identification of opportunities for collaboration, and the development of a core set of indicators will enable those taking action on MHHM to monitor and assess their program's progress and achievements, and can inform future programs and policy initiatives. Drawing upon the research and intervention literature on MHHM, as well as consultations with program implementers, stakeholders engaged in advocacy efforts, and policy makers, this chapter proposes a comprehensive framework to address MHHM in India, outlines key MHHM indicators, and discusses how these products can be used by various stakeholders in the country to improve MHHM in a comprehensive manner.

Keywords Menstrual health and hygiene management
Intersectoral approaches · Action and monitoring framework

A. Muralidharan (✉)
WaterAid India, New Delhi, Delhi, India
e-mail: ArundatiMuralidharan@wateraid.org

D. Nambiar and A. Muralidharan (eds.), *The Social Determinants of Health in India*, https://doi.org/10.1007/978-981-10-5999-5_9

Introduction

Girls and women of reproductive age menstruate, yet this normal, healthy physiological phenomenon is affected by sociocultural forces, the menstrual absorbents available and used, and the water, sanitation and hygiene services that determine how girls and women experience and manage their monthly period. In India, girls and women have low levels of knowledge about menstruation, the menstrual cycle and menstrual hygiene, with many lacking awareness about menstruation prior to menarche [1–7]. Mothers, who are often the primary source of information, are also limited in their ability to accurately communicate information about menstruation to their daughters. Underlying this poor awareness are deep-set sociocultural norms that regard menstruation as dirty or impure, and consequently affect if and how much information is shared and by whom, and how menstruation is managed [1–7]. Girls and women in the country use an array of menstrual absorbents, many of which are unhygienic or unsafe (e.g., old rags, synthetic materials, hay, ash) causing discomfort, and in some cases, even infections [2, 5, 8]. Poor water, sanitation, hygiene, and solid waste disposal facilities in homes, communities, schools, and worksites also make it difficult for girls to maintain hygiene during their menses, further compounding their risk of adverse health outcomes such as reproductive tract infections (RTI), stress and anxiety, and even gender-based violence. Girls drop out of school on attaining menarche or may miss school days during their periods [9]. Consequently, program implementers, researchers and policy makers are increasingly recognizing menstrual health and hygiene management (MHHM) as a critical issue facing adolescent girls, impacting their health and well-being, as well as the ability to pursue education and employment opportunities [8].

Actions to promote MHHM inherently embody a social determinants of health (SDH) approach—seeking to address the upstream forces that shape how girls experience and manage their menses. Social determinants, according to the World Health Organization (WHO) are the conditions in which people are born, grow, live, work and age [10]. The conceptual framework developed by Solar and Irwin for the Commission on Social Determinants of Health (CSDH) emphasizes the 'causes of causes', calling for action on the circumstances of daily life (e.g., the social and physical environment) and structural drivers (e.g., societal norms, economic environment). Drawing on this framework, the CSDH recommends actions on the following to improve health and reduce inequalities: (1) improve daily living conditions, (2) address and reduce inequalities in the distribution of power, money and resources, and (3) measure and understand the problem and assess the impact of actions [10]. These recommendations are relevant for programs, research, and policy on MHHM.

Interventions on MHHM are designed and implemented to equip girls with the necessary knowledge, skills and materials to manage their menses in a safe, hygienic and dignified manner, and to create a conducive social environment. Policies are being formulated to enable the effective implementation of such programs [8]. Thus far, action on MHHM has taken either a *hardware* or *software* approach, and at times, comprises a combination of the two [8]. A *software* approach typically involves awareness generation and behavior change activities. At times, interventions are also geared towards garnering social support to promote MHHM. A *hardware* approach relates to technology and/or infrastructure development, and involves one or more of the following: (1) production or procurement, and distribution of menstrual absorbents (sanitary napkins and cloth pads) and (2) water, sanitation, hygiene (WASH) services (or some combination of these). Advocacy on MHHM at the programmatic and policy levels boost both the *software* and *hardware* components. Over the past few years, a number of not-for-profit and for-profit non-governmental organizations, as well as the government sector have addressed either the *software* or *hardware* or both components to varying degrees [8, 11]. For instance, WASH United, an international organization working on water, sanitation and hygiene promotion through advocacy and programs, has developed an interactive menstrual hygiene management curriculum to create awareness and educate adolescents and teachers about menstruation, menstrual hygiene and reproductive health. EcoFemme, a women's empowerment initiative, develops and promotes affordable, high quality, reusable cloth pads. Government initiatives do address MHHM directly (e.g., the Menstrual Hygiene Scheme under the Ministry of Health and Family Welfare that provides both health education and distributes sanitary pads to adolescent girls) and indirectly (e.g., the erstwhile Nirmal Bharat Abhiyan under the Ministry of Drinking Water and Sanitation (MDWS) that supported toilet construction in communities, schools, and Anganwadis). These and other interventions are much needed and are commendable. Yet limited evidence exists on the effectiveness of, or the benefits conferred by, such efforts. Where monitoring or evaluations do take place, indicators to measure the effect of these programs typically focus on select *hardware* components, such as the number of sanitary pads distributed or sold, number of toilets constructed in schools, with little or no inclusion of the *software* elements [11]. During the Menstrual Hygiene Day Conference on 28 May 2014 in New Delhi, WASH program experts disclosed that monitoring and evaluation efforts are limited because few guidelines exist on what to assess or measure, and highlighted the need for a comprehensive, easy to use framework and indicators that will enable them to design, implement, track progress, and assess or evaluate the benefits of their initiatives.

Methodology

The development of a comprehensive framework for MHHM as well as a core set of indicators to measure MHHM comprised two steps. The first involved a review of grey literature and peer reviewed publications on MHHM in low and middle-income countries. Approximately 90 documents were identified and reviewed. These documents included formative research studies, program evaluations, intervention descriptions, and advocacy documents. The author looked for definitions and descriptions of conceptual frameworks on menstrual health and menstrual hygiene management in the documents, and well as for indicators used by research studies and evaluations to collect data on various aspects of MHHM. Based on this review, a conceptual model and draft list of indicators were developed. The second step involved sharing the draft framework and indicators with MHHM experts during a roundtable. The aim of this roundtable was to deliberate frameworks and indicators that can guide and inform MHHM programming at the community, state, and even national level. The main objective of this roundtable was to come to a consensus on a comprehensive framework for action on MHHM and a core set of MHHM related indicators.

The roundtable was to facilitate discussions on the following:

- Need for indicators on MHHM
- Definition or conceptualization of MHHM
- Key MHHM components
- A comprehensive framework for MHHM
- Program settings that MHHM indicators can be applied to
- MHHM related indicators related to software and hardware components

A day-long roundtable discussion was held in August 2014, involving 11 experts representing seven organizations working on MHHM. Not-for-profit organizations working on MHHM both in terms of direct interventions (e.g., Azadi, EcoFemme) as well as research and advocacy (e.g., DASRA, 2014, WaterAid, PATH), and multilateral organizations (e.g., UNICEF) attended the meeting. Donor agencies and government officials were also invited, but were unable to attend due to other events being held on the same day.

Results

The Need for MHHM Related Framework and Indicators

In addition to informing program design and aiding the monitoring and evaluation of MHHM related interventions, experts felt that a commonly agreed upon comprehensive framework and core set of indicators can play a role in facilitating convergent action on MHHM across relevant sectors, and build consensus among donors about what program implementers and researchers should report on.

Conceptualizing MHHM

The Water Supply and Sanitation Collaborative Council (WSSCC)[1] proposed that menstrual hygiene management be defined holistically, drawing attention to three key elements: '(i) articulation, awareness, information and confidence to manage menstruation with safety and dignity using safe hygienic materials together with (ii) adequate water and agents and spaces for washing and bathing and (iii) disposal with privacy and dignity' [12]. The framework proposed by WSSCC captures the three elements that address both hardware and software components—breaking the silence around menstruation, managing menstruation safely and hygienically, and safe reuse and disposal options [12]. The international organization, WaterAid, also proposed a framework in their landmark resource guide, Menstrual Hygiene Matters. This framework highlights the key elements of menstrual hygiene programming, including the provision of knowledge and information, creating positive social norms, and the provision of water, sanitation and hygiene facilities. Central to these elements is the creation of a supportive environment [13]. Both these conceptualizations encompass the software component (i.e., hygiene education) as well as the hardware component (i.e., production and supply of menstrual absorbents, and availability of WASH facilities).

Drawing upon their framework and initial conceptualization, WSSCC along with other organizations later proposed a revised definition of menstrual hygiene management that again underscores the rights of girls and women to manage menstruation safely and with dignity: 'Women and adolescent girls are using a clean menstrual management material to absorb or collect menstrual blood, that can be changed in privacy as often as necessary for the duration of a menstrual period, using soap and water for washing the body as required, and having access to safe and convenient facilities manage/to dispose of used menstrual management materials. They understand the basic facts, and can seek information linked to the menstrual cycle and how to manage it with dignity and without discomfort or fear' [14].

Deliberating on this definition, roundtable participants suggested that this definition be modified to explicitly mention the importance of self-efficacy and interpersonal communication skills among adolescents in maintaining health and hygiene, as well as the critical role of an enabling or supportive environment in reinforcing the software component and facilitating the availability, accessibility and use of the hardware components. The amended definition now reads (italicized section represents additions to the original definition by the Global Monitoring Working Group on Hygiene):

[1]WSSCC is a global multistakeholder partnership and membership organization that works to save lives and improve livelihoods, driven by the mission to achieve sustainable water supply, sanitation and hygiene for all people in the world.

> Women and adolescent girls are using a clean menstrual management material to absorb or collect menstrual blood, that can be changed in privacy as often as necessary for the duration of a menstrual period, using soap and water for washing the body as required, and having access to safe and convenient facilities manage and to dispose of used menstrual management materials. They understand the basic facts linked to the menstrual cycle and how to manage it with dignity and without discomfort or fear, *and have the self-confidence, agency, and inter-personal communication skills to seek information and help regarding the same. Additionally, women and girls enjoy a supportive socio-cultural environment at home, in their communities, at schools and at workplaces that enable the safe and hygienic management of menstruation.*

MHHM Framework for Action

Intervention efforts may respond to select aspects of MHHM; a comprehensive framework can guide more concerted action on MHHM, and also link the various MHHM components, enabling program implementers to see how their interventions may draw from and/or influence other software and/or *hardware* efforts. For this reason, the expert gathering reviewed the WSSCC framework as well as the framework in Menstrual Hygiene Matters, and proposed that a revised model be developed to comprehensively represent action on MHHM, detailing the different levels of outcomes in which interventions can affect change. Immediate outcomes are the first change or benefits that those exposed to an intervention experience, and typically relate to knowledge, attitudes, and skills. Intermediate outcomes relate to deeper attitudinal changes and behaviour change. Long-term outcomes imply changes in condition or status [15]. Detailing the different MHHM outcomes in a framework will enable program implementers to determine which level of outcomes their interventions will address, and linkages with other outcomes.

Figure 9.1 showcases the newly developed comprehensive framework for action on MHHM. The ultimate goal of MHHM interventions is to improve girls' and women's menstrual health and well-being. The interrelated set of long-term outcomes to achieve this goal are four-fold, relating to improved health (e.g., reproductive tract infections) and nutrition (e.g., anaemia) outcomes, as well as socioeconomic (e.g., school attendance) and other outcomes (e.g., self-efficacy). Intermediate outcomes feed into the four long-term outcomes, and relate to favorable attitudes towards MHHM and improved availability of and access to water, sanitation, and disposal facilities. Immediate outcomes pertain to increased knowledge about menstruation, the menstrual cycle, menstrual hygiene and menstrual problems. Both knowledge and attitude related outcomes are relevant for adolescent girls as well as stakeholders who impact their menstrual health and hygiene related practices, such as mothers, community members, and teachers.

This framework can be applied to settings in which MHHM interventions are typically delivered, namely communities and educational institutions. Other potential settings include health facilities that serve adolescents (e.g., adolescent friendly health clinics), worksites, transportation services and public spaces.

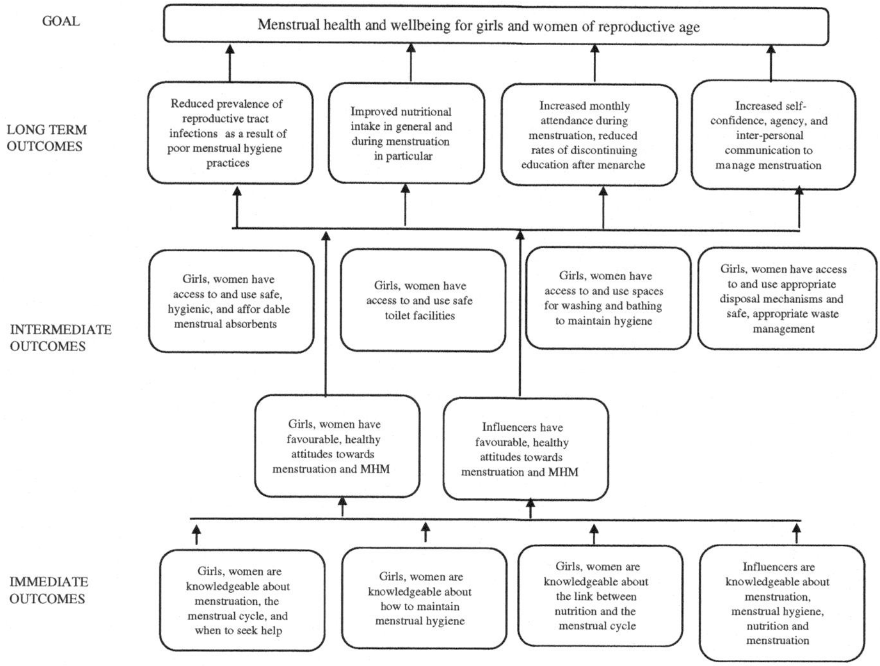

Fig. 9.1 MHHM framework

Core Set of MHHM Indicators

Drawing upon the logic model for action on MHHM, indicators address both the *software* and *hardware* components, and can be broadly divided into four categories: (1) health outcomes; (2) socio-economic outcomes; (3) knowledge, attitudes and practices related to MHHM; and (4) WASH infrastructure.

Knowledge, Attitudes, and Behaviours Related to Menstruation

Programs promoting menstrual hygiene among adolescent girls seek to increase knowledge, foster favorable attitudes, and promote hygienic and healthful behaviors related to menstruation and the use of menstrual absorbents. Adolescent girls in India are known to have poor knowledge, erroneous beliefs, and unfavorable attitudes about how and why menstruation occurs [1–7]. A systematic review pooled together evidence from much of the research on menstrual hygiene in India and found that only 48% of adolescent girls were aware of menstruation prior to menarche and less than a quarter knew that the uterus was the source of bleeding [16].

Sociocultural norms shape girls' understanding and management of their period [6, 7]. The deeply entrenched belief that menstrual blood is polluting, determines girls' choice of menstrual absorbents, hygiene practices, and observance of social, religious and food restrictions [1, 2, 4, 5, 17, 18]. Confirming this trend, the systematic review estimated that just 55% of girls in India considered menstruation to be normal [16]. On reaching menarche, girls typically learn about menstruation from their mothers, yet mothers themselves have low levels of awareness and may impart incorrect information to their daughters, highlighting the need to focus intervention efforts on this group as well. [4, 6, 16–20] Indicators, therefore, need to be developed, to assess knowledge related to menstruation and menstrual hygiene, as well as puberty and the menstrual cycle, and the sources of information on these issues. Given that attitudes towards menstruation underlie menstrual hygiene behaviors, the expert group felt that attitudinal indicators must also be developed.

During menstruation, girls may use homemade cloth pads, commercially available sanitary napkins, or even other materials such as hay, ash, sand, and dried leaves. Girls chose these absorbent materials based on the availability of, access to, and affordability of products, facilities, or services to wash or dispose of them, as well as the sociocultural acceptability of absorbent materials and WASH facilities. [2, 5, 16]. As a result, some may use unsafe and unhygienic materials, or use safe materials such as clean cotton cloth or sanitary pads in an unhygienic manner (i.e., not change the absorbent as regularly as is needed) which can cause infections and other adverse health outcomes. Evidence suggests that more adolescent more girls may use low-cost or no-cost menstrual absorbents as opposed to the more expensive commercially available sanitary pads—the reported use of commercially available sanitary pads according to a large survey was 12% [21]. Evidence also suggests that the product landscape is changing rapidly in India with greater penetration of sanitary pad brands as well as greater innovation in terms of disposable and reusable products by entrepreneurs. Indicators need to capture the type of menstrual absorbent girls use, how often they change reusable and disposable menstrual absorbents, and how they clean and dispose of used menstrual absorbents (Table 9.1).

Health Outcomes

The group identified three main health outcomes that MHHM related interventions focus on or should focus on: reproductive tract infections (RTI), menstrual problems and disorders, and nutritional outcomes. Literature on health outcomes related to menstrual health and hygiene among adolescents is limited to self-reported symptoms given the difficulty in clinically diagnosing conditions in this young population. Available studies primarily elicit reported symptoms associated with menstrual problems and poor menstrual hygiene, notably RTIs [22]. RTIs that are not sexually transmitted such as bacterial vaginosis and vulvovaginal candidiasis may result from poor menstrual hygiene practices or the use of unsafe, unhygienic

Table 9.1 Core indicators for knowledge, attitudes, and behaviors related to menstruation

Knowledge	• Proportion of girls who have correct information about: ○ Pubertal changes in girls and boys ○ Reproductive system ○ Menstruation and the menstrual cycle ○ Nutritious food to be eaten during adolescence, and during menstruation • Proportion of girls who report menstruation as a normal and healthy physiological phenomenon that occurs in women of reproductive age • Proportion of girls who report that the source of information on menstruation is: ○ Mother ○ Sister ○ Other female family member ○ Friend ○ Teacher ○ Other (specify) • Proportion of girls who report menstrual problems (specify menstrual problem: infrequent/scanty period, painful period, heavy bleeding etc.) • Proportion of girls who report seeking health care for menstrual problems • Proportion of girls reporting that they seek health care for menstrual problems from: ○ Mother ○ Sister ○ Other family member ○ Health care facility ○ Teacher ○ Others (specify)
Attitudes and menstrual norms	• Proportion of girls who believe that menstruation is normal and healthy, not unclean/polluting/impure/a curse • Proportion of girls who believe that girls/women can pray during menstruation/visit places of religious worship during menstruation • Proportion of girls who believe that girls/women can freely interact with others during menstruation • Proportion of girls who believe that girls can be active/engage in sports during menstruation • Proportion of girls who believe that girls/women can cook for and eat with the family during the menstruation • Proportion of girls who believe that girls/women should not be segregated during menstruation • Proportion of girls who believe that girls/women should eat normal, healthy food during menstruation • Proportion of girls who believe that menstrual norms and taboos can be questioned/challenged • Proportion of girls who believe that they can negotiate norms related to MHHM • Proportion of girls reporting that they received favorable/supportive responses from mothers, teachers, health care providers when they attained menarche or during menstruation • Sources of information of these menstrual norms and taboos

(continued)

Table 9.1 (continued)

Personal hygiene behaviours	• Proportion of girls who wash their genitals when changing menstrual absorbent/as often as required on a daily basis during menstruation • Proportion of girls who bathe daily during menstruation
Use of menstrual absorbents	• Proportion of girls who use ○ Reusable homemade cotton cloth pads ○ Reusable homemade cloth pads made of materials others than cotton ○ Reusable cotton cloth pads sold by NGOs, entrepreneurs, self-help groups etc. ○ Disposable sanitary pads (commercially available, manufactured by entrepreneurs, self-help groups) ○ Other materials (specify) ○ A combination of homemade/reusable cotton pads and disposable pads • Proportion of girls who change menstrual absorbents regularly every day (specify number of changes in the case of cloth pads and commercially available sanitary pads) • For girls who use homemade reusable cloth pads, proportion who: ○ Thoroughly wash used cloth with soap and water ○ Dry washed menstrual cloth in sun ○ Store washed menstrual cloth in a dry, clean place ○ Dispose of used menstrual cloth every few months ○ Dispose of menstrual cloth in dustbin ○ Reasons for preferring cloth over sanitary pads • For girls who use disposable sanitary pads, proportion who: ○ Dispose of sanitary pad in dustbin (probe for segregation of biodegradable and non-biodegradable components of menstrual pads) ○ Have knowledge of where to buy sanitary pads ○ Have knowledge of whom to ask for sanitary pads (e.g., ASHAs in rural areas) ○ Reasons for preferring sanitary pads over cloth ○ Affordability or ability to pay for sanitary pads

menstrual absorbents [22]. A recent systematic review examined the health and social effects of menstrual hygiene management, identifying studies that found a positive association between menstrual hygiene practices and the following outcomes: self-reported vaginal discharge, clinically confirmed bacterial vaginosis, and clinically confirmed RTI [22].

In addition to menstrual hygiene management, menstrual health is also an important consideration as menstrual problems can interfere with daily life, school attendance, and can even be a symptom of an underlying medical condition [23, 24]. Research on menstrual problems among Indian adolescents again elicited self-reported symptoms relating to common menstrual problems such amenorrhea, dysmenorrhea, and irregular menstruation [25, 26]. Survey items typically ask girls about the regularity and duration of their menstrual cycle and if they have pain or discomfort during menstruation.

Table 9.2 Core indicators for health outcomes

Reproductive tract infections	• Proportion of girls who report RTI symptoms (self-reported symptoms): ○ Abnormal (thick, curd-like) vaginal discharge ○ Itching/soreness of the vulva and vaginal area • Proportion of girls who have been clinically diagnosed with bacterial vaginosis or vulvovaginal candidiasis by a health care provider[a] • Proportion of girls who are aware that poor MHM can cause abnormal vaginal discharge and/or itching/soreness of vaginal area • Proportion of girls who report seeking help/health care/treatment for RTI symptoms: ○ Whom does the girl/woman tell/confide in about symptoms? ○ From whom does she seek treatment for RTI symptoms?
Menstrual problems/disorders	• Proportion of girls who report having a normal menstrual cycle (i.e., 21–35 days) • Proportion of girls who report the following symptoms: ○ Painful menstruation (specify time period) ○ Absence of menstruation (specify time period) ○ Excessive heavy bleeding (specify time period) ○ Scanty bleeding (specify time period) ○ Infrequent menstruation (specify time period) ○ Pre-menstrual symptoms ○ Combination of symptoms • Proportion of girls who have been clinically diagnosed with a menstrual disorder by a health care provider[a] • Proportion of girls who report seeking help/health care/treatment for menstrual problems: ○ Whom does the girl/woman tell/confide in about symptoms? ○ From whom does she seek treatment for menstrual problems?
Nutrition	• Proportion of girls who have correct knowledge of a balanced, nutritious diet • Proportion of girls who have correct knowledge about the importance of nutrition during adolescence and menstruation • Proportion of girls who are aware of the link between poor nutrition and anaemia • Proportion of girls who report following food taboos related to menstruation • Proportion of girls who have misconceptions regarding food intake during menstruation • Proportion of girls who restrict food and liquid intake during menstruation due to poor access to WASH facilities • Proportion of girls who report intake of nutritious food in general, and during menstruation in particular (self-report) • Proportion of girls who are anaemic[a]

[a]Only when clinical diagnosis is acceptable and possible

The link between nutrition and menstrual health, while grossly understudied, is important to explore, especially for adolescent girls, a significant proportion of whom are anaemic [27]. Limited research and programmatic anecdotes suggests that girls and women may constrain their food and liquid intake to limit urination and defecation, especially when they lack access to sanitation facilities [28].

Additionally, sociocultural food taboos are also imposed on menstruating girls. Such restrictions, whether self-imposed or normative, can impact adolescent girls' nutritional intake, having implications for their haemoglobin levels and perhaps other nutritional outcomes. The limited evidence on the association between nutrition and menstrual health is why the roundtable experts felt it necessary to develop indicators to learn more about this relationship and if programs are able to redress this in any way. Government programs, such as the SABLA scheme (Rajiv Gandhi Scheme for Empowerment of Adolescent Girls) do draw attention to the critical role of nutrition among adolescents, including during menstruation, yet do not have indicators that assess this relationship in any way [29]. Experts expressed the need to assess knowledge related to a nutritious diet and actual intake of a nutritious diet, the link between menstruation and nutrition, the observance of food restrictions, and the intake of restricted food during menstruation (Table 9.2).

Social Outcomes

The two key social outcomes, relevant for adolescent girls, were education status and gender.

For menstruating girls, the availability and accessibility of usable WASH facilities may play a role in them continuing their education [9, 30–32]. The association between school absenteeism and menstruation can be explained in two ways. The 'pull out' explanation proposes that girls may drop out of school when they attain menarche due to sociocultural constraints imposed on them, or they may miss school days due to menstrual problems. The push out' factor suggests that the unavailability of or inadequate WASH facilities, especially toilet facilities in schools, may force girls to drop out or remain absent during menstruation [9]. Key indicators include whether adolescent girls are enrolled in school, whether they discontinued their schooling or started to miss school days on a monthly basis on attaining menarche, and the reasons they drop out or remain absent from school. One caveat when looking at the link between menstruation, menstrual hygiene and education is to be careful when attributing absenteeism or dropouts to the inability to manage menses in a safe and hygienic way alone. Several interconnected issues related to puberty, menstruation and growing sexual awareness shape whether girls continue their education. Improving access to hygienic menstrual absorbents and safe spaces to manage periods may be important but alone is insufficient to address the range of barriers adolescent girls face in pursuing their education in school.

The limited literature on gender and menstruation highlights how menstruation can serve to reinforce gender inequalities experienced by girls curtailing their mobility and access to social capital, including education [33]. Jewitt and Ryley discuss how menstruation affects girls' 'spatial mobility' and reinforces 'wider gender inequalities'. With menarche, girls' freedom of movement is curtailed for two main reasons. First, menstruation is considered to be impure or dirty, and as a result, restrictions related to interactions and social activities, including religious

Table 9.3 Core indicators for social outcomes

Education	• Proportion of adolescent girls enrolled in: ○ Primary school ○ Secondary school • Proportion of adolescent girls discontinuing education after attaining menarche (either at primary school level or secondary school level) • Reasons for discontinuing schooling on attaining menarche • Proportion of school-going adolescent girls who miss school days on a monthly basis • Duration of absence from school during the month, on average • Proportion of girls who cite menstruation, menstrual problems, or the inability to manage menstruation as a reason for remaining absent from school on a monthly basis
Gender	• Gender equitable attitudes (includes items on promoting equity for girls) • Empowerment (includes items on mobility and economic security) • Decision-making (includes items on decision making related to purchases and to visiting friends and relatives) • Self-confidence/self-determination/self-efficacy (includes items on communication with mothers, teachers and other stakeholders to seek information and health care)

worship are imposed. Second, menstruation signals sexual maturity and gives rises to concerns regarding sexual activity and sexual abuse [33]. To promote menstrual health and hygiene behaviours, the expert group felt that interventions should seek to redress gender inequalities related to mobility, decision-making and self-efficacy, especially related to communication to seek information, help and health care. Resultantly, indicators should be developed to assess changes in these gender domains (Table 9.3).

WASH Infrastructure

The above mentioned literature clearly makes the case for available and accessible WASH facilities that meet the MHHM needs of adolescent girls. The WHO/UNICEF Joint Monitoring Programme on Water Supply and Sanitation (JMP) provides the most widely used hardware indicators for water and sanitation [34]. Sanitation-related indicators under JMP relate to the proportion of the population reporting practicing open defecation. Indicators for water include having access to a basic water supply and handwashing facilities in homes, educational institutions and health centers [34]. While these indicators do not explicitly refer to menstrual hygiene management, they do cover factors that enable girls to practice hygiene behaviors such as access to toilet and water facilities in various settings.

To develop WASH indicators relevant to MHHM, the expert group expressed that indicators should cover four hardware components: water supply, toilet facilities, bathing and washing facilities (includes handwashing stations and facilities to wash and dry menstrual cloths), and lastly disposal of menstrual waste under solid waste management. Additionally, indicators should cover four key aspects of each hardware component: availability, accessibility, acceptability and utilization, and affordability. Availability refers to whether WASH facilities are available in sufficient numbers. WASH facilities are accessible if they can be easily reached by girls when they need to use them. Acceptability relates to perceptions of quality; and utilization refers to the actual use of WASH facilities. Lastly, affordability is the ability of girls to pay for using WASH facilities (Table 9.4).

Table 9.4 Core indicators for WASH infrastructure

Availability	• Percentage of households, schools, health facilities/Anganwadi with WASH facilities: ○ Clean water for washing ○ Clean water for bathing ○ Handwashing station/space with water ○ Handwashing station/space with soap ○ Improved, functional toilets ○ Toilets with facilities such as latch, water, hook/shelves for storing personal items, dustbins ○ Dustbins or incinerators for the safe disposal of menstrual absorbents ○ Considerations: ▪ Toilet facilities should be broken down by type of toilet (individual household latrine and toilet blocks, improved and unimproved toilets) ▪ In certain settings such as schools, indicators for gender-specific toilets should be included (e.g., proportion of schools which have separate toilets for girls) • Percentage of girls practicing open defecation • Ratio of WASH facilities to people who need to use them in various settings • Proportion of bathing facilities that also have other amenities such as hooks/shelves for clothes and personal items, a place to wash and dry cloths, and disposal facilities
Accessibility	• Proportion of households, schools, health facilities with easily accessible WASH facilities as perceived by girls • Other considerations include: ○ Location of WASH facility/service ○ Time taken to reach WASH facility/service
Affordability	• Cost of constructing sanitation/WASH facilities (particularly in the case of households constructing toilets) • Proportion availing subsidy or scheme to construct or install sanitation/WASH facility ○ Government scheme/subsidy (specify) ○ NGO scheme/subsidy (specify) • Cost of operations and maintenance of sanitation/WASH facility (particularly in the case of institutional setting with such facilities) • Cost of using public WASH facility/service ○ Pay per use ○ Payment by other mode (e.g., monthly charges)

(continued)

Table 9.4 (continued)

Quality and utilization	• Proportion reporting that WASH facilities are clean (includes visible signs and odour) • Proportion reporting that WASH facilities are functional/in working condition • Proportion who state that toilet facilities are well maintained/regularly maintained • Proportion reporting that WASH facilities are safe or have safety provisions (e.g., door, door with lock, curtain, guard) • Proportion that report that WASH facilities have other related amenities (e.g., toilets have handwashing facilities, hooks or shelves, dustbins) • Proportion who use: ○ Clean water for washing ○ Clean water for bathing ○ Handwashing station/space with water ○ Handwashing station/space with soap ○ Improved toilets ○ Toilets with facilities such as latch, running water, hook/shelves for storing personal items, dustbins ○ Dustbins, incinerators for disposing of menstrual absorbents

Conclusion

MHHM is an important aspect of an adolescent girl's health and well-being. To improve MHHM, interventions must implement *hardware* and *software* elements, drawing upon the expertise of several relevant sectors such as health and nutrition, education, women's empowerment, and water and sanitation. To enable adolescents to have healthy periods, interventions must provide health education and basic WASH services that are responsive to MHHM needs, as well as engender favorable attitudes towards menstruation, encourage the utilization of WASH services and safe, hygienic menstrual absorbents. Although a comprehensive approach is desirable, there is not as yet a single program able to cover both the *software* and *hardware* MHHM components or for that matter, even all *software* or all *hardware* components. A comprehensive MHHM approach calls for collaborative action by stakeholders from different sectors who are experienced in implementing the key *hardware* and/or *software* components. A framework for action can promote such convergent action. Program implementers, and researchers and evaluators can place their specific intervention in this framework against the outcomes to be achieved. The framework will also enable them to locate their intervention in relation to other components needed to improve MHHM. This can lead to the identification of stakeholders, interventions, and consequently partnerships that will engender a holistic approach to MHHM. Indicators to assess MHHM programs by the government and non-governmental organizations do exist, yet are often limited to indicators for the *hardware* components. The core set of indicators proposed in this paper can be used by these interventions to assess their impact in a more nuanced and holistic manner, and also to see how action on one aspect links with action on and outcomes resulting from complementary efforts. For instance, the Menstrual Hygiene Scheme (MHS) and the Rashtriya Kishor Swasthya Karyakram (RKSK) under Ministry of Health and Family Welfare (MoHFW) identify menstrual health and hygiene as important for the health and well-being of adolescents and elucidate both health education and sanitary pad distribution as ways to improve MHM. [35–37] The indicators outlined in these government program documents are limited to the production, procurement, distribution and sale of sanitary pads. Given the focus on health education, more detailed indicators related to health, and knowledge, attitudes and behaviours, can be included. Additionally, program documents talk about convergence with other government agencies. The Ministry of Human Resource Development (MHRD) that implements the Sarva Shiksha Abhiyan (SSA) is partnered with MDWS to install toilets for girls and boys in schools. To address MHM more comprehensively, MHRD can also partner with MoHFW to have the MHS or RKSK impart health education sessions in schools, thereby enabling girls to benefit from both the *software* and *hardware* MHHM interventions. Using the MHHM framework and indicators can enable these programs to assess whether girls are benefiting from this collaborative approach.

India's Swachh Bharat Mission (SBM), launched in 2014, provides an ideal platform to catalyze action on the *hardware* and *software* components of MHM at scale. Key objectives of the Mission relevant to MHM are eliminating open defecation, creating awareness about the link between sanitation and public health, promoting healthy behaviors regarding sanitation, and creating effective solid waste management facilities [38]. MDWS spearheads the implementation of the Mission in rural India and in December 2015, launched the National Guidelines for menstrual hygiene management in schools [39]. The guidelines detail operational steps to be taken at various levels of implementation and suggests how various government departments, particularly MoHFW, MHRD, and Ministry of Women and Child Development, can work with MDWS to improve MHM. The framework proposed in these guidelines mirrors to some extent the framework presented here (but with a focus on educational institutions). The Guidelines also propose a set of performance indicators that government programs can use at scale to track program implementation. The Guidelines are valuable in that they provide concrete guidance to states on how they can develop and implement an MHM program with school-going girls. While the Guidelines have been launched at the national level, few states have adopted and rolled out the program in schools. However, moving forward, several organizations are advocating with state governments to review, adapt, and implement the guidelines, and this can provide a fertile opportunity to detail out the indicators to capture more than implementation related process indicators.

Several issues are emerging as critical for MHHM, particularly in relation to various institutional settings, intervention groups, menstrual hygiene products and the safe management of menstrual waste, emergencies and disasters, and policy action. With disposable sanitary pads becoming more available to girls in urban and rural India, we need to think through how menstrual waste products can be disposed of in a private and environmentally safe manner, and develop indicators that track their safe disposal and management. MHHM indicators must be adapted for use in institutional settings, including schools, residential schools for girls, worksites (for both formal and informal workers), health care settings, and Anganwadi centers. MHHM in institutional settings brings to light the need to work with key people who are, or will be, involved in the delivery of interventions—frontline health workers such as ASHAs and Anganwadi workers, teachers, peers in schools, and colleagues at worksites. MHHM is challenging not just for adolescent girls, but also for the influencers around them. In programs, indicators need to be developed to understand the four indicator categories from the perspective of critical influencers.

Some Indian states experience natural disasters such as droughts, floods, and earthquakes. During such events, women and girls are particularly vulnerable and lack even the most basic services to manage their periods. Organizations involved in disaster response can consider using select MHHM indicators to help direct response efforts to assist women and girls to gain access to safe products and WASH services.

Lastly, with increased policy attention to menstrual hygiene management in India, we must think about the development of indicators to track policy initiatives, budgetary allocations and expenditure on programs to ensure accountability.

The menstrual health and hygiene management landscape is changing in India with increasing interest and action by government, civil society organizations, research institutes, donors, media, activists, entrepreneurs, the private sector, and adolescent girls themselves. Consequently, this set of indicators must be a *living* document to respond to emerging issues, new evidence, policy advocacy, and programmatic learnings.

Commentary—Menstrual Health and Hygiene Management

Jashodhara Dasgupta
SAHAYOG, Lucknow, India

In many societies, menstruation marked the transition from being a girl to maturing into a young woman, and was traditionally celebrated with fertility rituals. For adolescent girls who had already been married, this was the signal for the formal departure to the marital family ('gauna' in Uttar Pradesh) to begin her sexual relations with her husband. It was important that her marriage be arranged before menarche; for if a girl had attained puberty and was still unmarried, it was seen as a high-risk situation. She could potentially become pregnant if she engaged in sexual relations, which would damage the natal family's honour, and no one would want to ever marry her. Even if these sexual relations were exploitative or non-consensual, as often faced by girls from Dalit families, the possibility of pregnancy would tarnish the family's honour. So it was even more important for those from socioeconomically weaker sections to marry off their daughters before menarche.

Today in many parts of India there is a social aspiration to educate daughters, even if they have attained puberty. Marriage is thus delayed, and the potentially fertile young woman enjoys some degree of mobility and freedom to mingle with those outside the family. But the latent anxiety about her sexuality continues and results in a number of restrictions being imposed upon girls after they begin menstruating. In its most extreme form, it may result in stopping her from attending classes as a regular student, or in closely monitoring her movements even though she attends school. In addition there are strictures about social interactions, especially with men or boys, and rules about modesty in clothing (wearing a scarf or veil to cover the shoulders and breasts), about public places where she may not go, and what games or activities are now unsuitable for her. Her future responsibilities as someone's wife and homemaker are a looming reality, and the family may direct her to learn various home-making skills rather than engage in games or spend time with friends.

Thus the onset of menstruation for young girls in India is not only the start of many physical discomforts as they struggle to manage hygiene without water or sanitation facilities at home or in schools, and without convenient and affordable sanitary protection; it is also marks the unpleasant onset of a large number of social controls imposed upon them. These controls, which basically stem from efforts to monitor and control their sexuality, result in loss of her mobility to a limited or large extent and in restrictions upon her social interactions, entertainment options or sports. In their worst forms, these controls may lead to loss of access to education and career opportunities and into an early or forced marriage. Overall the onset of menstruation marks the loss of independence and agency, and may also lead to frustration and stress through suppression of all natural urges.

For the mothers of girls who attain puberty, it is a time of anxiety and close monitoring, since any evidence of sexual activity on the part of the daughters will result in shaming and insult of the mothers. Mothers transmit key social messages to daughters such as the importance of chastity, dutifulness and submission to family norms; knowing that they will face the family's anger and be blamed if the unmarried daughter demonstrates any sexual agency.

An intervention that aims to improve menstrual health and hygiene management (MHHM) needs to incorporate these important aspects of gender and sexuality, so that menstruation is seen as a positive life-transition and not one that signals the end of autonomy and self-esteem. Education around menstruation should incorporate not only the biological aspects including the links with conception, but also enable analysis of the social controls upon sexuality. In addition the key messages of consensual, respectful and safe sexual relations have to be included within age-appropriate comprehensive sexuality education.

Therefore the Social Outcomes indicators for assessing effectiveness of such an intervention could include the component of 'reduction in the number of early/forced marriages' of girls before or just following menarche. The Social Attitudes indicators could also include the extent of 'fertility awareness and sexual responsibility' among adolescent girls and boys.

References

1. Garg S, Sharma N, Sahay R. Socio-cultural aspects of menstruation in an urban slum in Delhi, India. Reprod Health Matters. 2001;9(17):16–25.
2. Narayan KA, Srinivasa DK, Pelto PJ, Veerammal S. Puberty rituals, reproductive knowledge and health of adolescent schoolgirls in South India. Asia Pac Popul J. 2001;16(2):225–38.
3. Khanna A, Goyal RS, Bhawsar R. Menstrual practices and reproductive problems: a study of adolescent girls in Rajasthan. J Health Manag. 2005;7(1):91–107.
4. Dasgupta A, Sarkar M. Menstrual hygiene: how hygienic is the adolescent girl? India J Community Med. 2008;33(2):77–80.
5. Nemade D, Anjenaya S, Gujar R. Impact of health education on knowledge and practices about menstruation among adolescent school girls of Kalamboli, Navi-Mumbai. Health Popul Perspect Issues. 2009;32(4):167–75.
6. Jogdand K, Yerpude P. A community-based study on menstrual hygiene among adolescent girls. Indian J Matern Child Health. 2011;13(3):1–6.
7. Kumar A, Srivastava K. Cultural and social practices regarding menstruation among adolescent girls. Soc Work Public Health. 2011;26(6):594–604.
8. Dasra. Spot On! Improving menstrual health and hygiene in India. http://www.dasra.org/research/flip/report/spot-on-improving-menstrual-hygiene-management-in-india. Accessed 28 Oct 2014.
9. Birdthistle I, Dickson K, Freeman M, Javidi L. What impact does the provision of separate toilets for girls at schools have on their primary and secondary school enrolment, attendance and completion? A systematic review of the evidence (internet). London: EPPI-Centre, Social Science Research Unit, Institute of Education, University of London; 2011. http://eppi.ioe.ac.uk/cms/LinkClick.aspx?fileticket=aX5WKT1UsKo%3d&tabid=3098&mid=5766. Accessed 14 Feb 2014.
10. WHO Commission on social determinants of health. Closing the gap in a generation: health equity through action on the social determinants of health: commission on social determinants of health final report. World Health Organisation; 2008.
11. Muralidharan A, Patil H, Patnaik S. Unpacking the policy landscape for menstrual hygiene management: implications for school WASH programmes in India. Waterlines. 2015;34(1):79–91.
12. Patkar A. Preparatory Input on MHM for End Group (Internet); 2010. http://www.wssinfo.org/fileadmin/user_upload/resources/MENSTRUAL-HYGIENE-MANAGEMENT-Paper-for-END-group-1.pdf. Accessed 2 Feb 2014.
13. House S, Mahon T, Cavill S. Menstrual hygiene matters: a resource for improving menstrual hygiene around the world; 2012. http://www.popline.org/node/579119. Accessed 31 May 2015.
14. Global Monitoring Working Group on Hygiene. Meeting report of joint monitoring program post-2015 global monitoring working group on hygiene. Washington DC; 2014. www.wssinfo.org/fileadmin/user_upload/resources/Meeting-Report-of-the-JMP-Post-2015-Hygiene-Working-Group-May-2012.pdf.
15. Way U. Measuring program outcomes: a practical approach. United Way of America; 1996.
16. van Eijk AM, Sivakami M, Thakkar MB, et al. Menstrual hygiene management among adolescent girls in India: a systematic review and metaanalysis. BMJ Open. 2016;6:e010290. doi:10.1136/bmjopen-2015-010290.
17. Omidvar S, Begum K. Factors influencing hygienic practices during menses among girls from South India: a cross sectional study. Int J Collab Res Intern Med Public Health. 2010;2(12):411–23.
18. Deo DS, Ghattargi CH. Perceptions and practices regarding menstruation: a comparative study in urban and rural adolescent girls. Indian J Community Med. 2005;30(1):33.

19. Kamath R, Ghosh D, Lena A, Chandrasekaran V. A study on knowledge and practices regarding menstrual hygiene among rural and urban adolescent girls in Udupi Taluk, Manipal, India. Glob J Med Public Health. 2013;2:1–9.
20. Shanbhag D, Shilpa R, D'Souza N, Josephine P, Singh J, Goud BR. Perceptions regarding menstruation and practices during menstrual cycles among high school going adolescent girls in resource limited settings around Bangalore city, Karnataka, India. Int J Collab Res Intern Med Public Health. 2012;4(7):1353–62.
21. Sinha K. 70% can't afford sanitary napkins, reveals study. Times of India. 23 Jan 2011. http://timesofindia.indiatimes.com/india/70-cant-afford-sanitary-napkins-reveals-study/articleshow/7344998.cms. Accessed 18 Feb 2014.
22. Sumpter C, Torondel B. A systematic review of the health and social effects of menstrual hygiene management. PLoS ONE 2013; 8(4). http://dx.doi.org/10.1371/journal.pone.0062004. Accessed 8 May 2015.
23. Ali TS, Rizvi SN. Menstrual knowledge and practices of female adolescents in urban Karachi, Pakistan. J Adolesc. 2010;33(4):531–41.
24. Sommer M. Where the education system and women's bodies collide: the social and health impact of girls' experiences of menstruation and schooling in Tanzania. J Adolesc. 2010;33(4):521–9.
25. Joshi BN, Chauhan SL, Donde UM, Tryambake VH, Gaikwad NS, Bhadoria V. Reproductive health problems and help seeking behavior among adolescents in urban India. Indian J Pediatr. 2006;73(6):509–13.
26. Sharma P, Malhotra C, Taneja DK, Saha R. Problems related to menstruation amongst adolescent girls. Indian J Pediatr. 2008;75(2):125–9.
27. Toteja GS, Singh P, Dhillon BS, Saxena BN, Ahmed FU, Singh LR, et al. Prevalence of anemia among pregnant women and adolescent girls in 16 districts of India. Food Nutr Bull. 2006;27(4):311–5.
28. Das B, Das P, Dutta A, Misra PR, Pradhi B, Sahoo K, et al. Social and psychological impact of limited access to sanitation: the link between MHM and reproductive tract infections, and between WASH practices and pregnancy; 2015. http://www.shareresearch.org/LocalResources/Limited_Access.pdf. Accessed 2 Feb 2015.
29. Ministry of Women and Child Development. Rajiv Gandhi Scheme for Empowerment of Adolescent Girls (RGSEAG): SABLA implementation guidelines; 2010. http://wcd.nic.in/schemes/SABLA-guidelines141210.pdf. Accessed 2 June 2014.
30. Sommer M, Kjellén M, Pensulo C. Girls' and women's unmet needs for menstrual hygiene management (MHM): the interactions between MHM and sanitation systems in low-income countries. J Water Sanit Hyg Dev. 2013;3(3):283.
31. Jasper C, Le T-T, Bartram J. Water and sanitation in schools: a systematic review of the health and educational outcomes. Int J Environ Res Public Health. 2012;9(8):2772–87.
32. Water Aid India, Centre for World Solidarity. Study on status of school sanitation in Andhra Pradesh. 2012.
33. Jewitt S, Ryley H. It's a girl thing: menstruation, school attendance, spatial mobility and wider gender inequalities in Kenya. Geoforum. 2014;56:137–47.
34. WHO/UNICEF JMP. India: estimates on the uses of water sources and sanitation facilities (1980–2012); 2014. http://www.wssinfo.org/documents/?tx_displaycontroller%5Btype%5D=country_files&tx_displaycontroller%5Bsearch_word%5D=India. Accessed 5 Oct 2014.
35. WHO/UNICEF JMP. Post-2015 WASH Targets and Indicators; 2013. http://www.unicef.org/wash/files/4_WSSCC_JMP_Fact_Sheets_4_UK_LoRes.pdf. Accessed 5 Oct 2014.
36. Ministry of Health and Family Welfare. National rural health mission—operational guidelines: promotion of menstrual hygiene among adolescent girls (10–19 year) in rural areas; 2010. http://indiasanitationportal.org/sites/default/files/Menstrual/Hygiene_Operational/Guideline_Eng_25-08-10.pdf. Accessed 2 Feb 2014.

37. Ministry of Health and Family Welfare. Rashtriya Kishor Swasthya Karyakram strategy handbook; 2014. http://www.nhp.gov.in/health-programmes/national-health-programmes/rashtriya-kishor-swasthya-karyakram-rksk. Accessed 2 Feb 2014.
38. Ministry of Drinking Water and Sanitation (2014). Swachh Bharat Mission (Gramin) Guidelines.
39. Ministry of Drinking Water and Sanitation (2015). Menstrual Hygiene Management—National Guidelines.

Chapter 10
Chhattisgarh Swasth Panchayat Yojana: Convergent Community Action for Health and Its Determinants in Rural India

Samir Garg

Abstract This chapter provides the implementer's perspective on the Chhattisgarh Swasth Panchayat Yojana as an example of convergence on a single, decentralized action platform for health and its determinants. The rationale for this initiative was the wide-ranging participation of community institutions like the Panchayat (an elected Village Council) in coordination with the Village Health, Sanitation, and Nutrition Committees (VHSNC), and Mitanins (Community Health Workers or CHW), stewarded by the State Health Resource Centre of Chhattisgarh in collaboration with the state Government. From 2006 onwards, there has been active community engagement in the collection of data on indicators of health status, access to health services, and determinants of health (nutrition, water, gender, employment). Indicators have been designed so that the community can record, understand and make use of the data to advocate for and monitor improvements in public service delivery. The challenges and lessons are many, including the fact that poor progress on indicators can sometimes reflect the severity of social determinants and not merely the lack of progress or success of any action. The process has seen several iterations and revisions, and the addition of new components to compile and use the data at levels beyond the village. This chapter attempts to describe how multiple interventions were brought in at various stages. The impact is a result of the mutually-reinforcing, interlinked and therefore integrated set of interventions, with some interventions being seen as more successful than others. The community platform was strengthened at each stage, where further components were added based on a periodic analysis of what worked and what did not. The process of analysis and the adding of components was also guided by a vision of community empowerment and a holistic definition of health that specifically included SDH. The complex and interlinked nature of interventions were crucial to achieving convergent action on health and Social Determinant of Health (SDH) and its scaling-up. Chhattisgarh has scaled-up the Swasth Panchayat program across the state and has institutionalized its implementation and facilitation arrangements. The National Health Mission has included the essential components in its guidelines.

S. Garg (✉)
State Health Resource Centre, Raipur, Chhattisgarh, India
e-mail: koriya@gmail.com

D. Nambiar and A. Muralidharan (eds.), *The Social Determinants of Health in India*, https://doi.org/10.1007/978-981-10-5999-5_10

The adequacy of arrangements for the facilitation of community-level structures and the autonomy of key actors will be crucial to the success of its replication.

Keywords Rural health · Village health · Sanitation and nutrition committees Healthy panchayat · Chhattisgarh

Introduction

Chhattisgarh state was formed in 2000 when it was carved out of the state of Madhya Pradesh. The state had a population of around 21 million, with nearly 80% being in rural areas. The state also had a substantial population of indigenous tribes forming 32% of its population, most of which were distributed in forested areas away from the centre of the state. The state had inherited a health system severely deficient in health human resources and was at the bottom in terms of indicators of health status and health care services. For example, its rural Infant Mortality Rate (IMR) in 2000 was 95 per 1000 live births, and the full immunization rate measured in 1998 was 21%. In this context, the state was willing to try out new initiatives to improve health. One such key intervention was the Mitanin Program, a CHW program initiated by the Government of Chhattisgarh state in 2002.

The Mitanin Program currently has nearly 70,000 CHWs (called Mitanins) covering almost all of the rural habitations and urban slums of the state. The word Mitanin literally means a friend in the local dialect of Chhattisgarh. The Mitanin program was unique as it was initiated by government but its design consciously included the essential features drawn from earlier successful models of NGO-run CHW programs in India [1]. It was further significant as it had mechanisms for a fast scale-up and it actually spread to all rural areas of the state within two years of its beginning in 2002. It has been credited with the unprecedented decline achieved by the state in its rural IMR [2, 3]. The national policy environment on health in India underwent a similar change in 2005 with the launch of National Rural Health Mission (NRHM). The NRHM initiated a national CHW program called ASHA (Accredited Social Health Activist) and further interventions for community participation in health along with the strengthening of health care services. The Mitanin initiative of Chhattisgarh, being an up-scaled CHW model promoted by government, served as an important reference for ASHA. Mitanins were recognized as ASHA by the NRHM.

The Foundation Laid by the Mitanin Program for Convergent Action on Social Determinants of Health

The Government of Chhattisgarh state launched the Swasth Panchayat Yojana in 2006. The literal translation of the phrase is the healthy village scheme. This scheme was built upon the foundations laid by the Mitanin Program.

The role defined for the CHWs in the Mitanin Program laid down the path, which led to emergence of the Swasth Panchayat or the Healthy Panchayat scheme. The concept of health as taught to Mitanins in their curriculum, included an emphasis on the Social Determinants of Health (SDH). There was a definition of health prominently stated in the Mitanin Program's first training module [4]. Health was defined as the physical, mental and social well-being of a person. 'Good Health' includes the following:

- Adequate food
- Secure and equitable work environment
- Safe drinking water, sanitation, housing, clean environment
- Access to preventive and curative health care services
- Well-being: rest, entertainment and human relations
- Gender equity

The role of Mitanins therefore extended far beyond health education and the curative elements. The stated objectives of the Mitanin Program also included (a) Organizing women and weaker groups to secure their rights related to health and (b) Promoting involvement of locally elected bodies (Panchayats) in the health sector and facilitating systematic local health planning and action [4].

Experiments in the Koriya district of the state had shown the success achieved by Mitanins in organizing a community watch on nutrition programs through neighborhood committees [5]. This experience was expanded into other parts of the state through the design of a nutrition security initiative in 2006 with two main components (a) Direct counseling or Behavior-Change-Communication on nutrition, and action on the prevention and control of infections amongst young children, and (b) promoting community awareness and action to access food and nutrition entitlements from government programs. Quantitative evaluations have shown that the above Mitanin-led interventions were effective in achieving a very significant state-wide reduction in child malnutrition rates [6]. More recently, the Mitanin program has been playing a key role in the implementation of the Fulwari Scheme—a program for community-managed child crèches and spot-feeding centers under the ownership of local elected Panchayats [7]. There have been efforts to carry out an in-depth analysis of action by Mitanins on SDH and to understand the factors contributing to its efficacy. They show that the way objectives were stated, along with the way that the selection was done, the training curriculum was designed and how supportive supervision was provided in the Mitanin program, led to the activeness of Mitanin CHWs on SDH issues [8]. The seeds of an initiative like Swasth Panchayat were always there in the way wider community involvement in action on health and SDH was emphasized in the design and the processes of the Mitanin program.

In terms of the involvement of local elected bodies called Panchayats, there were significant attempts right from the start of the program. When the program was launched, a large social mobilization campaign was taken up across the state through cultural troupes to convey the message of the need for community participation in health. This campaign was facilitated in most places by Panchayats. The selection of Mitanins was based on consensus decisions taken by meetings of citizens at habitation level, which was ratified by a Gram Sabha—the general body of the village recognized by the Constitution of India. Beyond selection, Panchayats were also involved in local planning for vector control in the prevention of malaria, and received joint-training with Mitanins on this in 2004.

Another feature of the program that strengthened the possibility of facilitating a community platform and action on SDH, was the Mitanin support system built into the program right from its beginning. Each cluster of 20–25 Mitanins is supported by a nearly full-time Mitanin Trainer. Thus, an average block has around 450 Mitanins supported by around 20 Mitanin Trainers who in turn receive supportive supervision from two block coordinators. The above teams are guided by the State Health Resource Centre (SHRC) through its District Coordinators. The SHRC is an autonomous organization created through collaboration between the state and civil society. It has been facilitating the Department of Health and Family Welfare in implementing the program and other initiatives aimed at strengthening health systems.

The Start of Swasth Panchayat Yojana

With the aim of strengthening the involvement of Panchayats in the health sector, the Swasth Panchayat scheme was launched by the state Government in 2006. The objectives were to enable local communities and elected Panchayats to assess the situation of their health and SDH, and identify gaps, and then to plan and execute multisectoral collective action to address those gaps. One of the mechanisms to build the involvement of Panchayats in the health sector was to institute awards for those Panchayats showing a better performance of health and SDH. It required the ranking of Panchayats in each administrative block. A Panchayat-level Health and Human Development Index (Panchayat-HHDI) was conceptualized to measure performance and rank Panchayats based on objective indicators. The Swasth Panchayat indicators and HHDI was thus meant to serve twin purposes: to (a) encourage Panchayats through awards based on objective health performance and (b) involve communities in collecting information on SDH for assessing health performance—including any gaps—thus putting into motion a process of dialogue, understanding and action on SDH.

In order to start implementation of the intervention, a dedicated training module was designed as training had been the preferred strategy and practice for introducing anything new in the Mitanin Program. In order to give a boost to this message, another strategy adopted was to organize large gatherings at district level of Panchayat representatives in 2006–07. The training module conceptualized what constitutes a 'healthy village' and the role that elected Panchayats had in achieving it. It questioned the conventional narrow understanding of the role of Panchayats as implementation agencies for construction-based rural development schemes.

It attempted to convey the message that a Panchayat addressing the gaps in SDH is a 'Healthy Panchayat' [9]. Mitanins and members of Panchayats across the state were trained together on this module, which also included critical aspects of community health and the collection of data on those aspects. The involvement of the local community in data collection was aimed at creating an opportunity for them to assess their health situation.

It included the collection of data on 26 Indicators covering SDH, such as access to the local public health care services, status of nutrition and sanitation, and access to food and nutrition programs.

The Evolution of Swasth Panchayat

Beginning in 2007, disaggregated data were collected annually from each habitation on the above indicators and recorded on a Panchayat scorecard. The data set was computerized to allow the calculation of Panchayat-level composite scores. Awards were given to the top ranking Panchayats in each block. The scheme covered all 146 rural blocks of the state and Swasth Panchayat data collection took place in nearly 80% of the 70,000-odd rural habitations in the state. Four rounds of the Swasth Panchayat survey and HHDI were carried out between 2007 and 2011.

One of the strengths of the methodology was that for the first time, it enabled comparison across habitations on objective health indicators. It brought out the sharp inequalities that existed between habitations in terms of their access to health, nutrition, drinking water and education services. Habitations with poorer communities often had lower access to services. Inter-Panchayat comparisons were also very instructive with Panchayats located in more remote locations and having a predominantly tribal population usually got very low scores. The scores therefore did not realistically reflect a Panchayat's performance in acting on health issues. The score was much more a reflection of the severity of the inequity faced by a Panchayat in comparison to others. Thus, it was always debatable whether the award-winning Panchayat was actually making a greater effort to improve SDH or whether it had benefited from being more favorably located with respect to available services.

Nevertheless, the Swasth Panchayat scheme was able to collect and compile data to highlight local inequities in health. The next and more difficult challenge for the scheme was to enable the local communities to understand and make use of the information. While implementation mechanisms were available for collecting data and computing Panchayat-wise HHDI, the mechanism for creating a community dialogue through which to make use of the information had yet to evolve. It also required ways of communicating the quantitative information to Panchayats and other stakeholders in community, including Mitanins. The attempts to communicate in form of Panchayat scorecards or through creating grades of performance with an associated color-coding did not bear the desired fruit. The intended practice of assessing situations based on quantitative data seems to have remained alien to the rural stakeholders. The strategy of giving awards also seemed ineffective in making a serious impact on the involvement of Panchayats in health. It did, however, contribute to keeping the issue alive in discussions and in the minds of Mitanins and Panchayats at the local level, and policymakers and planners at state level.

Village Health, Sanitation and Nutrition Committees (VHSNCs)

There were other changes happening in that period which guided the evolution of Swasth Panchayat. In 2008, the state constituted Village Health, Sanitation and Nutrition Committees (VHSNCs) as a key intervention promoted through the National Rural Health Mission (NRHM). VHSNCs provided the ideal platform for promoting action on SDH as the name itself conveyed that its role was in multiple sectors. It showed the potential to be able to fill the gap in Swasth Panchayat on a community-level platform, which focused on health and encouraged the participation of Panchayats in it. VHSNCs could carry out a 'Community Watch and Action' on health and social determinants. In 2008, the NRHM introduced another component called 'Community Based Monitoring' (CBM) which brought in civil society groups with the primary objective of organizing a community watch on health services.

Chhattisgarh had begun an intervention on Nutrition Security in 2006 through Mitanins, which by 2009 had created an implementation structure capable of facilitating local health monitoring, planning and action. Realizing the complementarities and overlaps in the Swasth Panchayat HHDI and ranking, VHSNC-based action and CBM, and the Nutrition Security initiative, it was decided to integrate all of them under the umbrella of the Swasth Panchayat scheme from 2009 onwards. The constitution process of VHSNCs was built on the participation of Gram Sabhas and Gram Panchayats (village general assemblies and elected councils) and it helped to eliit their involvement in VHSNCs right from the beginning.

For two years, VHSNCs tried to utilize the information available through Swasth Panchayat indicators to identifying local health gaps and plan collective action to address them. Based on that experience, the indicators used in the Swasth Panchayat survey were simplified and the number of indicators was reduced so that rural stakeholders had a better chance to understand them. In 2011, the annual Swasth Panchayat survey was transformed into a Village Monitoring Register (VRM) that was updated monthly in VHSNC meetings. It allowed communities to have more continuous monitoring on key issues.

These VRMs monitored health status, service access and determinants using basic counts in the previous month of the following:

(1) Health status (comprising mortality—infant mortality, maternal mortality, and by common causes like malaria, diarrhea, TB, pneumonia etc.; morbidity—due to common causes; malnutrition; and violence against women);
(2) Access to local health services (including immunization, free drug provision, referral transport, and use of bed nets); and
(3) Access to underlying determinants of health including food, water, sanitation and education, again linked to government schemes and entitlements (including functionality of hand pumps, toilets, out-of-school girls, midday meals, rural employment guarantee wage payment, and provision of food under the Integrated Child Development Scheme).

The VRM data were connected to Village Health Action plans in a stepwise process of identifying a gap and its cause, along with the response and responsibilities of different stakeholders and a timeline for joint action. Studies have shown that by 2012, around two-thirds of the villages in the state had started using this methodology [10].

It was a challenge to sustain the link between monitoring and planning. The assumption was that the monitoring register would lead to the identification of gaps to address which the VHSNC would then plan to act on. In actual practice, it was found that around one-third of the problems were identified through registers. Other ways of deciding the topics of action were spontaneously expressed problems by a community-participant in a VHSNC meeting, topics decided by the support-structure at state level from time to time and topics that were more convenient for the facilitator to incorporate. The last method produced the least value-addition but was common enough to be a concern.

It was seen that the majority of monitoring registers tended to under-report the gaps across sectors. Facilitators found it difficult to have an adequate discussion on 29 indicators in every meeting. The presence of a service-provider in the meeting e.g. an Anganwadi worker also reduced the chances of recording her performance negatively, but did result in the development of an unrecorded understanding with her to address gaps to the extent that she was able. Despite the under-recording of problems, the monitoring registers still led to the identification of more issues than the VHSNC or its facilitators could take-up.

The tools given to enable the community showed some drawbacks. In some situations they tended to be used mechanically by the facilitators. Recording is useful but it runs the danger of becoming the central feature of VHSNC facilitation rather than ‘action’. In order to overcome this, periodic issue-based campaigns involving action on a specific SDH were introduced. It helped to rejuvenate community involvement in VHSNCs to some extent though carried the risk of being seen as imposed from the top at the cost of local priorities. In order to reinforce the idea that ‘action’ is the essential purpose of VHSNC meetings, it was decided to try to mobilize the community in the course of a VHSNC meeting itself to initiate their action there and then.

The VHSNCs enjoyed leadership from Mitanins and elected women representatives. The attendance of workers representing Integrated Child Development Services (ICDS) in VHSNC meetings was also found to be good. The ward Panchs, the lowest level of elected representatives (elected from a population of around 200) contributed significantly to VHSNCs. In 2014, a drive was taken up to increase membership of VHSNCs, as a result of which it went up from 11 members per committee to 20 [11]. However, there are variations across villages in the level of active participation of local communities in VHSNCs. In some committees, Mitanins end up doing all the work due to the limited attendance of others in VHSNC meetings. This has been a persistent challenge for the facilitation process. Another attempt was therefore made in 2015 to expand the membership of VHSNCs and to improve their representation of all habitations in a village. Further measures to improve attendance included: (a) using more formal ways of reminding VHSNC members of upcoming meetings by circulating a register, (b) conducting meetings in the open so as to attract attendance, and (c) shifting the meeting to days other than the immunization day in order to allow greater time for Mitanins to mobilize attendance and for the VHSNC to discuss and act on issues.

Building Further on the Swasth Panchayat and VHSNC Program—Community Monitoring of Mortality and Facility Level Health Care Services

The monitoring data available from VRMs of VHSNCs presented an opportunity for extending the feedback to government beyond local (village and block) to state level. Further, this data has also been combined with community feedback data gathered on health care expenditure and facility level care. The first state report on community monitoring was produced in 2011. The state level sharing of reports strengthened the legitimacy of the community monitoring process and helped in articulating some gaps at the program planning and policy levels. Feedback on the services of Health Sub Centers and Primary Health Centers (PHCs) was gathered from concerned VHSNCs. Exit interviews of outpatients and inpatients were performed to get feedback on services of CHCs and District hospitals. In terms of eliciting action from government on the gaps, feedback taken on specific services such as the availability of anti-snake venom, anti-rabies vaccine, emergency obstetric care and referral transport was more effective than feedback on health facilities covering a large number of aspects. Thus, the government response was more forthcoming when one problem was taken at a time. The structure of the community monitoring reports evolved according to such experiences.

The mortality data from death registers kept by VHSNCs is being compiled at state level. This process began in 2012. It is used to triangulate government data of both all-cause and specific-cause mortality. It thus creates an alternative evidence of inequity especially where governments often grossly under-report cause-specific mortality e.g. for malaria or diarrheal diseases. It has helped in bringing back the focus to key health problems that the poor face. E.g., state action has become stronger in order to ensure essential health care services for malaria, one of the biggest public health issues in the state [14]. A total of 40,000 deaths were covered in 2012 and the coverage of deaths has been improving each year. In 2016, around 100,000 deaths were covered, thus capturing information on more than two-thirds of the total expected rural deaths in the state.

While the Government has a process of auditing maternal deaths and child deaths through Medical Officers, followed by a review involving a committee of senior district officials, in 2013 a need was felt to augment it through community audits of deaths as the child death audits by medical officers had not taken off as expected. Apart from the implementation gaps in medical officer-led audits, the key reason for instituting community audits was to involve the voice of community or families through verbal autopsies. It was felt that biases in the medical officer-led audits were inevitable as the medical officers would avoid recognizing the gaps in facilities as contributors to preventable mortality. Also, audits done by the officers were good at finding the clinical causes of deaths but often missed the systemic causes. After the state Government asked the SHRC to initiate community audits, a social autopsy tool was created. Block coordinators of the Mitanin program were trained to collect further information on gaps leading to maternal or child deaths using the social autopsy tool. They present the information back to the VHSNC in the following monthly meeting and a common understanding is arrived at regarding what gaps led to the death and how such gaps can be prevented in future. From 2014 onwards, around 400 maternal deaths and 3000 child deaths (0–5 years) have been audited by communities through this process. This has now emerged as a system of community audits, providing valuable feedback on gaps in health care.

In order to ensure inputs to more VHSNCs and to create a sense of solidarity amongst them, VHSNCs were federated into clusters with monthly meetings introduced in 2011. This created a supportive network around VHSNCs and their action on SDH. It helped VHSNCs to escalate the complaints to higher levels and to look at issues which were common across villages.

By 2015, it had become a regular practice in more than 15,000 of the state's villages to monitor using the register, to record and discuss deaths and their probable causes, and to plan and act on two or three problems identified each month. Assessments showed that around 50% of the collective action undertaken resulted in success [10].

It has now become difficult to draw a line between action on SDH by Mitanins and by VHSNCs. Each month they monitor more than 100,000 service providing institutions at village level including ICDS centers, government schools, 'fair price' shops, immunization sessions and health centers. They played a successful role in promoting access to the Public Distribution System (PDS) [6]. Getting access to safe drinking water by ensuring the repair of hand pumps has been another very common feature of action. Mitanins and VHSNCs together account for opposing domestic violence in around 25,000 to 40,000 cases annually [12]. They took up a campaign on the rights of disabled people in 2014, which resulted in more than 15,000 disabled people being able to demand and secure their entitlements from the Government.

In terms of addressing gaps through local collective action, a need was felt for a block-level platform where any unresolved issues could be raised to demand accountability from higher officials (block/district level). To this end, public dialogue events known as Jan Samwads were initiated at block level. Though this component had been in practice in some blocks since 2007, it was institutionalized in 2013 when more than 100 blocks held such events. Elected representatives of state legislature and even the national Parliament supported many such events by attending them and creating pressure on government service provider departments to address public complaints. Public dialogue events have been documented and it has been shown that each of them attracted 500–1000 people, mostly VHSNC members attending voluntarily and presenting 100–1000 complaints each covering a variety of issues involving access to health, safe drinking water and food and social security entitlements [15]. These gatherings strengthened the network and solidarity amongst Mitanins, VHSNC members, Panchayat representatives and individuals. By 2015, 137 of the 146 blocks in the state had started organizing annual public dialogues. Mitanins and their local facilitators gained significant capacity to gather and present evidence and to articulate demands along with the organizational skills needed for the public dialogues. These gatherings continued to attract the participation of elected representatives. As these dialogues became a regular annual feature, they gained acceptance with government officers at the local level and they started responding better to collective demands.

An innovation was introduced in 2016, as a strategy cutting across many of the above activities. It was the use of street theatre to train Mitanins to articulate certain issues in public dialogues and to communicate them to the wider community through VHSNCs. It also shows promise as another tool to rejuvenate community engagement. Mitanins and community committees as the support structure, tried street theatre and were soon taken in by its power to communicate and engage.

The program ensured that underprivileged areas were included in the facilitation process and got equal attention compared to other areas. Mechanisms like the Swasth Panchayat facilitators, VHSNC cluster meetings and block-level public hearings were first introduced in tribal blocks. The program, however, is yet to evolve mechanisms to provide additional inputs and priority to such areas in terms of ensuring actual improvements in services. It has mobilized communities in underprivileged areas to air their grievances and demands collectively. There is some movement in recognizing the needs of such areas and not considering all of their problems as given constraints.

Institutional Arrangements for Implementation

Mitanins and the Mitanin support system played a central role in facilitating each phase of implementation. The Swasth Panchayat survey was led by Mitanin trainers. It was compiled by the SHRC, with the help of block coordinators of the

Mitanin program. SHRC conceptualized the HHDI methodology and implemented it directly with funding from the state health department.

VHSNCs were formed by mobilizing local communities and their elected bodies. Mitanins and their support system carried out the mobilization and formation of VHSNCs. The SHRC helped the state Government in formulating the structure and function of VHSNCs in the form of guidelines and it also implemented a round of training Mitanins and VHSNC members on those guidelines. The capacity-building strategy borrowed heavily from the large-scale multilevel training cascade used in the Mitanin program. However, with the number of VHSNC members being around 4 times the number of Mitanins, it posed a daunting challenge in terms of funding as well as for creating an adequate number of trainers. It was resolved by deciding to train around one-third of the membership of VHSNCs in formal training workshops and leaving the rest to be oriented through monthly meetings of VHSNCs facilitated by Mitanin trainers.

It was realized that VHSNCs require active facilitation by trained facilitators in order to be able to monitor and plan action on SDH in a systematic manner. It was felt that VHSNCs relied heavily on inputs from Mitanins and therefore should share the support structure of Mitanins instead of having their own. Therefore, from 2011 onwards, the role of the support structure of the Mitanin program explicitly included the facilitation of VHSNCs and was institutionalized though guidelines issued by the Government. Systems were created for the allocation of adequate time for facilitation, training of facilitators and their monitoring through a block-level coordinator focusing on VHSNCs. The job charts of Mitanin trainers were tweaked so as to have a fixed schedule of monthly VHSNC meetings. Their job charts allocated around 35% of their time to VHSNCs. The Mitanin program monitoring system was also altered to cover the essential processes in VHSNCs as well as the role of Mitanins and trainers in them. The involvement of Mitanin trainers in facilitating VHSNCs definitely improved the regularity of meetings and the completion of monitoring registers and the recording of action plans. It did, however, in some VHSNCs create a problem of dependence on the Mitanin trainer and stifled the 'natural' community process. Another related critique of the strategy was that Mitanin trainers tended to impose the priorities given from the top. On the other hand, there were some areas where the VHSNCs did not receive the required attention from the Mitanin support system. Ensuring the quality of facilitation was a challenge for the up-scaled program. Continued emphasis on the facilitation of village monitoring and planning for more than three years helped in improving the capacity of facilitators and the monitoring of its quality.

The State Health Resource Centre (SHRC) has played a key role in designing the Swasth Panchayat initiative and the various iterations and additions in its evolution. Its unique governance structure and its role as an innovative institution improving the effectiveness of community-based interventions on SDH have been documented by researchers [16]. The SHRC conceptualized the interventions and created a composite approach by synthesizing elements from the National Rural Health Mission (NRHM), views of the state health department and experiences of civil

Table 10.1 Cost estimates and source of funds for Swasth Panchayat

Year	Annual direct cost (rupees million)		Annual indirect cost (rupees million)		Total annual cost (rupees million)
	State share	Central share (NRHM)	State share	Central share (NRHM)	
2007	8	0	0	0	8
2014	16	6	15	45	82

society initiatives and tuning them to the context of Chhattisgarh. The SHRC designed and implemented all the capacity-building required. It compiled and shared data at state level and it helped in getting the state on board.

Financing of Swasth Panchayat

The Swasth Panchayat Yojana was fully funded by the state Government at the outset. The direct costs of the program in 2014 was 22 million Indian Rupees (Rs.). The indirect annual costs in terms of time allocated to the Mitanin support structure on facilitating its various interventions described here were close to Rs. 60 million in 2014. The intervention covered a population of around 20 million across 19,000 villages. Thus, the total estimated annual cost per capita is around Rs. 4 and per village covered is Rs. 4200. It is around five times more economical when compared with costs to the NRHM for community monitoring and action in some states [17]. What helps it to be cost-effective, is the integration of its activities with the processes of Mitanin program. As a result, the requirement of additional human resources is limited to one facilitator per block. The table shows the costs at different stages of the initiative (Table 10.1).

Conclusion

Swasth Panchayat Yojana has evolved into a program which enables citizen involvement in activism on entitlements. Activism, even though funded by the state in this case, can still be resented by many government officials when they have to face questions, and when CHWs and VHSNCs supported by the health department are raising those questions. But in actual experience, the process has not been stifled. It has been able to grow and the articulation of issues in public dialogue events has been gradually becoming sharper as the teams gain more experience and confidence. The factors that enable it seem to be:

(a) In Chhattisgarh, the process being led by the SHRC has been a key factor. The SHRC has a civil society character as well as that of a parastatal. It has a governing board with a majority of members and a chair drawn from civil society. The structural autonomy that the SHRC enjoys has enabled its work on SDH and entitlements. The SHRC has characteristics of a boundary organization that bridges the gap between government and community and between design and implementation.

(b) The articulation of Mitanins' role as activists in government guidelines has been strong and consistent for more than a decade. Mitanins have also enjoyed a fair bit of autonomy as volunteers.

(c) Involvement of Panchayats and other elected representatives has won it the space for raising grievances and demanding accountability from officials.

That the SHRC is providing leadership, however, results in it remaining the prime mover and the ownership of the overall initiative by government is limited as a result. However, despite this limitation, the state has managed to arrange adequate facilitation to community-based structures on a long-term basis to undertake action on SDH. The program involved periodic creation of some buy-in from government, followed by its scale-up and gradual acceptance by the Government. The process was aided by the continued political support given to Mitanins through elected representatives, irrespective of their political party affiliations.

In 2013, the state transferred the responsibility of paying Mitanin incentives to Gram Panchayats. This move had the potential to improve the autonomy of Mitanins further and is likely to strengthen the Mitanin-Panchayat relationship that is critical to the Swasth Panchayat program. However, it was perceived by the health department as a loss of control over payments to Mitanins. The decision was rolled back and block officials of the health department are now responsible for paying Mitanins. The implications of the rollback on the autonomy of Mitanins is yet to be fully understood, but the early indications show that Mitanins are still able to maintain autonomy to a great extent.

In terms of achieving involvement of Panchayats in the health sector, VHSNCs seem to be relatively more successful compared to other attempts. The VHSNC-based processes have allowed representatives from most of the Panchayats to participate and contribute to action on SDH. Their involvement has been more noticeable in addressing issues such as drinking water, the functioning of nutrition programs, and domestic violence. The involvement of Panchayats in paying incentives to Mitanins and in the implementation of Fulwari crèches has provided them with a well-defined role in continuous work on health and nutrition. Thus while traditional roles still dominate the agenda of Panchayats, they have begun to engage with SDH issues. This has allowed Panchayats to realize some of their role in the social sector and to exercise a limited accountability over local service providers from government departments. A quantum jump is possible in this aspect if the state guidelines and actions encourage genuine decentralization and actually allow Panchayats to assert their control over the decision-making of most departments. The implementation of the 73rd amendment of the constitution in spirit, can thus take the convergent action on SDH far beyond where it stands today.

The impact achieved on SDH in the form of action and improvements in the PDS, ICDS, school meals program, domestic violence, and drinking water etc.

is a result of a combination of approaches tried out over a decade. This impact was initiated by the Mitanin program and built on by Swasth Panchayat and its various interventions at different stages. The factors that were crucial for the impact achieved on SDH and its scaling-up seem to be:

- The interventions were complex, interlinked and mutually reinforcing.
- The approach was to integrate each new intervention with the existing platform.
- The integrated set of interventions evolved through field experience and reflection. Some interventions were assessed as more effective than others. Such interventions were given more attention and they were scaled-up across the system. This led to the periodic strengthening of the community platform.
- The process of analysis and adding of new interventions and components was also guided by a vision of community empowerment and a holistic definition of health that specifically included SDH.

Frequent reflection on field experience, based on dialogues with local facilitators and visits to VHSNCs has been a feature of this effort. Innovation while being a force taking the program forward, has almost been a necessity in Swasth Panchayat. Sustaining the active participation of rural communities required reflection and innovation.

There have been efforts to replicate the Swasth Panchayat experience in other states and domains. Mitanins and VHSNCs from Chhattisgarh continue to be seen as national best practices [18]. In Chhattisgarh, similar processes have been introduced in urban slum communities through organizing Women's Health Committees called Mahila Arogaya Samitis (MAS) and getting them facilitated through urban Mitanins. Though urban areas do not have mechanisms like the Gram Sabha (general assembly) and Panchayats, they have elected councilors for urban wards. MAS fill these gaps to some extent and show potential to emerge as a platform for promoting participatory democracy in urban slums. They have started maintaining monitoring registers and death registers and have begun to undertake action on SDH. Chhattisgarh started it in urban areas in 2012, a couple of years earlier than the effective launch of the NUHM. Currently, there are around 3700 such committees actively engaged in SDH across 19 cities in the state. The replication in urban areas involved some modifications to the VHSNC-based design, but it benefited a great deal from the experience of Swasth Panchayat. Urban slum communities as represented through MAS show a faster trajectory to achieving significance in their work on SDH issues such as violence against women, and drinking water. They seem to fill a big vacuum in community participation in urban areas. They also seem to be facing far fewer challenges in staying relevant and energetic when compared to VHSNCs in rural areas, though the reasons for this crucial difference are yet to be understood.

Most of the components of the Swasth Panchayat program including the facilitation process and the tools used have been included the national guidelines of NRHM and NUHM on Community Processes [19, 20]. The training modules designed at the national level have also been guided by the experience [21].

It remains to be seen how other states respond to the opportunity. The lessons that the Swasth Panchayat experience offers will be critical while replicating and adapting the initiative in other states. It also offers a fertile ground on which to explore the complex issues of promoting community participation and the role of government in SDH, issues of autonomy, and the accountability and governance of community programs.

Commentary—Swasth Panchayat Yojana

Rajani Ved
National Health Systems Resource Centre, Delhi, India

In India, where decentralization to local government up to the *Gram* (village or cluster of villages) level is a constitutional mandate, other than in a few states there is a paucity of evidence to demonstrate the processes by which such decentralization can be effected for improved health care and action on Social Determinants of Health (SDH). The implementation framework of the National Rural Health Mission (NRHM), launched in 2005, envisioned the Communitization component as a key part of the health systems reform process, creating a Community Health Worker—the Accredited Social Health Activist (ASHA), rooted in the community, supported and strengthened by a Village Health Sanitation and Nutrition Committee (VHSNC) to undertake community monitoring as a way of improved accountability and village-level planning and implementation. The document also envisaged the creation of planning and monitoring committees at various levels of the health system to enable people's participation in health and health care [1].

The chapter on convergent community action for health and its determinants in Chhattisgarh state throws up several useful lessons for other states in the country and indeed globally. This article provides a historical trajectory of the intervention, commencing with the Mitanin or Community Health Worker to the establishment of Village Health, Sanitation and Nutrition Committees involving broader community participation including members of local government and implementation at scale. Including SDH, equity and the involvement of local self-government as an inherent part of the model design and ensuring that this vision was an integral part of all processes—creation of institutional structures, development of training modules and the very orientation of the stakeholders involved demonstrates that this factor, notwithstanding the intensity of process, has made scaling-up possible. The model, in fact, demonstrates a promising alternative to engaging elected representatives in addressing issues of SDH, through action on health and its determinants as a way of promoting local action and accountability, on a basket of determinants ranging from food security to the maintenance of hand pumps.

There are two noteworthy aspects of the intervention that attest to the particular strength of the model in addressing SDH and the capacity for decentralized action.

The first is the discussion on the ability of the VHSNC to address issues of disability and domestic violence which are both completely bypassed by the public health system. The model demonstrates that the VHSNC is an effective platform with the potential to identify cases of disability and domestic violence and demand action. Thus it becomes an important first step in formulating a strategy for the health system to mount a comprehensive response in both areas.

The second appealing facet of the model is the use of village monitoring registers by the VHSNC to record deaths and undertake community audits of maternal and child deaths. The focus on collection of mortality data enables a form of step by step approach to community monitoring, and allows for a causal analysis that is linked to the specific event of death, but which could be attributed to the health system response, to social or environmental determinants or a mix of all three. This component of the model enables a focus on largely preventable deaths and builds the VHSNC's perspective on causes of mortality and the accountability of the health system and their own responsibility. The article is an important contribution to understanding the value of mortality audits as an early step in village health planning.

The role of village health committees in promoting the accountability of service providers and the health system while increasing community capacity to take action on SDH, is an area of considerable study. The article adds to this body of literature and the focus on process provides insights for policymakers and programs on implementation and scaling-up. Two aspects of this intervention need further investigation. One is the understanding of service provider perspectives and responses to community demand for action, which is key to creating a broader and sustained health system response. The second is the nature of power relationships between members of the VHSNC and the extent to which this affects participation and action.

References

1. State Health Resource Centre (SHRC). Mitanin programme: conceptual issues and operational guidelines. Raipur: State Health Resource Centre; 2003. http://www.shsrc.org/pdf/MitaninProgramme/ConceptualIssuesandOperationalGuidelin.pdf. Accessed 10 Mar 2015.
2. Sundararaman T. Community health-workers: scaling up programmes. Lancet. 2007;369:2058–9.
3. European Union State Partnership Programme (EUSPP). Draft report on evaluation of the community health volunteer (Mitanin) programme. Raipur: Department of Health, Chhattisgarh; 2011. http://health.cg.gov.in/ehealth/MitaninFinalReport11thMarch2011.pdf. Accessed 4 Jan 2012.
4. State Health Resource Centre (SHRC). People's health in people's hands (Janata ka Swasthya Janata ke haath) Mitanin module-1. Raipur: State Health Resource Centre; 2002.
5. Garg S. Grassroots mobilisation for children's nutritional rights, Econ Polit Wkly. 2006. 26 Aug 2006: 3694.
6. Vir SC, Kalita A, Mondal S, Malik R. Impact of community-based Mitanin programme on undernutrition in rural Chhattisgarh State, India. Food Nutr Bull. 2014;35:83–91.

7. Garg S. Panchayat led nutrition and daycare centres—fulwari scheme of Chhattisgarh; 2014. Implementation note No. 9 POSHAN led by IFPRI Oct 2014.
8. Nandi S, Schneider H. Addressing the social determinants of health: a case study from the Mitanin (community health worker) programme in India. Health Policy Plann. 2014;29:ii71–81. doi:10.1093/heapol/czu074.
9. State Health Resource Centre (SHRC). Together we will build a healthy village (Judmil Banabo Swasth Panchayat Mitanin) module-7. Raipur: State Health Resource Centre; 2007.
10. State Health Resource Centre (SHRC). Village health sanitation and nutrition committees in Chhattisgarh, An assessment; 2012. www.shsrc.org. Accessed on 15 Feb 2015.
11. State Health Resource Centre (SHRC). Campaign to increase Participation (Sahbhagita Badhao Abhiyan); 2015. www.shsrc.org. Accessed on 14 Apr 2015.
12. State Health Resource Centre (SHRC). State level MIS report of the Mitanin programme: Report 2011, 2012, 2013 and 2014. Raipur: State Health Resource Centre; 2014.
13. State Health Resource Centre (SHRC). Community based monitoring of health in Chhattisgarh, Report 2013; 2013. www.shsrc.org. Accessed on 15 Feb 2015.
14. Garg et al. Documentation of deaths by local communities to counter severe under-reporting of deaths by government: experiences from a community based monitoring process from India. Poster presentation at the Third Global Symposium on Health Systems Research: The Science and Practice of People-Centred Health Systems 30 Sept to 3 Oct 2014, Cape Town, South Africa. 2014. Abstract available: http://hsr2014.healthsystemsresearch.org/sites/default/files/Poster-Presentations.pdf. Accessed on 15 Feb 2015.
15. State Health Resource Centre (SHRC). Public Dialogue events Report 2013–14. (Swasth Panchayat Sammelan—Jan Samwad). 2014. www.shsrc.org. Accessed on 14 Apr 2015.
16. Kalita et al. Role of innovative institutional structures in integrated governance. J Health Organ Manage. 2012;26(6).
17. National Rural Health Mission. Approval of State Programme Implementation Plan; 2013.
18. 2013–14 Maharashtra. http://nrhm.gov.in/nrhm-in-state/state/programme/implementation/plans/Maharashtra/html. Accessed on 15 Feb 2015.
19. National Rural Health Mission. 6th common review mission report; 2012. http://nrhm.gov.in/images/pdf/monitoring/crm/6th-crm/6th_CRM_Main_Report/pdf. Accessed on 15 Feb 2015.
20. National Rural Health Mission. Guidelines for community processes; 2013.
21. National Urban Health Mission. Guidelines for community processes; 2014.
22. National Health Systems Resource Centre. Training module for VHSNCs; 2014.

Chapter 11
When People Wake up the Anganwadi—Community Monitoring and Action in Maharashtra Is Making Child Nutrition Services Accountable and Effective

Shweta Marathe and Abhay Shukla

Abstract Ensuring community accountability of social services is a major challenge in India, with few proven and effective models at scale. In this context, Community Based Monitoring and Planning (CBMP) of health services in Maharashtra, implemented with support from the National Rural Health Mission (NRHM) since 2007, has emerged as a large scale, effective model for the 're-claiming' of public health services. Several organizations involved in CBMP in Maharashtra considered social determinants of health (SDH) as an important allied area, requiring similar community interventions, and child nutrition was a logical area in which to implement similar processes. Hence, Community Based Monitoring and Action (CBMA) to strengthen Integrated Child Development Services (ICDS) has been implemented on a pilot basis in six rural and urban areas of Maharashtra covering 114 habitations since mid-2013. Development of this process includes developing an operational framework based on an official mandate, capacity building of NGOs and field-level activists, formation of multi-stakeholder monitoring committees at various levels, periodic community monitoring of Anganwadi services using data collection tools, preparing public report cards, discussing issues identified in block-level public hearings, and ongoing facilitation at state level. Implementation of this process over nearly two years has yielded significant positive results. Analysis of data over successive rounds of monitoring shows substantial improvement in nutrition and health-related services provided by ICDS in CBMA areas. This paper is an attempt to describe and analyse the process of CBMA of ICDS services in Maharashtra, as a participatory approach to promote the accountability and improved delivery of ICDS services, exploring the positive impacts, as well as discussing challenges and lessons emerging from this process.

S. Marathe (✉) · A. Shukla
Support for Advocacy and Training to Health Initiatives (SATHI), Pune, Maharashtra, India
e-mail: shweta51084@gmail.com

A. Shukla
Advisory Group on Community Action (AGCA), New Delhi, India

D. Nambiar and A. Muralidharan (eds.), *The Social Determinants of Health in India*, https://doi.org/10.1007/978-981-10-5999-5_11

Keywords Community-based monitoring and action
Integrated child development scheme

Background

It is important that public services such as health care, education, food security and nutrition are delivered in a responsive manner, addressing the needs of communities, especially the marginalized communities that are the intended beneficiaries of the services. However, significant gaps have been observed in delivery systems for various public social services, which often remain unaccountable to the communities which are supposed to be served. While there is a clear need to substantially improve the supply side of services in terms of adequate funds, improved infrastructure, quality, and increased human resources etc., at the same time the demand side must also be strengthened to ensure active community involvement in the implementation, as well as to ensure the responsiveness of the services towards the community.

Integrated Child Development Services (ICDS) is India's largest community based outreach program, a public system designed to address the issues of child nutrition, health and other aspects of child welfare in India, which has been implemented over last four decades. One key objective of ICDS is to improve the nutritional and health status of children in the age group of zero to six years. This objective is hoped to be achieved by providing a package of six services comprising of supplementary nutrition, early childhood education (pre-school education), nutrition and health education, immunization, health check-ups, and the provision of referral services to children below six years, pregnant women, and lactating mothers.

Despite several achievements that the ICDS scheme has witnessed during the span of its implementation, there are large and glaring inefficiencies in the delivery of health and nutrition-related social services, leading to the underutilization of services, and as a result the issue of malnutrition remains unresolved. Several studies have been conducted to assess different aspects of the program, which clearly indicate gaps between the program and its beneficiaries.

In this context we may note that National Family Health Service—3 (NFHS) data [1] shows that supplementary nutrition on almost daily basis is available to only 11.86% children. In a Situational Analysis study [2] conducted by the Nutrition Rights Coalition in Maharashtra, it was observed that 73% of the respondents reported that the hours of the Anganwadi are not convenient to them. Out of those, 82% of the respondents wanted to increase the hours of the Anganwadi.

A study by Kumar et al. [3] in 2008 showed that about 40% of the Anganwadis in Maharashtra worked for fewer than 300 days. The same research also showed that in 21% of the cases, the food supplied was not edible and in one-third of cases was not considered tasty. Put together, the quality of food was poor in 20% of the centers. In a way, these findings indicate the need for active community participation in the monitoring of the ICDS program. There are certain studies [4, 5] which clearly document the current lack of community participation in the ICDS program. A rapid assessment of the ICDS project in Bihar has revealed that in 34 villages (60.7%) community members were found to be unaware of the recently introduced decentralized guidelines. Only in nine villages were people somewhat aware of the guidelines and their provisions.

Furthermore, there are studies [6–9] which have specifically mentioned and endorsed the same facts in their report. A National Institute of Public Cooperation and Child Development (NIPCCD) program evaluation report [6] states that community participation is a very weak link of the ICDS program. It recommends that it is imperative that community representatives should be involved right from the preparatory stage of initiating a project. Effective ways of augmenting participation need to be found. Another report [7] by the Center for Development Finance (CDF) also provides recommendations on similar lines. It states that involving local communities in the delivery and monitoring of the scheme is widely held to be the best way to improve its performance. A study [8] on the ICDS and child survival issues in Madhya Pradesh discussed ICDS centers, where the occurrence of malnutrition has been controlled through proper implementation of the ICDS scheme and most importantly by promoting community participation. This indicates the potential of the ICDS scheme in improving child nutrition, if implemented appropriately.

International reviews have noted that mechanisms such as social audits and community monitoring have significant potential to promote accountability and to improve the provision of public services, however, the impact of such mechanisms on the provision of nutrition services has not been empirically evaluated and further work is required to identify models that work best when applied to nutrition service delivery [9].

In view of this entire context, social accountability is being increasingly recognized worldwide as a means of enhancing community participation, empowering citizens, and improving service delivery. Though ensuring community accountability of social services is a major challenge in India, there are currently few proven and effective models which are being implemented at scale. Today, the most extensive community accountability initiative underway in the health sector in India is Community Based Monitoring and Planning (CBMP), which is being implemented within the framework of India's National Rural Health Mission (NRHM). Nine states of the country, including Maharashtra, were selected to implement CBMP on a pilot basis between 2007 and 2009. At the time of writing (early 2015) in Maharashtra the process is being implemented in 13 districts, 41 blocks and 141 Primary Health Centres (PHCs) covering 860 villages, and 25 civil society organizations (CSOs) are involved in facilitating CBMP processes in various blocks across these districts [10, 11]. External evaluations [12, 13] of this process have shown very promising results in terms of strengthening health services and improving the quality of care.

Drawing upon the successes of CBMP of health services and adapting this approach to a key SDH in the form of nutrition, the Nutrition Rights Coalition[1] (NRC) initiated the process of Community Based Monitoring and Action (CBMA) related to ICDS in Maharashtra in June 2013.

Community Based Monitoring and Action—Evolution and Process

In late 2012 and early 2013, a group of civil society organizations involved in CBMP in Maharashtra, considered SDH as an important allied area, requiring similar community interventions. Nutrition is one of the key SDH and hence child nutrition was considered as a logical area in which to apply similar processes, especially given the malnutrition figures for Maharashtra. It has been shown through considerable evidence that despite high economic growth rates, the situation regarding nutrition in Maharashtra is unsatisfactory. In this 'developed' state, almost half of the children are stunted, one-fifth are severely stunted and around two-thirds of children are anemic [14]. Given this situation, the coalition of organizations felt the need to ensure community participation, accountability and ownership of the ICDS services, the key strategy which is being used by the government in the battle against malnutrition. Despite various limitations in the design and implementation of the scheme, ICDS is probably the most important public system with which to deal with the issue of nutrition of young children, and we see public systems as a crucial fulcrum to act upon SDH. ICDS targets the most vulnerable and dependent groups in the society, which further emphasizes the importance of the scheme.

If malnutrition in rural, tribal areas and urban slums is to be addressed effectively, and if ICDS services are to be utilized by the community in an optimal fashion, then the poor and vulnerable population must reclaim ICDS services as their right, regular dialogue between providers and people should be ensured, and ICDS functionaries need to start responding to the genuine expectations of the community. As a step towards this, a state-level workshop was organized in

[1]The 'Nutrition Rights Coalition' is a coalition of six civil society organizations working on Nutrition Rights in Maharashtra,—Amhi Amachya Arogyasathi (Nagpur and Gadchiroli), Janarth (Nandurbar), Rachana Trust (Pune), Lok Seva Sangam (Mumbai) and Khoj (Amaravati)—which are involved in carrying out the activity of CBMA, and a network of CSOs coordinated by SATHI, Pune.

December 2012 on 'Extension of Community Based Monitoring and Planning to ICDS services in Maharashtra'. In the workshop, the idea of piloting a model of CBMP in Maharashtra was shared. The Principal Secretary, WC&D and other state-level officials participated in the workshop and expressed an interest to extend administrative support to the pilot project that was to be implemented in select districts in Maharashtra. The department also issued a Government Resolution to that effect on 23 June 2013. At present, the CBMA process is being implemented in five rural blocks (with 15 villages in each block making a total of 75 villages) and two urban areas (with a total of 39 clusters), which includes selected rural areas in Amaravati (two blocks), Nandurbar, Gadchiroli, and Pune (one block each) and selected urban slum areas of Nagpur and Mumbai, covering a total of 114 habitations.

The approach that has been deployed for CBMP of health services has been adapted and modified in the context of child nutrition, keeping in mind the specific framework and features of child care and nutrition services delivered by ICDS.

Promotion of Community Action as a Component of Community Based Monitoring and Action (CBMA)

In the first one and half years of CBMA, the emphasis was on community-based monitoring, however, while implementing community monitoring, it was felt that along with promoting community monitoring, encouraging community and household-based actions is also important for improving nutrition practices, and as in monitoring, the role of community is limited to giving feedback about services delivery, but community action would allow the extending of the community's role to allow it to take the initiative on actions towards improving child nutrition. Taking this into account, in late 2014, community-based monitoring was combined with community action.

Key Processes Related to CBMA

Development of the CBMA process includes developing an operational framework with an official mandate, capacity building of NGOs and field-level activists, community assessment of service delivery, discussing issues identified in block-level public hearings, and facilitation at state level. Brief details about these processes are as below:

(a) **Developing an organizational framework for CBMA of ICDS**

Prior to the implementation, preparatory processes were conducted at different levels. Meetings and workshops with key stakeholders were held at different levels to orient them to the CBMA process, to share the concept and ensure broad-based participation and cooperation from all those expected to be involved in the implementation of the emerging CBMA process. A state-level workshop was organized with academicians and CSOs for the conceptualization and finalization of the operational framework. Block/Project-level workshops were organized in the intervention areas involving diverse stakeholders such as ICDS officials, PRI members/corporators, and NGO representatives. Capacity building workshops were also held with a group of CSOs (NRC) who are involved in the overall facilitation of the CBMA process.

In addition to this, situational analysis was conducted in order to better understand the current status of utilization of anganwadi services prior to commencing the process. This study focused on understanding peoples' current perceptions as they related to child nutrition, their awareness concerning nutrition-related government services, and their experiences related to access and utilization of these services, mainly the anganwadi, Village Child Development Centres (VCDC) and NRC. One-third of the intervention villages in each block were covered by the study.

(b) **Community awareness, strengthening and capacity building of various stakeholders**

Creating environment and building awareness was important to help facilitate the CBMA process, while ensuring cooperation from the different stakeholders. Various innovative processes have been promoted for community awareness on nutrition issues such as Kala Jathas, demonstration through pictorial stories and community meetings. Training and capacity-building workshops were organized in all of the intervention areas for different stakeholders such as community members, members of Village Health Nutrition and Sanitation Committees (VHNSC), and anganwadi workers etc.

(c) **Community assessment of ICDS services using an Anganwadi tool for data collection and preparation of report card**

In order to understand the present status of ICDS services especially at the Anganwadi level, a specific tool was developed. A short tool for monitoring—which was used in CBMP of health services—was modified and elaborated in the context of ICDS services and a comprehensive tool was produced which includes infrastructural issues, delivery of various services from Anganwadi such as growth monitoring, supplementary food, immunization, health checks, medicines, health and nutrition education, and referral services as well as issues related to the utilization of Anganwadi services. The experiences and feedback of the community are collected by the community itself on quarterly basis using this specific tool along with the help of a field facilitator from a NGO, through various methods such as group discussions with community members, interviews with Anganwadi workers and direct observations. The data collected are analyzed in a standardized manner to present a public document in the form of report card.

Based on the various problems reported through the process of monitoring, regarding the overall Take Home Ration (THR) scheme, a separate study was conducted to help understand the ground-level situation regarding usage of THR-packaged foods among children under three, and the report has been published in the form of a policy brief.

(d) **Multi stakeholder dialogue**

Issues which were identified through data collection such as the poor quality of cooked food, irregularities in the distribution of cooked food and THR, non-availability of medicines, and irregularities in the functioning of Anganwadi, were presented and discussed during the dialogue with AWW (Anganwadi Worker)/supervisor, CDPO and CEO to resolve the problems and address gaps in the Anganwadi services. A block-level 'Jan Samwad' is organized once a year in each block. As mentioned above, issues identified through data collection, especially those which have remained unresolved at various other levels, are raised in Jan Samwad and corrective actions are sought.

(e) **Promoting community and household-based action for improved nutrition practices**

While implementing the process of CBMA-ICDS, it was felt that to improve child nutritional status, along with promoting community monitoring, then encouraging community and household-based actions and practices for improved nutrition practices is important. A child attending an Anganwadi remains there for around four hours only. Furthermore, there is a considerable number of children who do not avail themselves of the ICDS services in terms of attending an Anganwadi. An evaluation study commissioned by the Programme Evaluation Organization of the Planning Commission (PEOPC), shows that around half of the total eligible children are currently enrolled at Anganwadi centers, and the effective coverage as per norms is only 41% of those registered for ICDS benefits. Furthermore, considerable evidence [16–18] from initiatives in various Indian states exists to show that complementary interventions, based on resources within the community and families, can contribute to substantially improving child nutrition and health. Such expectations were also repeatedly expressed by community members in project areas. Hence in response to this, the promotion of community and household-based actions to improve nutrition practices was introduced as a small pilot intervention in mid-2015 in all seven project areas (urban and rural) where CBMA-ICDS is being implemented.

This intervention included two focused activities: (a) Individualized counseling of mothers and carers of malnourished children, in order to improve household child nutrition practices along with a follow-up related to each of these children. (b) Building general community awareness about key nutrition issues using various innovative processes, and promoting collective community actions especially involving mothers of young children. This was focused on the nutrition of young children below three years of age, promoting desirable food practices and the avoidance of junk foods. The main strategy utilized was organizing periodic awareness events in each village involving groups of women and members of Mother's committees etc. Field facilitators from CSOs provided training through a series of capacity building workshops regarding healthy nutrition practices, based on which field facilitators from the involved CSOs shouldered the responsibility of the implementation of this newly introduced process. A list of children who were severely underweight (SUW) and moderately underweight (MUW) was taken from the Anganwadi register. From this list, a total of 409 children was particularly focused upon in this intervention between September 2015 and March 2016.

Preliminary Evidence for Positive Impacts of Community Based Monitoring and Action (CBMA)[2]

Implementation of this process over one and half years appears to have yielded significant positive results. Analysis of the data from successive rounds of monitoring shows substantial improvement in nutrition and health-related services provided by ICDS in the intervention areas. Analysis also shows that most of the issues pertain to Anganwadi functioning and could be raised and resolved at village level, which underlines the fact that the CBMA process has contributed to increased community awareness, participation and a sense of ownership towards ICDS services. Various innovative steps taken by the community as well as 'stories of change'—stories of resolving issues through community action—are being observed in the intervention areas, and can certainly be treated as positive impacts of the process, enabling the community to begin taking ownership of the ICDS program, and establishing forums for dialogue at multiple levels, contributing to improved ICDS services.

[2]So far, in the span of one and half years, the CBMA process has not undergone an external evaluation to assess its impact. Preliminary observations on the positive impact of the process as described in this section have mainly drawn upon analyzing data from successive rounds of monitoring, and numerous positive stories of resolving issues through community action. However, we look forward to conducting an external evaluation soon.

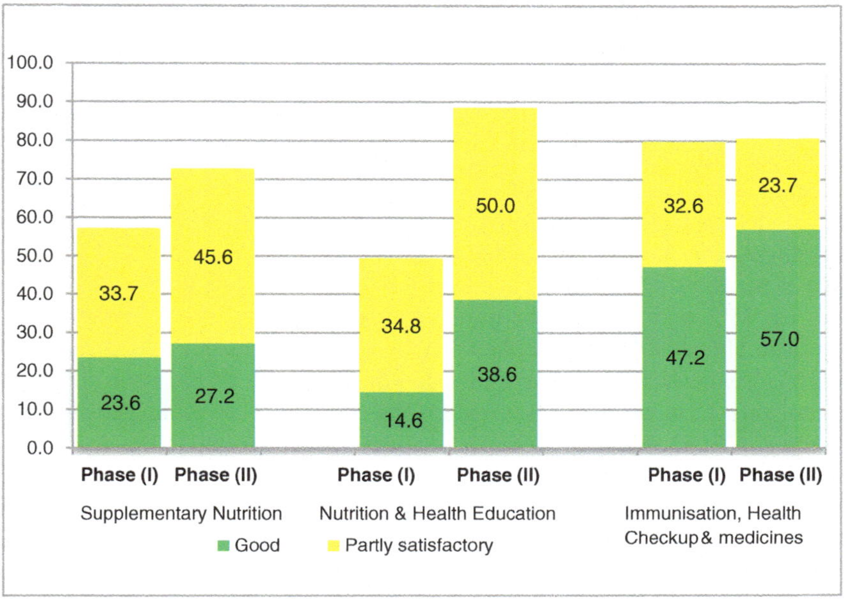

Fig. 11.1 Overall improvement in anganwadi services across CBMA areas from Round I to II (*based on group discussions*). *Source* Derived from data collected from Round I and II of the CBMA process

(a) **Analysis of data from reports cards: change from phase 1 to phase 2**

The first round of community-based data collection using a standardized tool and report card was undertaken between August and November 2013, following which the data was shared with Anganwadi workers and ICDS officials at various levels, and was also presented at well-attended Jan samvads. Over time, these accountability processes led to certain improvements in the functioning of Anganwadis in project areas. This was followed by a second round of community data collection from February to April 2014. The rating of key services as 'good' and 'partly satisfactory' (as opposed to 'bad') had clearly gone up during this roughly six-month period of intervention, as illustrated in Diagram-1.

There was a substantial improvement in nutrition and health education, with a 24% improvement in 'good' rating in round II. As emerged from these data, much more frequent and systematic nutrition demonstrations are being conducted in the CBMA areas. There has also been a moderate improvement in the provision of supplementary nutrition and various health services such as immunization, health checkups and medicines from Anganwadi due to continuous monitoring and visits by mothers' groups to the Anganwadi. These initial changes within a short period of community-based monitoring intervention are expected to deepen over time, with successive rounds of data collection and multistakeholder accountability dialogues aimed at improving the Anganwadi services (Fig. 11.1).

(b) **Analysis of data regarding issues raised and resolved from 114 Anganwadis in intervention areas between April 2014 and Sept 2014**

As a part of the CBMA process, different issues related to Anganwadi functioning are raised at different levels. It was observed that within a span of around five months 2221 issues were raised at different levels. Considering the huge number of issues raised within such a short timeframe, data were analyzed further to better understand the proportion of resolving different issues at different levels. Interestingly, this analysis shows that the maximum number of issues (1317) were raised at the local level (village and Anganwadi), out of which nearly half of the issues i.e. 45% were found to be resolved at the local level itself. Furthermore, it shows that almost 90% of the issues pertaining to supplementary food and cleanliness in Anganwadi have been resolved, while only 5% of the issues related to infrastructure have been resolved. More importantly, 37% of the issues raised concerned VCDC (Village Child Development Centres) and NRC (Nutritional Rehabilitation Centres), which come under the health department. However, none of these issues was resolved, due to the poor coordination between ICDS and health departments. Demand for such convergence is being continuously raised by the group of CSOs involved (for further elaboration, refer to Section "Challenges".c). This exercise could guide the development of appropriate strategies towards resolving various issues related to Anganwadi functioning.

(c) **Preliminary findings related to the impact of community and household-based actions for improving nutrition practices**

After a period of just six months from the intervention (September 2015–March 2016) related to nutrition practices, analysis of nutritional data has shown significant improvement in the grade of nutrition of children in intervention areas. Of the total of 409 children across seven blocks/habitations, the grade of nutrition improved in 58% (236 children), with 193 children improving to normal and 43 children improving from SUW to the MUW category. On disaggregating the data to district level, the Nagpur and Amravati areas have shown maximum improvement. In Amravati, out of 88 MUW children, 69 moved to the normal category, while in Nagpur out of 58 SUW children, 17 moved to the normal category and 14 to the MUW category. Subsequent follow up of these children in early-2017 has shown that their improved nutritional status has been well sustained even after one year.

(d) **Stories of change**

Case 1 [15]—Campaign for weighing machines

Well-equipped Anganwadis with proper services are key to resolving malnutrition among small children. However, the CBMA process in the Dhadgaon block of Nandurbar district, revealed the sorry state of affairs regarding Anganwadis. During the routine visits for preparing report cards of Anganwadis, under the CBMA process, it was discovered that many of the weighing scales were non-functional. On reporting this to ICDS authorities, they argued that the weights of children were regularly being noted, so how could the scales be non-functional? Finally, upon the insistence of Janarth, ICDS authorities visited the Anganwadis, and Janarth activists were equipped with their own weighing scales. The difference in weights taken by the Anganwadi scales and the proper scales was between 400 and 500 g. There was also an issue over the lack of electricity in villages with which to charge the electronic weighing scales, and in addition to this, all of the AWWs were not trained to handle the electronic weighing scales. The issue was taken up at the block level by the monitoring committee members, but this did not yield timely results. Then the ICDS authorities began to morally question the AWWs, saying that by writing false weights they were cheating the villagers who trusted them. The AWWs in turn started reporting on the performance of the scales to their supervisors, and ultimately by December 2014, all the Anganwadis in Dhadgaon were given new weighing scales.

Case 2 [15] *Gandhigiri*—Silent protest to ensure punctuality of Anganwadi staff
In the Shivajinagar area of Mumbai, which is often in the news for its serious problem of malnutrition, the *Lok Seva Sangam*—the nodal civil society organization—faced an uphill battle while implementing CBMA in 17 Anganwadis. In their daily struggle for survival, the people from this largely slum area had never paid attention to the functioning of the Anganwadis. In fact, during one of the community meetings regarding CBMA, it came to light that they were not even aware of the working hours of the Anganwadi! To them, the opening times were whenever the AWW chose to come and open the Anganwadi. When the community members were informed by the organization that the Anganwadi should be open for at least four hours a day, they were shocked, since it was only being run for an hour or two. The local monitoring committee members decided to tackle this in a unique manner, by adopting a peaceful *Gandhigiri* approach. All they did was that one of them turned up every day when the Anganwadi opened, equipped with a register to note the time of opening of the Anganwadi and the reason for the delay. Initially the AWW came up with several excuses, but she soon started running out of explanations. To see the children gathered around the Anganwadi before her arrival was also embarrassing and finally the ploy worked and the AWW started coming to the Anganwadi punctually, providing services for the entire required period.

Case 3 [19]: Improving household nutrition practices is both necessary and possible …
Sangita, from the Kurkheda block in Gadchiroli district, was born with a low birth weight (1.6 kg) and used to fall sick quite often with a fever, cold, cough or diarrhea.

In her village, as a part of the CBMA process, when parents along with active community members started gathering in the Anganwadi, the AWW began to weigh every child in front of them, explaining the nutritional grade of each child to their parents. At the same event, demonstrations of nutritious recipes were also performed. Sangita and her mother also participated in one such event, and her mother was told that Sangita's weight was very low for her age (3.7 kg at an age of nine months). After this, the local CSO facilitator made home visits to Sangita's and started regular counseling along with nutritious food demonstrations with her mother and *aaji* (grandmother). In the meantime, the CSO organized a heath checkup camp at block level, where the doctor advised admitting Sangita to the NRC. Accordingly, with active facilitation by a CSO facilitator, she was admitted to the district NRC for 14 days, and as a result her weight increased by a kilogram. After being discharged from the NRC, the CSO facilitator continued individualized counseling with her carers. When asked, Sangita's parents stated that, '*Sangita's health is relatively improved now; her junk food intake has also reduced. Her appetite is notably improved and as suggested by Meenatai (the CSO facilitator) we have modified her diet with inclusion of egg, milk, fruit, peanut laddu, edible oil, etc*'.

The major positive change in Sangita's nutritional status seem to be a combined result of regular weight monitoring from the AWW, individualized counseling, improved household nutritional practices and timely medical treatment. Inspired by her positive story, other parents in the village have now also started approaching the AWW, asking her about the nutritional grade of their children, and seeking her guidance regarding household nutritional practices.

(e) **Key Innovations**

- '*Bal hakka Gat*' (Child rights group) were formed in the Kurkheda block in Gadchiroli and Velhe block in Pune, where the high school children were actively involved in Anganwadi monitoring.
- In Gadchiroli district, a ritual custom called '*Chatavani*' was used to create an awareness program in the community, where a nutritionist was invited to provide information related to how to prepare nutritious food items with the help of available local food grains.
- In the Velhe block of Pune district, at the *Raksha Bandhan* event, members of the *Bal Hakka Gat* tied threads to the government officials working in ICDS. This was their unique way of appealing to these authorities to protect the children of the village from malnourishment.

Challenges and Lessons

Challenges

The wide range of positive impacts of the CBMA process within such a short period, demonstrates the potential of this process in ensuring the responsiveness of ICDS services, as well as in increasing community participation and a sense of ownership of these services among community members. However, the implementation of such a complex and multidimensional process through a coalition of civil society organizations has not been an easy task. Despite the undoubted positive impacts, there are certain challenges in the implementation of this process. Key challenges which need to be specifically addressed during the further development of this process are as described below:

(a) **Need for strong official support and a clear formal mandate from the Women and Child Development (WCD) department, for the continuation and expansion of the CBMA process related to ICDS in Maharashtra**

The CBMA process has shown its potential for ensuring the delivery of ICDS services in a community-oriented and sensitive manner in the pilot phase. However, continued support and a mandate from the WCD department in the post-pilot phase would be crucial and important for expansion of the CBMA process in Maharashtra. Such support may be in the form of a government sanction for the continuation and geographical expansion of the CBMA process in various areas of Maharashtra, along with the need to provide an official mandate by issuing Government Resolutions (GRs) and important letters at state level, which will ensure the smooth implementation of this process with the cooperation of officials at various levels.

If there is clear a government sanctioning, it becomes mandatory for public officials and staff at different levels to participate in, as well to cooperate with, the implementation of the process. Furthermore, such an official mandate being provided to civil society organizations enables their involvement in decision-making processes, and ensures their access to relevant information etc. Also, in some of the areas, ICDS officials and staff responded or participated in the CBMA process solely because of the GR. However, after a certain point, when there was a delay in extension of the GR from the state level, a CDPO in Mumbai refused to provide access to basic information, and declined to cooperate with the CSOs in any other manner, displaying a typical bureaucratic approach. This incidence of the CDPO's non-cooperation after completion of the official period of the GR, reiterates the necessity for such an official mandate to ensure effective implementation of the CBMA process. Drawing upon the experience of CBMP of health services, one of the crucial elements in the successful implementation of this process over the last eight years in Maharashtra has been the government's support for the process in terms of inclusion of CBMP in the framework of implementation of the NRHM.

Hence, recognizing the need and impact of the CBMA process, it should be included as a core component in the framework of ICDS at national level.

(b) **Addressing systemic and structural issues raised through the CBMA process**

The CBMA process has been conceptualized as a mechanism for making ICDS services responsive to the community which they serve. However, this process can effectively function only in tandem with supply side changes such as improvements in infrastructural facilities, human resources, and delivery systems etc. For example, vacancies for Anganwadi workers and the bad condition of basic amenities in Anganwadis etc. are issues which cannot be solved at the local level. In the slum areas of Mumbai, most of the Anganwadis do not have their own place for carrying out their activities, which are instead held in somebody's house. In such cases there is no point questioning the Anganwadi worker for not maintaining basic infrastructural facilities in the Anganwadi, as per the guidelines. All of these issues are crucial and directly affect the delivery of ICDS services. Hence all the systemic and structural issues which have emerged from the CBMA process need to be addressed at the state level and on a priority basis.

Another relevant example pertains to the scheme of supplementary nutrition in the form of the Take Home Ration (THR) for children under three years of age. A study conducted by the NRC in Maharashtra has shown that only 11% of children were frequent users of THR, while 79% of respondents said that they feed it to animals or use it for fishing. Where the policy or scheme itself is flawed, mere monitoring of the services rendered is insufficient, unless there is a process of acting upon suggestions emerging from the community and modifying the scheme based on the community's feedback.

(c) **Need to strengthen coordination between WCD and health department**

Certain services in the Anganwadi are provided with the help of Public Health Department, such as regular health checkups of Anganwadi children and the admittance of Severe Acute Malnourished (SAM) and Moderately Acute Malnourished (MAM) children to Public Health Institutions etc. However, since these two departments come under two separate ministries as well as being separate functional bureaucracies, it is observed that there are significant issues related to coordination between the two. As mentioned earlier, analysis of issues raised and resolved have shown that none of issues related to VCDC and NRC were resolved. Hence steps must be taken to ensure effective coordination between both of the departments at all levels, which will help in the effective delivery of ICDS as well as health services to the community. These issues can be addressed by strengthening existing spaces, as well as developing additional platforms for accountability and regular dialogue, involving officials of both of these departments as well as PRI members and civil society organizations, where pressure for 'convergence from below' can lead to improved coordination from village to district level.

Lessons

Below are some of the key lessons emerging from the experience of implementing CBMA—ICDS in Maharashtra over a period of almost two years:

(a) **Involvement of CSOs with a Rights-based approach, and participatory spaces created by CBMP of health services, has considerably facilitated the implementation of CBMA**

As mentioned earlier, the process of CBMA has been operationalized in Maharashtra through the NRC, which is a group of seven CSOs working with a rights-based approach on health services and social issues. Most of these CSOs have been involved in the implementation of CBMP of health services, hence this experience as well as the spaces created by CBMP has considerably facilitated the implementation of CBMA at various levels in terms of ensuring community participation in the activity of monitoring, attending village level meetings, and public dialogues etc. It has also been found helpful in ensuring the participation of ICDS officials in public dialogues, in monitoring committee meetings, and overall in ensuring responses to the issues raised through CBMA from local to district and state levels.

(b) **Targeting the vulnerable frontline Anganwadi worker is not an appropriate strategy**

While implementing CBMA of ICDS, it has been widely recognized that the Anganwadi worker is a very vulnerable worker, and is in a very different situation compared to Medical Officers in health services. Therefore, the exclusive targeting or holding her primarily responsible is not a useful strategy for the resolving of issues. The CBMA process aims to address gaps in the delivery of services with community participation, rather than blaming frontline providers. When services are provided at a community level through a person who belongs to the same community, then ensuring responsiveness of the delivery system cannot be achieved merely through confrontation or the pressurizing of such frontline workers, but rather through an approach of 'social supervision' and dialogue, which values her work and takes cognizance of her problems, while ensuring that she fulfils her responsibilities as best as possible within the given constraints.

(c) **Sensitization of ICDS officers regarding CBMA, ensuring a positive response by the system to issues raised through the CBMA process**

As a part of the CBMA process, when community members give critical feedback to the system or hold concerned staff or officials accountable, the system should not respond mechanically by taking blanket disciplinary action against frontline staff. Recently, in the Nandurbar district Jan samvad, various positive changes were presented, while certain areas requiring improvement were also raised. After the Jan samvad, the CDPO issued a letter to all the AWWs in the block, asking for a written explanation regarding various issues raised by the CSO in the Jan samvad, failing which their honorarium would be kept on hold. Following this, AWWs totally stopped cooperating with the local CSO related to CBMA processes.

Such knee-jerk reactions are potentially harmful to the dialogue process, and underline that implementation of this process cannot be done without informed support from officers and staff members, across various levels of the ICDS system. Resistance or non-cooperation of ICDS officials or staff at any level, or misdirected action as in the above case, would adversely affect implementation of the entire process. Hence the state needs to place more emphasis on providing proper and regular orientation and sensitization regarding the CBMA process to ICDS officials and staff at various levels. This would certainly help in reducing their resistance to the process and reshaping attitudes, ensuring their response to accountability processes in a positive manner.

Appropriately dealing with each of the challenges mentioned above is a complex exercise, which depends on effective intervention by diverse stakeholders. The lessons learned from the early phase of the CBMA process would definitely be useful inputs for the further development and generalization of this process across the state.

On the whole, the emerging initiative of CBMA of ICDS in Maharashtra has demonstrated its significant potential to ensure improved and accountable Anganwadi services, based on community activism and the improved responsiveness of providers.

Taking a broader view, while seeking improvements in child nutrition by strengthening access to various SDH, a two-level approach is required. The strengthening of ICDS as a key public program dealing with child nutrition is an important starting point, but obviously this would address only a part of the problem. The existing form in which ICDS is functioning is certainly not adequate to fulfil even the primary objectives of the scheme. In this context, community processes like CBMA could certainly play a critical role in improving the functioning of ICDS with community participation, along with ensuring accountability of the services. However, beyond this, comprehensive efforts are essential to improve overall socioeconomic conditions, combined with a range of interventions such as promoting improved community and household nutrition practices, along with an awareness of proper breastfeeding and complementary feeding, and ensuring complete immunization and the prompt treatment of children for any illness. The processes outlined in this chapter, which have attempted to reorient the functioning of the ICDS program in pilot areas through community action, are one of the many efforts in India that could contribute to improving child health and nutrition in the coming years.

Acknowledgements The authors would like to thank Deepali Yakkundi for data analysis, Renuka Mukadam for editing and other SATHI team members, especially Vinod and Shailesh for their inputs in developing this write up. The authors would like to specifically acknowledge member organizations of the 'Nutrition Rights Coalition' for their commitment and active involvement in the overall implementation of the CBMA process, without which this process would not have had the desired impact. Our sincere acknowledgements to the Ministry of Women and Child Development, Maharashtra, for the administrative sanction and facilitative framework being provided for CBMA, and to the Narotam Sekhsaria Foundation for their financial support of this process.

References

1. Ministry of Health and Family Welfare. Government of India. National Family Health Survey 3. Ministry of Health and Family Welfare, 2005–06.
2. Nutrition rights Coalition, Maharashtra. Situational analysis of anganwadi services in selected areas of Maharashtra (unpublished); 2013.
3. Kumar S, Kamble M, Joseph J. Food to the poor: a study of Implementation of the food related schemes of the Government of India in Maharashtra. National Centre for Advocacy Studies, 1 Feb 2008.
4. ICDS Directorate Department of Social Welfare Government of Bihar and Unicef Bihar. Rapid assessment of ICDS project in Bihar; 2007.
5. Working Group for Children Under Six (of the Right to Food Campaign and Jan Swasthya Abhiyan). Strategies for children under six update and recommendations for the 12th plan; 2012.
6. National Institute of Public cooperation and Child Development. National evaluation of the integrated child development services. New Delhi; 1992.
7. Center for development finance. Integrated Child Development Services (ICDS) scheme brief; 2009–10.
8. Right to Food Campaign Madhya Pradesh Support Group, Vikas Samvad and Sanket-Centre for Budget Studies, Bhopal. Moribund ICDS (a study on the ICDS and child survival issues in Madhya Pradesh. Bhopal; 2009.
9. International Food Policy Research Institute. Global nutrition report: actions and accountability to accelerate the world's progress on nutrition. Washington, DC; 2014. p. 64.
10. Shukla A, Saha S, Reclaiming public health through community based monitoring: the case of Maharashtra. In: McDonald DA, Ruiters G, editors. Municipal services projects. Occasional paper no. 27; 2014.
11. Shukla A, Saha S, Jadhav N. Community based monitoring and planning in Maharashtra: a case study. Pune, India: SATHI and COPASAH; 2013.
12. Khanna R, Pradhan A, Evaluation of the process of community based monitoring and planning of health services in Maharashtra. Evaluation carried out under guidance of NRHM Advisory Group on Community Action (AGCA). Pune, India: SATHI; 2013.
13. State Health System Resource Centre (SHSRC). Evaluation of community based monitoring and planning of health care services under National Rural Health Mission, Maharashtra. Pune, India; 2013.
14. SATHI, Pune, Maharashtra. Nutrition crisis in Maharashtra; 2009.
15. SATHI. Anganwadila jevha jag yete (When Anganwadi wakes up). Marathi collection of stories of change in context of CBMA. Pune; 2015.
16. Tripathy P, et al. Effect of a participatory intervention with women's groups on birth outcomes and maternal depression in Jharkhand and Orissa, India: a cluster-randomised controlled trial. Lancet. 2010;375(9721):1182–92.

17. Prasad V, Sinha D. Potentials, experiences and outcomes of a comprehensive community based programme to address malnutrition in tribal India. Int J Child Health Nutr. 2015;4: 151–62.
18. Unicef, Fulwari: providing care and nourishment to tribal children in community-managed crèches in Chattisgarh. http://www.unicef.in/tribalchildren/Story-Fulwari-Providing-care-nourishment-to-tribal-children-in-community-managed-cr-ches-in-Chattisgarh.html. Accessed 19 April 2017.
19. SATHI. Marathi collection of stories of change in context of promoting community and household based nutrition practices (unpublished). Pune; 2017.

Chapter 12
Social Determinants of Maternal Health: Dead Women Talking

Renu Khanna and B. Subha Sri

Abstract This chapter presents an understanding of maternal health from a perspective of social determinants of health (SDH). It is based on an analysis of maternal deaths performed by 23 collaborators who came together as part of an initiative named 'Dead Women Talking', to document maternal deaths across 31 districts in 10 states of India. The collaborating partners developed a social autopsy tool based on a framework that they named SSSR (**S**ocial factors, Health **S**ystem-related factors, **S**cience (or Technical) factors, and **R**ights violations). Each maternal death was analyzed using this framework. Dead Women Talking emerged out of a critique of the Government of India's maternal health policy and programs, which are heavily oriented towards the biomedical framework and the health care delivery system. Although Maternal Death Reviews are mandated by the Government of India, information from the analysis of these reviews is not available in the public domain either at the national or the state level. Maternal death reporting is inadequate and most maternal deaths in the community are not captured let alone reviewed. We use an adapted World Health Organization (WHO) framework on social determinants of maternal health to report our findings from the analysis of 124 maternal deaths. In addition to the individual attributes of women that may contribute to maternal deaths, we highlight the community factors—their historical disadvantages such as belonging to the scheduled caste and scheduled tribes social groups—as well as health system factors and structural determinants, that contribute to their deaths. Recognition of the social and structural determinants is the first step to begin addressing the reasons underlying maternal deaths. Action is required at all levels—at level of the individual woman and her family and community, the health systems level, and at the structural level in terms of developing the requisite policies and programs.

R. Khanna (✉)
CommonHealth: Coalition for Maternal-Neonatal Health and Safe Abortion,
Society for Health Alternatives (SAHAJ), Vadodara, Gujarat, India
e-mail: sahajbrc@yahoo.com

B. Subha Sri
CommonHealth: Coalition for Maternal-Neonatal Health and Safe Abortion,
Rural Women's Social Education Centre (RUWSEC), Chengalpattu, Tamil Nadu, India

D. Nambiar and A. Muralidharan (eds.), *The Social Determinants of Health in India*, https://doi.org/10.1007/978-981-10-5999-5_12

Keywords Maternal death review · Social autopsy · Conceptual framework
Human rights · Health system

The death of Urmila

Urmila was a 32-year-old adivasi woman from Panchmahals in Gujarat—she was a migrant worker in cotton mills and had a history of tuberculosis. She had delivered her first child at a construction site where she had been working and the next two at home. This was her fourth pregnancy. She had only one antenatal visit at a Primary Health Centre (PHC), but her haemoglobin was not checked. The only antenatal services she received were tetanus toxoid and 10 iron folic acid tablets. When she developed breathlessness in the eighth month, her family first took her to the local PHC on a motorbike. From here, she was referred to the taluk hospital—the 108 service was arranged for this, however she had to be taken three kilometres across a river on a bike to reach the 108 pick-up point. From the taluk hospital, she was referred further to the district hospital. Here, the doctor told them he would not be available at night, so the family took Urmila to a private hospital nearby. However, she was refused care here and told to go to a higher facility, so the family took Urmila back home to arrange for more money—this journey was by a chakda,[1] *bus and then a rickshaw. It took three days for the family to arrange the money by which time Urmila's condition had worsened. This time, the family decided to take her to a private hospital in another town—she was refused care here and also in another private hospital where she was taken next. So the family arranged for a private ambulance and took her to the medical college hospital. She was admitted here and investigations done, but the next morning, the doctor told them that treatment at the medical college would not be possible and that she should be taken to a private hospital. At this point, Urmila's family gave up and decided they could not afford any more care and decided to bring her back home, where she died that night. She had been to seven different facilities over five days with no definitive care being given, even in tertiary level public institutions (S No. 4—Dead Women Talking).*

The death of Nayana

Nayana lived in the Azamgarh district of Uttar Pradesh and belonged to a scheduled caste community. She had been married at the age of 14 and was now 25 years old. This was her fifth pregnancy—three of her previous children are alive.

Nayana and her husband had migrated to Delhi in search of a job. While there, Nayana was diagnosed with tuberculosis and received treatment. Once better, Nayana returned home. She did not realize she was pregnant until six months later. By then, her husband had lost his job and this made food availability in the family a problem. The lack of nutrition made her weak and tired. As Nayana's condition

---

[1]An adaptation of a motorbike with a passenger compartment attached and used for transporting people in parts of rural India.

worsened, her family took her for a check-up—she was diagnosed to have tuberculosis again, for which treatment was begun in the nearest Community Health Centre (CHC). In the meantime, Nayana went into labor—she was taken to the CHC by the 108 ambulance and had a normal delivery. The baby's birth weight was found to be low and after a day's treatment with oxygen, both Nayana and her baby were discharged the next day.

Once home, Nayana developed fever—she was taken to the PHC on the second day where she was given some medicines by the doctor and sent home. However, her condition kept worsening. About a week later, she was taken to a private hospital in the nearby town and admitted—treatment was begun, however Nayana died a few hours later.

Urmila's and Nayana's tragic stories show how a host of factors—their socioeconomic status, the fact that they had to migrate for work, had to endure hunger, lived in remote inaccessible areas, had medical histories of tuberculosis and obstetric histories of multiple pregnancies and lost children, were married young, health system factors like the non-availability of health services, poor antenatal care as well as postnatal care, weak accountability resulting in multiple referrals—all interacted to produce fatal health outcomes, namely preventable maternal deaths.

It is increasingly being recognized that health outcomes are a result not only of biological and individual risk factors but also of other factors like wealth, ethnic background, gender, education and so on (see Annexure III). This understanding is termed as a Social Determinants approach to Health. Inequalities in people's access to information, decision-making and life opportunities contribute to their ill health and levels of well-being. Political choices and social organizations that distribute power and resources unequally across populations produce unequal health outcomes. 'Together, the structural determinants and conditions of daily life constitute the social determinants of health and are responsible for a major part of health inequities between and within countries' [1]. Just as these social determinants shape unequal health outcomes and produce health inequities, it is being recognized that it is possible to improve health outcomes by analyzing and acting upon salient social determinants [2].

This is the essence of the social determinants approach that we use to analyse maternal health in this paper. The paper is based on an initiative, led by CommonHealth, named 'Dead Women Talking'[2] (DWT) through which more than 124 maternal deaths were identified and documented between January 2012 and December 2013 by 23 collaborators [3].

[2]The 'Dead Women Talking' process is a civil society initiative led by CommonHealth that aims to look at maternal mortality in India from a social determinants and human rights perspective. This process has led to the development of a social autopsy tool and a collaborative civil society effort across several states to document maternal deaths.

Context

Although there has been a decline in India's maternal mortality ratio (MMR) from 254 per 1,00,000 live births in 2004–06 to 178 per 1,00,000 live births in 2010–12, this is far behind the fifth Millennium Development Goal (MDG) target of 109 per 100,000 live births by 2015 [4–8] This is in contrast to other smaller countries in South Asia like Nepal, Bangladesh and Bhutan that have already achieved or are well on track to achieve MDG 5 [9–11].

Although MMR is accepted as an indicator of a country's maternal health status, aggregate MMR figures do not tell us which women are dying. Small studies from various parts of the country show a disproportionate representation of women from marginalized groups, such as scheduled castes and scheduled tribes, in maternal death statistics [12–14].

Several efforts have been made in the last few years to analyze causes and contributors to individual maternal deaths and use lessons from this exercise to improve health systems. The WHO has published guidelines for verbal autopsy of maternal deaths and this has been used in several countries across the globe [15, 16]. In India, Tamil Nadu has been conducting verbal autopsies of maternal deaths followed by a district-level Maternal Death Review since the late 1990s [17]. Based on this successful initiative, the Government of India (GOI), in 2010, mandated Maternal Death Reviews at the district level across the country and published guidelines for the same [18]. The GOI efforts on institutionalizing Maternal Death Reviews (MDR) have faced significant challenges. As of March 2012, only 18% of all expected maternal deaths were being reported under the MDR process, and of these, only two-thirds were being reviewed by the district-level committee for MDR. Also, this exercise was largely restricted to finding a medical cause for death rather than identifying gaps in the health system and instituting corrective action [19].

Another initiative of documenting maternal deaths to inform policy and intervention is the Maternal and Perinatal Death Enquiry and Response (MAPEDIR), led by UNICEF, to identify the household, community and environmental factors underlying a maternal death [20]. Using a specially developed MAPEDIR verbal autopsy tool, trained frontline health workers collect information on maternal deaths from households. Between 2005 and 2009, the MAPEDIR initiative was implemented in 18 districts across eight Indian states with high maternal mortality. The initiative yielded many insights into the non-medical determinants of maternal deaths and demonstrates the potential of meticulously collected information to catalyze change within households and communities, and within the health sector.

The Dead Women Talking Initiative

It is in this context of persistently high maternal mortality, ignored social disparities in mortality, a lack of transparency in the documentation of maternal deaths, and a governmental focus on institutional delivery rather than safe delivery, that several civil society organizations in the country came together in 2012 as 'Dead Women Talking'. The initiative recognized that those affected by maternal deaths were disproportionately the poorest and most vulnerable groups, and that existing verbal autopsy tools focused largely on technical issues while systemic and social causes behind maternal deaths went largely unaddressed. DWT sought to center-stage the lived experiences of communities and families of women who die unnecessarily, and amplify the narratives of the women who died. The initiative aimed to examine maternal mortality in India from a social determinants and human rights perspective.

This paper based on maternal deaths documented across diverse settings in India, is an effort to focus attention on social determinants highlighted by these maternal deaths. We hope that this paper will result in the addressing of social determinants, both by the state and the community, to prevent avoidable maternal deaths in future.

Social Determinants of Maternal Health

A discussion paper by the United Nations Development Programme (UNDP) [2] describes a framework through which to analyze the structural and social determinants of maternal health. Figure 12.1 shows the elements of the framework. The categories of factors as described in the framework are: **individual attributes** of women such as age, parity, knowledge of services, previous obstetric history and so on; **family characteristics**—economic status, access to resources, support from natal and marital family, marital relationship; **community context**—(rural, urban, tribal), social position (class, caste, ethnicity), social capital, distance to facilities; **culture and social values**—women's status, gender norms, religion, health beliefs, social cohesion; **health services**—availability of services (emergency obstetric care, blood availability), skilled staff, acceptability of services, fees and charges for services; and **structural determinants**—laws, policies, budgets, education, social protection, and so on.

In the framework proposed by the WHO described (Fig. 12.1), although cultural and social norms are presented under structural factors, we believe that they also stem from the community context and can also be considered as intermediary factors.

Methodology

The 124 maternal deaths included in the DWT analysis were from 31 districts across 10 states of India.

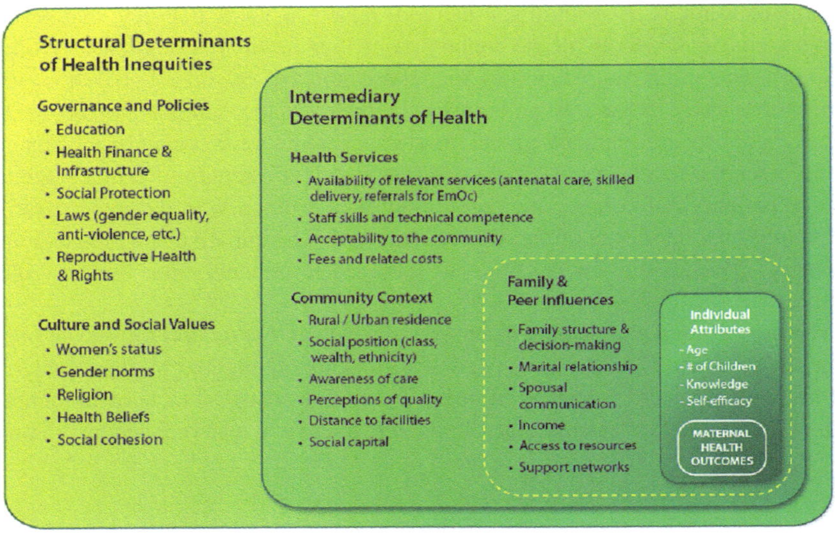

Fig. 12.1 The social determinants of maternal health. Adopted from [21]. Geneva: World Health Organisation: Page 7. *Source* (2, Page 8)

Overall Process and Tool Development

A social autopsy tool (see Box 12.1) was developed by a group of maternal health activists and academicians based on a framework that was developed to look at maternal mortality in the Indian context. This tool was designed to capture social determinants that contribute to maternal deaths, as well as to identifying a probable medical cause of death.

The tool included sections on: background information on the family, personal history of the deceased woman, story of the events leading up to the woman's death, her reproductive history, medical history, details of the current pregnancy, relevant details for death in the antenatal or postnatal period or intranatal death, her rights violations—in the family and vis-a-vis the health system. The tool also included issues to be explored in community-level discussions, like sociocultural practices, discrimination and HIV or disability-related exclusion, and geography related-exclusion from health services.

Box 12.1: Social Autopsy

Social autopsy is defined as 'an interview process aimed at identifying social, behavioural, and health systems contributors to maternal and child deaths' [22].

Social autopsies are meant to complement verbal autopsies for maternal/child deaths which, through interviews with the members of the dead woman/child's household, draw conclusions about the clinical cause of death.

Social autopsy has been recognized as a tool with the potential to provide information to policymakers and program managers to develop better strategies and interventions that would prevent avoidable deaths, and also as a tool that would provide communities with the information to make changes in behaviors within households and communities on the one hand, and demand greater accountability of health programs on the other.

Teams participating in DWT were trained to analyze each death across the four domains of the SSSR framework described in Box 12.2. They listed the gaps that were found to contribute to the death along with the actions that could address them. These actions or recommendations for all deaths in a particular geographical area were compiled periodically and discussed as actionable recommendations with both the local health system and the community leaders.

Box 12.2: SSSR Framework for Analysis

The SSSR framework to analyze maternal deaths was based on our earlier experience of documenting maternal deaths where we categorized factors contributing to maternal deaths across four domains:

1. Technical Factors (or Science Related Factors)
2. Health System Factors
3. Social Factors
4. Human Rights.

Thus, it was dubbed the SSSR Framework.

Training of Investigators

After the development of the tool, teams from different organizations in the 10 states, were trained by medical doctors (obstetricians), reproductive rights activists and public health researchers, to conduct social autopsies. Training included sessions on the epidemiology of maternal deaths, technical inputs on common obstetric complications and their management, rights-based perspectives on looking at maternal deaths, and skill based training on the actual use of the social autopsy tool.

Identifying and Documenting Maternal Deaths

The maternal deaths were initially identified and reported by members of several community-based organizations. The death was then verified as a maternal death by trained staff from these community-based organizations through a house visit. Following this, the families of the deceased women were contacted by members of these organizations in order to do a social autopsy.

The interviews with the family were done by a team of two to five trained investigators, usually after the initial mourning period was over. Following a verbal, informed consent process that detailed the objectives of the exercise and assured confidentiality, details of the death were collected using the social autopsy tool. Interviews were conducted with the marital as well as natal families of the deceased women, depending on whether she was at her natal or marital home during the pregnancy. Efforts were also made to contact other community members to understand the local social and cultural issues, and issues regarding health and other public services. Where possible, interviews were also conducted with frontline health providers like ASHA, ANM and the medical officer of the PHC concerned. Thus, multiple visits by the investigating team to the family and the community had to be made to document one maternal death.

During the whole process, senior members from both CommonHealth and individual civil society organizations engaged in the process, periodically met with those actually collecting data to ensure that technical and ethical standards were maintained. All those engaged in the process participated in two workshops during active data collection in order to examine the data and fill in gaps. These workshops also served to understand and address challenges in the field during data collection.

Compilation and Analysis

The details of the maternal deaths were compiled both state-wise and all together. Analysis was undertaken using the SSSR framework to identify health system gaps, social determinants and rights violations leading to the death.

Ethical Considerations

DWT was not designed as a research study to exclusively advance generalizable knowledge, but rather as a tool for advocacy by organizations with long-standing commitment to improving health and with close relationships with the communities in which deaths were investigated. Thus, no formal ethical clearance was sought from an external body. Despite this, all efforts were made in data collection and analysis, to maintain rigorous ethical standards. Verbal informed consent was taken from all those interviewed. Confidentiality was ensured by suitably anonymizing the deceased women and informants. Ethical issues that were likely to come up during data collection, and how to address them, were part of the initial training and subsequent workshops. Finally, the results of this work were shared with local communities and policymakers alike.

Limitations

Access to medical records was difficult, except where the family could provide copies of some of these records—thus the analysis draws largely from the narrative of events provided by the family and others. However, we believe this provides sufficient material from which to draw conclusions regarding contributors to these women's deaths.

Challenges

(a) Community-based members from these organizations needed to be trained to recognize maternal deaths according to the standard definition as well as record information about the deaths. It was also found that one-off training on conducting social autopsies was insufficient to train staff of civil society organizations. Furthermore, the tool evolved as it was used in the field, requiring repeated orientation to the additions/modifications.

(b) It was found that families often provided incomplete information for a social autopsy. For example, on many occasions the family would not share details about issues like abortions due to the preference for sons, violence, and nutrition and domestic workload. Family members were also often not allowed inside the labor room or were not given details of events that led to the death, and hence were not able to give sufficient information when the death was in a health facility. Thus, information needed to be triangulated to arrive at a point as close to the reality as possible: frontline health workers like ASHAs and ANMs needed to be interviewed, every facility the woman had been to or was referred to, needed to be visited, and the natal family needed to be interviewed. Each social autopsy thus took a minimum of three visits to the field and each interview with the family took at least an hour. It is thus an intensive process requiring investment in both transportation costs and personnel time.

(c) Deaths due to unsafe abortions, deaths due to home deliveries and late maternal deaths were likely to have been missed despite our efforts in obtaining complete information. Special efforts needed to be made to recognize these, including training of community-based organizations.

Results

In this section, we use the social determinants framework described earlier to present the determinants of maternal health at the individual, family, community and health system level. We also highlight how certain structural factors—policies and programs—resulted in system induced vulnerabilities.

Individual attributes

Age and parity: A majority (78 out of 124) of the women who died were very young, at less than 25 years old and 26 of them were between 16 and 20 years of age. All except one of them were married. Almost 40% of the women died during their first pregnancy and another 38% during their second or third pregnancy. At the other end of the spectrum were older women with a history of multiple pregnancies.

Work: Most of the deceased women were wage laborers or agriculture workers, in addition to being responsible for daily household chores. Six women were migrant laborers and four home-based *beedi* (Indian cigarette) workers. Some of them worked till the last month of their pregnancy, indicating that these women were extremely poor. Two of the women were ASHAs[3] themselves, one was a Sahayika in an Anganwadi[4] and one, a person incharge of a school midday meal programme[5]—and while these women were workers in public institutions, they were the lowest and most peripheral workers in the hierarchy of these institutions.

Community factors

Caste and Religion: Almost 45% of the women who died were from scheduled tribes and a further 17% were from scheduled castes.[6]

Migrants: At least six out of the 124 women who died in this sample were migrants. A special group of migrants were those in tea estates, two of whom were tribals. (Civil society organizations working in these estates have observed that health facilities for these tribals are almost non-existent).

Geographical location: Another group of women who were especially vulnerable and were excluded from care were those in remote hamlets. Families revealed that these hamlets did not receive any services at all. Rupa's story below shows how multiple vulnerabilities compounded the risks—young age, adivasi antecedents, and residence in a remote location in an economically backward state with poorly functioning health systems.

---

[3]ASHA or Accredited Social Health Activist is the name given to the Community Health Worker under the National Rural Health Mission. ASHAs are selected by the community and trained under the NRHM.

[4]An *Anganwadi* is a village facility under the Integrated Child Development Scheme (ICDS) that addresses early childhood nutrition and education. Each *Anganwadi* is staffed by an *Anganwadi* worker and an assistant (Sahayika).

[5]The midday meal programme addresses nutritional needs of schoolchildren by providing one fresh cooked meal in public schools at lunch.

[6]Scheduled castes and scheduled tribes are historically disadvantaged groups in India that are recognized and given a special status under the Indian constitution for affirmative action.

Box 12.3—Rupa's Story

Rupa was a 17-year-old adivasi girl in Chhattisgarh. Her family had been resettled because her village was in an area declared a tiger reserve. The resettlement village was 10 km away from the road and was inaccessible during the rains. There was no ICDS centre in the village, the ANM did not visit there and no immunization took place. Rupa, pregnant with her first child, did not therefore have any antenatal care. She delivered at home, developed a post-partum haemorrhage and died before the family could get a vehicle to transport her to a facility (S No. 99).

Gender as a cross-cutting issue: Women's secondary status, lack of involvement in decision-making, the lower value placed on their lives, and the health system's neglect of issues affecting women, all came up in the narratives. The preference for sons as a determinant of maternal death came up in the stories of Shanta (Box 12.4) as well as Baria from Banaskantha district in Gujarat. Baria was diagnosed with a heart ailment in her earlier pregnancy. She had three children including one son earlier but a desire for two sons, propelled her to her fourth pregnancy despite her family being aware of the risk. Social stigma attached to a pregnancy out of wedlock and resultant lack of care, was highlighted in the story of Neeru from Poreyahat in Jharkhand, who died as the result of an unsafe abortion after getting pregnant before marriage.

Health system factors

Lack of availability of emergency obstetric care: The poor quality of such emergency care emerged as a significant issue. This contributed in many cases to the loss of the life of the woman in spite of her reaching a health facility. In at least 38 of the 124 maternal deaths documented, there was a clear third phase delay [23]. Very often, the providers of immediate care were nurses, who seemed not to be able to recognize complications, and doctors were either not available, or not called, or were called too late. Providers sometimes seemed too over pressured and understaffed to pay enough attention to a woman with an emergency.

Another reason for the lack of emergency obstetric care was that health facilities at various levels seemed poorly prepared to manage emergencies. In addition, health care providers often did not seem prepared to even do what was possible at their level to manage an emergency. Women often went from facility to facility without even being given first aid, contributing to further delays. When treatment was finally initiated, many times it seemed that standard protocols were not followed, resulting in inappropriate and inadequate treatment.

In addition to the poor quality of emergency care, some narratives seemed to illustrate poor adherence to standards of care in general. Seven women died of sepsis in this sample of 124 deaths—all seven had had institutional deliveries. This points to either poor adherence to sterile precautions during labor and delivery, or a failure to identify women who were at high risk for sepsis and treat them appropriately. Irrational practices such as the augmentation of labor with intramuscular oxytocin also seemed prevalent.

Blood—a critical gap: Blood seemed to be unavailable in emergencies—blood transfusions were either delayed or inadequate—and the responsibility of arranging for blood was often put on the family. Blood was not seen as a critical emergency supply whose availability the facility had to ensure. Families of the deceased women often had to pay large sums of money and locate blood donors at short notice.

Absent or inadequate antenatal care: At least 12 of the 124 women who died had not received any form of antenatal care at all. In many cases, antenatal care was restricted to receiving tetanus toxoid injections or iron folic acid tablets—and even here, several families reported that the women were given 10–50 tablets only. Anaemia was the cause of 22 deaths out of the 124 women and contributed to at least four more deaths. Detection and treatment of anaemia did not seem to be a priority during antenatal care.

Absence of post-partum care: Out of 124 deaths, 82 were in the post-partum period, with 52 of these happening in the first 24 hours after delivery. Post-partum care largely seemed to be absent in facilities, and women were discharged soon after delivery. The case of Sarita from Chhattisgarh highlights how post-partum care is neglected even when the woman continues to be in the facility. Sarita delivered normally in the medical college, but her baby needed to be shifted to the Neonatal Intensive Care Unit (NICU)—she was discharged on the second day after delivery and stayed outside the NICU in order to look after the baby. When she developed a fever on the third day, she was readmitted to the postnatal ward, but no treatment was initiated. Her family got her some medicines from the medical store. She was attended to only after she fainted on the seventh day, by when it was too late and she died soon after.

Post-partum care in the community was worse. Narratives of women show that there was a lack of any form of care in the community after childbirth and that frontline workers failed to recognize post-partum complications.

Referrals and emergency transport: Of the 124 maternal deaths documented, 104 women attempted to seek care in a health facility and died either in a facility or on the way, or in the case of 12 women, at home, after deciding not to seek any further care and returning home. The stories of women's efforts to seek care reveal that they were shunted from facility to facility. Of the 124 women, 36 women visited three or more facilities seeking care when they were faced with an obstetric emergency, with one woman (Urmila whose story is presented at the beginning) visiting as many as seven facilities in search of care.

While there was difficulty in getting vehicles to transport women from one facility to another, families also stated that they faced difficulties in getting designated ambulances or vehicles to come to their homes to take women for emergency care. Often, the vehicle came much later than the assured 30 min, leading to a delay in transporting the woman to hospital.

Structural factors

Several system-induced vulnerabilities could be seen in the narratives. Policies and programs of the government actually affect the most vulnerable most adversely. The impact of the family planning program and the two-child norm on frontline workers and how it affects maternal health is highlighted by the case of Shanta, an *adivasi* woman in the Gadchiroli district of Maharashtra (see Box 12.4).

Box 12.4: Shanta's Story

In her third pregnancy with two previous daughters, Shanta was under tremendous pressure to produce a son. The ANM however insisted that her husband should undergo sterilization as they already had two children. In this scenario, no antenatal care was provided to Shanta this time, nor did she seek any. She later delivered a boy who died of prematurity. Shanta went into depression and died four months later of a worsening infected ulcer on her leg.

Another example is the Janani Suraksha Yojana (JSY)—a cash incentive to promote institutional deliveries. As we saw earlier, more than half of the women who died were either under 25 years of age or were older women. Both young and older multiparous women were until recently excluded from the Janani Suraksha Yojana [24, 25], which in many states, still requires documentary proof of poverty that many poor women may not possess. Thus, the most vulnerable women do not receive benefits.

The narratives showed that migrant women were not covered by antenatal services or ICDS services and when they died, their deaths were not officially documented because they did not belong to any service provider's 'area.' Portability of services is an issue for migrant women.

Discussion

The social determinants approach to maternal deaths described in the previous sections shows that many young women tragically lost their lives while fulfilling their social role of reproduction, due to structural, social and health system related reasons. Many of these deaths could have been averted with actions at various levels—family, community, health system, policy and program.

In the sections above, we described how individual, family, community and health system as well as structural factors interacted to produce adverse—in fact—fatal consequences for women. Many of the women whose stories we documented were socially and economically vulnerable, and from social groups that have been historically deprived of fruits of modern development. In several of their lives, multiple vulnerabilities came together to produce cumulative effects. Previous studies have also shown that these groups have a disproportionately higher maternal mortality [12, 13]. These vulnerable women, faced severe challenges in accessing health care. From the narratives, it seems that women with vulnerabilities are actually getting left out of antenatal and post-partum care because of the way health services are structured and delivered. We argue that a rights-based approach and a focus on equity and social justice would make special provisions for women with vulnerabilities to ensure their access to care.

Maternal Health services cannot be improved in isolation. 'Silo'ed approaches that narrowly focus on one specific area such as maternal health will result in the inefficient investment of resources and a weakening of health systems. Maternal health services must be implemented within a broader Universal Access to Health Care (UAHC) intervention. For social determinants of maternal health to be addressed maternal health care services have to be situated within the broader comprehensive primary health care approach. This will ensure the addressing of health issues such as anaemia and infectious diseases convergent with maternal health care. Similarly maternal health services also need to be located within the reproductive health continuum.

The social determinants' approach suggests that structural factors as well community and sociocultural factors are equally important. Longer-term policy action is required to address the social inequities that disadvantage the scheduled castes and scheduled tribes, to invest in programs that will improve their education and health status—more facilities and delivery points, and additional skilled providers in remote areas. Strong and effective governance is required to ensure that equity policies and programs introduced by the government, for example, the Janani Shishu Suraksha Karyakram (JSSK) and the VHNDs (Village Health and Nutrition Days) are implemented well and actually deliver. Accountability has to be ensured —multiple referrals in the stories that we documented highlight Governance is also required to regulate the private sector and ensure that it provides quality essential maternal health services, free from corruption. Intersectoral coordination is required to address several intermediary factors such as roads and transport systems, nutrition and food security, safe and healthy workplaces, and violence against women. The intersectoral coordination has to permeate from the policy and program design level to the community level.

Community-based approaches to empower families and women's collectives, with information about danger signs in pregnancy and birth preparedness are important. Women's organizations and collectives need to be recognized as critical actors to ensure that women have voice and agency in all matters affecting them and that they have a place in all decision-making and review bodies of the government [26]. There is a growing body of literature to suggest that making maternal health an agenda that community leaders need to engage with, has led to improved maternal health outcomes [27, 28].

While the empowerment of women in terms of their improving their self-efficacy is extremely important, there is also a need to work on gender issues. Cultural norms that govern women's and men's behavior and roles, and gender power relations that adversely impact women's health need to be challenged and transformed [26]. Men as partners and decision makers within families and communities, need to be addressed so that they become caring and supportive of women's self-determination. Studies have shown that interventions with men, designed with women's participation and implemented with their consent, have resulted in positive maternal health outcomes [29].

The paper also shows that guidelines and tools that enquire into women's position and condition within the family and society are required to identify the specific gender and other social determinants that contribute to maternal deaths.

Conclusion

In this chapter, we presented an analysis of maternal deaths documented by the 'Dead Women Talking' initiative, through a social determinants perspective. A framework developed by UNDP was adapted to present the analysis. In addition to the individual attributes of women that may contribute to maternal deaths, we highlighted the community factors—mainly their historical disadvantages like belonging to the scheduled caste and scheduled tribes social groups—as well as health system factors and structural determinants, that contributed to their deaths. Recognition of the social and structural determinants is the first step to begin addressing the reasons underlying maternal deaths. Action is required at all levels—at the level of the individual woman and her family and community, at the health systems level, and at the structural level in terms of developing the requisite policies and programs.

Commentary—Dead Women Talking

R. Srivatsan
Anveshi Research Centre for Women's Studies, Hyderabad, India

I have always been a little uneasy with the free and easy use of the term 'social determinants of health' because it carries the danger of becoming a shorthand phrase that defers the hard work of thinking about what exactly the problem is. It is also easy to say this or that outcome is because of 'social determinants' and cluck ones tongue at the sad state of affairs. It is true that social determinants may well be difficult to solve, and this explanation also ensures that the victim is not blamed for his or her death or suffering—the social structure is the culprit. This is no doubt important.

But if one were to think a bit more aggressively, 'determinant' is a neutral term which has no specific agent. The 'social situation' is the 'determinant (i.e., the ground) for this or that tragedy. Even a slight turn of phrase would change this—for example, if we say instead that the pregnant woman's death was 'socially determined'—it would cause us to squirm as a possible member of the collective agent of that death. The term 'determinant' is the kind of umbrella term that the World Health Organization (WHO) would use to ensure that pointed reference to questions of race, ethnicity, tribe, religion and caste (not to mention the question of economics, which I reserve for my last paragraph) are avoided. Given WHOs position of speaking to governments and large bureaucracies, it is a kind of minimum level terminology to get the widest consensus. And yet, it seems likely that this dilution of a critical perspective to get a wider consensus may well be counterproductive.

To push the argument further, the term 'social' too, is one that tends to be apolitical. The use of the term 'social' indicates a reality that is greater than individual, but also tends to signal a perspective that observes a situation passively. When a given health catastrophe is attributed to 'social determinants' it hides what society, government and state ought to have done, but have failed to do. This masking is problematic where there is a constitutional promise to eradicate social discrimination (as in India). It is to be expected that the government will use this term to shift blame to those aspects of its functioning that are mired in 'society' and are beyond governmental control. It suggests what is called 'implementation failure' of planned intentions with respect to health care. For example, if a tribal woman who delivers at a governmental facility is refused physical contact by the functionaries of the hospital due to 'uncleanness', is it 'implementation failure', a 'social determinant' or a crime? What if she dies as a result?

If health activism and a politics of health were to look at health care with a transformative agenda (rather than a liberal ameliorative one), what would a useful way to look at social determinants be? What is a critical perspective on 'social determinants'? This is something that voluntary workers and health activists need to think about with great care.

Some steps would be:

1. The term 'social determinant' signals that forces larger than individual intentions are at work. The immediate response should be the attempt to characterize these forces in some detail so that the processes become more evident. In other words, the term social determinant should be an investigative trigger rather than an explanatory seal.
2. The term 'social determinant' should not automatically absolve individuals of criminal culpability for serious acts of commission or omission. Social determinants are not some superhuman forces that act independently of human conduct. They act through human action. The law and the processes of protecting rights should work toward discouraging such actions.
3. Even when the determinants of exclusionary, discriminative and oppressive practices in health care are social (and in some cases without overtly injurious actions of specific individuals), the end result is that an individual person dies or suffers catastrophic loss in the process. What needs to be addressed in each case is the issue of justice. How would a law that is based in a constitution that is

dedicated in spirit and in theory to equality be applied in practice to expand (and also plug loopholes in) that equality?

4. All the above responses will need to be driven by political processes that define what progress means in each specific situation. These processes will have to act in several registers—individual, institutional, political and cultural.

Finally, the use of the term social determinant should be seen as expressing the economic dimension. This is to strain against the liberal tendencies of the term which in effect point a finger away from the economic determinants of ill-health (i.e., systematic impoverishment under capitalist development) towards that somewhat pre-modern culprit out there: the 'social' (even though paradoxically the 'social' is very much a modern category). One implication of using the term 'social determinant of health' is that there are interests and forces in society that go beyond the economic dimension and force a situation of illness in spite of governmental efforts to oppose that situation: thus it points to the very real discrimination against dalits, minorities, tribals, and women. However, we should insist on the broader picture here, that social determinants most often have catastrophic results for individuals only in their intersection with economic deprivation and systematic impoverishment. In India, current historical conditions of rampant liberal capitalism coupled with caste-Hindu cultural hegemony establish the social determinants of all atrocities in the domain of health. Thus the struggle against social determinants has to be simultaneously a struggle against systematic economic impoverishment.

References

1. CSDH. Closing the gap in a generation: health equity through action on the social determinants of health. Final Report of the Commission on Social Determinants of Health. Geneva: World Health Organization; 2008.
2. UNDP. A social determinants approach to maternal health: roles for development actors, discussion paper. Bureau for Development Policy; 2011.
3. Subha SB, Khanna R. Dead women talking: a civil society report on maternal deaths in India, common health and Jan Swasthya Abhiyan; 2014.
4. RGI. Sample Registration system: maternal mortality in India: 1997–2003. Trends, causes and risk factors. New Delhi: Registrar General, India; 2003.
5. RGI. Sample Registration system: special bulletin on maternal mortality in India, 2004–06. New Delhi: Registrar General, India; 2009.
6. RGI. Sample registration system: special bulletin on maternal mortality in India, 2007–09. New Delhi: Registrar General, India; 2011.
7. RGI. Sample registration system: special bulletin on maternal mortality in India, 2010–12. New Delhi: Registrar General, India; 2013.
8. Millennium Development Goals: India country report. New Delhi: Social Statistics Division, Ministry of Statistics and Programme Implementation, Government of India; 2014. http://mospi.nic.in/Mospi_New/upload/mdg_2014_28jan14.pdf.

9. Nepal Millennium Development Goals Progress Report. Kathmandu: Government of Nepal, National Planning Commission; 2013. http://www.npc.gov.np/new/uploadedFiles/allFiles/mdg-report-2013.pdf.
10. Millennium Development Goals Bangladesh progress report 2012. Dhaka: General Economics Division (GED), Bangladesh Planning Commission, Government of the People's Republic of Bangladesh; 2013. http://www.bd.undp.org/content/dam/bangladesh/docs/MDG/MDG%20Report%202012.pdf.
11. MDG 5 Improve maternal health: where we are. United Nations Development Programme. http://www.bt.undp.org/content/bhutan/en/home/mdgoverview/overview/mdg5/. Accessed 22 Aug 2014.
12. Sri BS, Khanna R. Maternal health policy in India: from institutional deliveries to safe deliveries. Vadodara: CommonHealth, Jan Swasthya Abhiyan; 2012. http://www.commonhealth.in/report-pdf/4a.%20monograph%20Maternal%20Health%20Policy%20in%20India-2012.pdf.
13. UNICEF. Maternal and perinatal death inquiry and response. New Delhi: UNICEF; 2008.
14. Sri BS, Sarojini N, Khanna R. An investigation of maternal deaths following public protests in a tribal district of Madhya Pradesh, central India. Reprod Health Matters. 2012;39(12):11–20.
15. Campbell O, Ronsmans C. Verbal autopsies for maternal deaths: report of a WHO workshop, London, 10–13 January 1994. Geneva: World Health Organization; 1995.
16. Verbal autopsy standards. The 2012 WHO verbal autopsy instrument. Geneva: World Health Organization; 2012.
17. Padmanaban P, Raman PS, Mavalankar DV. Innovations and challenges in reducing maternal mortality in Tamil Nadu, India. J Health Popul Nutr. 2009;27(2):202–19.
18. MoHFW. Maternal death review guidebook. New Delhi: Maternal Health Division, MoHFW, Government of India; 2011.
19. Malhotra M. Maternal death review—country perspective: presentation at WHO multicountry workshop, Bangkok, Thailand. September 24–28, 2012. New Delhi: Deputy Commissioner, Maternal Health, MoHFW, Government of India; 2012.
20. Kalter HD, Mohan P, Mishra A, Gaonkar N, Biswas AB, Balakrishnan S, et al. Maternal death inquiry and response in India—the impact of contextual factors on defining an optimal model to help meet critical maternal health policy objectives. Health Res Policy Syst. 2011; 9 (41).
21. WHO. Closing the gab: policy into practice on social determinants of health. Discussion documents for the world conference on social determinants of health. Geneva: World Health Organization; 2011.
22. Kalter HD, Salgado R, Babille M, Koffi AK, Black RE. Social autopsy for maternal and child deaths: a comprehensive literature review to examine the concept and the development of the method. Popul Health Metrics 2011; 9(45).
23. Thaddeus S, Maine D. Too far to walk: maternal mortality in context. Soc Sci Med. 1994;38 (8):1091–110.
24. Janani Suraksha Yojana: features and frequently asked questions and answers. New Delhi: Maternal Health Division, MoHFW, Government of India; 2006. http://mohfw.nic.in/WriteReadData/l892s/file28-99526408.pdf.
25. Sri BS, Khanna R. Maternal health policy in India: from institutional deliveries to safe deliveries. Vadodara: CommonHealth, Jan Swasthya Abhiyan; 2012. http://www.commonhealth.in/report-pdf/4a.%20monograph%20Maternal%20Health%20Policy%20in%20India-2012.pdf.
26. Sen G, Östlin P, George A. Unequal, unfair, ineffective and inefficient gender inequity in health: why it exists and how we can change it. Final Report to the WHO Commission on Social Determinants of Health, Sept 2007. Women and Gender Equity Knowledge Network.

27. Sinha D. Empowering communities to make pregnancy safer: an intervention in rural Andhra Pradesh. New Delhi: Population Council; 2008.
28. Mullany BC, Becker S, Hindin MJ. The impact of including husbands in antenatal health education services on maternal health practices in urban Nepal: results from a randomized controlled trial. Health Educ Res. 2007;22(2):166–76. doi:10.1093/her/cyl060.
29. Davis J, Luchters S, Holmes W. Men and maternal and newborn health: benefits, harms, challenges and potential strategies for engaging men. Melbourne: Compass: Women's and Children's Health Knowledge Hub; 2012.

Chapter 13
Weaving It Together: Concepts, Methods and Indicators

Devaki Nambiar and Arundati Muralidharan

As noted at the outset, the World Health Organization's Commission on Social Determinants of Health (CSDH) sought to foster and augment the attention of the public health community towards the pivotal role of social determinants of health in shaping health outcomes and inequalities in health. The Commission's work drew on global experiences, yet emphasized strongly the importance of locating SDH in national contexts while contributing to global practice. To catalyze action on SDH, the CSDH put forward three key recommendations:

(1) Improve daily living conditions;
(2) Tackle the inequitable distribution of power, money and resources; and
(3) Measure and understand the problem and assess the impact of action [1].

This volume speaks to the third recommendation proposed by the CSDH, that is—to 'measure and understand the problem, and assess the impact on action' [1]. Through this recommendation, the Commission calls for the assessment of health problems, the appraisal of action taken to mitigate problems, the development and capacity building of health professionals at different levels on SDH, and the spreading of awareness about SDH among the general population. We note that the chapters in this volume actualize one or more of these recommended actions, serving as a valuable resource to both the Indian and global communities working on SDH. Some contributions apply a nuanced SDH lens through which to study critical health concerns or determinants of health, contributing evidence to how well-recognized as well as less-explored social determinants can shape health outcomes and health inequalities in India (see Yumnam and Dasgupta, Bhan, Chakravarthi, Goswami,

D. Nambiar (✉)
The George Institute for Global Health, New Delhi, Delhi, India
e-mail: devaki.nambiar@gmail.com

A. Muralidharan
WaterAid India, New Delhi, Delhi, India
e-mail: arundatimuralidharan@wateraid.org

D. Nambiar and A. Muralidharan (eds.), *The Social Determinants of Health in India*, https://doi.org/10.1007/978-981-10-5999-5_13

and Khanna and Subha Sri B). Going forward, select chapters examine or suggest ways to assess action on SDH at various levels, including the community, state, and national levels (see Marathe and Shukla, Desai, Garg, Khanna and Subha Sri B, Ganesan and colleagues, and Muralidharan). These chapters offer important lessons on how large scale government programs and non-governmental initiatives can measure or evaluate action on SDH and health inequalities. These chapters also have implications for how assessments of SDH can be integrated into existing data collection platforms in the country. While not explicitly stated, some of the methodologies deployed to both assess the problem and the action taken have simultaneously enhanced the capacity of stakeholders to appreciate SDH through data gathering and analysis. Of particular relevance is the fact that these stakeholders include not only academics and researchers, but also civil society organizations, frontline health workers, and the community (see Goswami, Marathe and Shukla, Desai, Khanna and Subha Sri B, and Garg). Lastly, some chapters allude to generating awareness about SDH through the community-based and led approaches used to appreciate action on SDH (see Garg, Marathe and Shukla). These chapters underscore the need for capacity building to study action on SDH in a concerted manner, and to explore platforms to effectively disseminate information on SDH and health inequalities to relevant stakeholders. Taken together, the chapters present a rich patchwork of how SDH is understood, acted upon, and assessed in India, highlighting the importance of locating global conceptualizations and recommendations regarding SDH in the unique Indian context.

What's in a Name?

The chapters in this volume attempt to unpack the complexity of different social determinants of health (SDH) working at multiple levels, including nutrition, health systems, conflict/violence, occupation, social status, rural-urban residence, and water, sanitation, and hygiene (WASH). In so doing, we see implicit and often explicit challenges to the existing conceptualizations of the concept of SDH itself. Srivats points out that SDH 'carries the danger of becoming a shorthand phrase that defers the hard work of thinking what exactly the problem is'. Perhaps this is common sense in India, as we found it to be rarely the case that the frame of SDH was used as a starting point for thinking or research.

Instead, we found that each chapter made mention or drew attention to action on SDH through a focus on a particular population, institution, health issue, or intervention/process. Additionally, authors of each piece present a powerful rationale that explains their chosen focus. Goswami's work on the occupational health of women in the informal economy in rural Bihar draws attention to SDH primarily with respect to a particular population. This emphasis on a population facilitates the appreciation of multiple adverse health outcomes (such as hearing loss, malnutrition, gastrointestinal problems, and skin disorders) that these women face as a consequence of their occupational status and constraints as informal workers. Desai demonstrates how this focus, even for what may be considered a single group of self-employed women, may vary based on geography and circumstance, and must be commensurably prioritized in each specific context. Khanna and Subha Sri B, and Muralidharan's chapters centre on health issues, namely maternal mortality and menstrual health and hygiene respectively. Attention on a specific health issue fosters the identification of SDH at different levels (e.g., individual, household, community, health systems, and structural forces). Two papers highlight the role of institutions (Garg, Ganesan et al.). While Ganesan and colleagues look historically at the institution of the Municipal Health Officer as a locus of convergence, Garg's contribution further describes a community-based intervention process of action on SDH. Along lines similar to Garg, Marathe and Shukla also deliberate on the process of community monitoring and action for nutrition. Bhan considers urbanization as a determinant of health, deconstructing the urban transition in India and its implications for health while Chakravarthi raises distal determinants as harder to measure, but nonetheless critical antecedents to understand and act on health. The emphasis on institutions and processes suggest how various stakeholders or agencies are implicated in SDH—both in constructive and potentially destructive ways. Yumnam and Dasgupta's piece is unique in that the focus is on an event as a social determinant of health—conflict.

Looking at our commentary contributions, we move further away from the girding logic of SDH. Instead, complexity and context are highlighted in particular, giving concurrence to or seeking to deepen the arguments made by authors. On the one hand are efforts to situate the work presented in larger canons of work (equity, peace and disaster studies in relation to conflict, feminist epistemology in relation to work on labor), while other commentaries reflect on experiences and grassroots realities linked to chapter themes (how the vacuums of the urban health sector are experienced by low income workers, or the strictures governing the mobility and sexuality of adolescent girls). Other commentaries situate chapters in the larger context of political developments (such as India's move towards decentralization and the design of the National Rural Health Mission (NRHM), or the WHO's motivation in using such a generic SDH frame in the interest of universal application and relevance). It is clear to see that this is an area of rich ferment, and indeed of dialogue that this volume has modestly helped advance.

In reviewing these contributions, certain themes emerged as salient, that speak to what the Indian idiom or discourse on SDH could be, and what novel or unexpected themes were presented. We describe these in the following sections.

Conceptualization as Expansion, Operationalization as Convergence, Oversight to Widen Participation

As aforementioned, eschewing the meta-framework of SDH per se, most contributions sought to develop bespoke frameworks with corresponding methodologies. Mishra seeks to unpack the SDH framework, demonstrating how its unraveling and adaptation offers the greatest changes of applicability. Importantly, she underscores the need for dialogue between and across disciplines that will necessarily be in opposition from time to time—particularly in the mythical tussle between understanding the complexity of SDH and acting on it. There is a cost, as she points out: 'research and practice (focus on actions) are spurious distinctions that harm the cause of health equity'.

Ganesan and colleagues, drawing upon their work as members of the Technical Resource Group (TRG) to the National Urban Health Mission (NUHM), deploy a historical perspective to unpack the role of an institutional structure in taking action on the SDH of urban health. The authors critically review the evolving role and responsibilities of the Municipal Health Officer (MHO) over almost 250 years. Furthermore, they use data collected from various stakeholders in three types of cities in present-day India to underscore the effect that an institutional role can have on catalyzing multisectoral action on SDH in urban settings. Based on their historical analysis and assessment of the current scenario, the authors suggest that despite several constraints and competing interests, the role of the MHO is imperative in implementing an integrated approach to addressing the social determinants of urban health. Bhan unpacks the complexity of urbanization in India by discussing how urbanization is conceptualized, how it impacts health and health behaviors, and methodologies for studying urbanization and health. She emphasizes the characteristics of both people and place in understanding urbanization, and also presents nuances of speed, spread and style in studying the trajectory of urbanization in India. Yumnam and Dasgupta examine conflict as an SDH as well as a factor that strengthens the effect of existing SDH to further undermine health, enhance inequalities in health, and challenge health systems. They discuss the SDH of conflict in the case of Manipur, a state in North-East India, plagued by internal conflict and a battle between society and the state. This chapter ends by urging health systems to recognize conflict as an emerging determinant of health, and support research that will inform a SDH approach to interventions addressing conflict. Chakravarthi builds an argument for why typical SDH discourses—particularly in the global arena—tend to focus on more measurable, proximal determinants, while also highlighting the more vexed and ephemeral—but nonetheless critical determinants of health. She also notes the highly political nature of these distal determinants; power imbalances are played out in the very lack of attention given to some of these distal determinants and the preference given to more proximal depoliticised, 'risk factor' type determinants. Desai presents the Self Employed Women's Association's (SEWA) approach to addressing SDH in practice. In their chapter, they underscore how an underlying philosophy, one that keeps social determinants at its core, has enabled the scale up of a community health worker-led intervention. Critical to their success has been the element of responsiveness, whereby community-based programs have addressed social determinants in a dynamic and needs-based manner. Khanna and Subha Sri B share, create and demonstrate the SSSR (social factors, health system related factors, science/technology, rights violations) framework, using it to develop a social autopsy tool with which to assess the social determinants of maternal deaths. Such a framework and tool enable an in-depth exploration of the causes of maternal death, as well as the gaps and opportunities for action in various domains. Muralidharan presents a comprehensive framework for action on the software (awareness and behavior change) and hardware (infrastructure/technology) components to improve menstrual hygiene management, emphasizing the opportunities for intersectoral action to improve health.

Five chapters in this volume describe how data has been, or can be used, to assess and/or inform action on SDH. Four chapters discuss findings based on the analysis of SDH data, while one chapter presents a core set of indicators to measure action on SDH. Khanna and Subha Sri B in 'Dead Women Talking' presented an analysis of 124 maternal deaths using key indicators in the four domains outlined in the SSSR framework, namely individual attributes, community factors, health system/services, and structural determinants. This analysis was used to identify gaps and areas for intervention to avert maternal deaths. Goswami's study, 'Voices of Women', used a mixed methods approach employing a survey and focus group discussions to explore the status of female informal workers in Bihar related to the type of informal work and related health impacts, and issues related to physical security. These findings were then used to propose recommendations to improve the working conditions, occupational health hazards, and health systems response to women in the informal economy. Two chapters describe participatory methods of collecting data on SDH, and simultaneously show how action on SDH has improved health over time. Marathe and Shukla discuss and analyze the community-based monitoring and action (CBMA) as applied to the ICDS program in Maharashtra. Two rounds of data were collected using a standardized tool and report card related to supplementary nutrition, nutrition and health education and health services, and were analyzed to track improvements over a six-month period. Garg explains how community involvement in collecting, recording, and analyzing data on key health and SDH indicators (e.g., access to health services, food, water, sanitation, education, and government schemes) in Chhattisgarh has bolstered convergent action for health. While Muralidharan does not present an analysis of data, she draws upon the menstrual health and hygiene management (MHHM) framework and literature on MHHM to suggest a core list of indicators across four key domains—health outcomes, socioeconomic outcomes, knowledge, attitudes and practices, and water, sanitation and hygiene (WASH) infrastructure.

What one is left with, therefore, is a multiplicity of frameworks, not unlike what happened with the CSDH knowledge networks, (as discussed in the introduction). Thus, in India we see a replication of the global tendency to work within a context and build frameworks in a bespoke fashion—to link knowledge and action in meaningful ways. Throughout all of the chapters, rather than a larger meta-framework per se, we saw unique frameworks and linked methodologies. And yet, we also saw emerging a possible idiom with which to think about SDH in India: convergence.

		Convergence of:	
		Decision-making (e.g. Village Health Nutrition and Sanitation Committee)	**Services delivered** (e.g. Non-Governmental Organisation)
Convergence for:	**Population** (e.g. Rural, tribal, women)	• Municipal Health officer • Swasthya Panchayat • Task force on women workers	• Community-based approach to SDH for informal women workers
	Issue (e.g. Violence, HIV/AIDS)		• Social factors, (Health) System related factors, Science/technology, Rights violations Social Audit • Menstrual Health and Hygiene Management indicators • Community-Based Monitoring of Nutrition

Fig. 13.1 Tendencies of convergence. *Source* Authors [2]

The Idea of Convergence

Chapters focused on methods and indicators suggest that the notion of convergence may be a conceptualization useful to address health inequality and work across SDH sectors in India. It is not the multiplicity of determinants per se that is focused upon, but rather their coming together that is emphasized [3]. Convergence is defined as 'coordinated policy decisions and programme actions in multiple sectors [fields that have proximal or distal effects…]…to achieve a common goal' [4]. We mapped our chapters in relation to the notion of convergence (Fig. 13.1). We found that two tendencies emerge: one, when considering issues (such as nutrition, maternal mortality, menstrual hygiene and management), convergence of services is either monitored or sought. In contrast, when considering a population (such as rural, urban, or women workers), we see an emphasis on convergent decision-making, i.e. either within a single individual like a MHO or joint decision-making by a village committee or a state-level task force.

On the face of it, these may seem like natural, neutral and distinct pairings: population—decision-making, and issue—services. Yet, they may be drawn upon to point to areas for action and further consideration. For example, the challenge facing a population-focused strategy is ensuring comprehensiveness of attention to an adequately wide range of determinants or services, for which responsibility may be distributed by line or sectoral departments. Here, developing a multilevel framework (individual, household, community) may reveal a logic whereby determinants and the services providing them, could be organized. On the other hand, when looking at an issue-based approach, one has to contend with coalescing services under a single rubric (of that issue) and enabling joint or coordinated decision-making. Here it makes sense to think of institutional roles and processes, such the Village Health and Sanitation Committee (VHSC) or the modality of a Task Force, to advance action.

That said, here again, there is complexity. For one, it is usually the case that an issue will have a commensurate population of focus (e.g. maternal deaths link to pregnant women, while MHHM draws attention to adolescent girls, and nutrition monitoring largely focuses on children). Furthermore, there will be priority issues for populations of focus (maternal and child health in rural areas, and occupational health among workers).

Further light may be shed in looking at differences of scale and geographies of implementation of methodologies and indicators across chapters. Four of the seven chapters located their application of methodologies and/or indicators in rural India; three of these focused on a specific state (Garg, Marathe and Shukla, Goswami) and one garnered and analyzed data from across the country (Khanna and Subha Sri B). Of the remaining three, two directed attention to the urban context across different types of cities in the country (Bhan, Ganesan et al.), two discussed a national application irrespective of an urban or rural setting (Chakravarthi and Muralidharan), and the last positioned itself in a particular state (Yumnam and Dasgupta). This in part reflects the recent history of health system strengthening in India, which has placed a greater emphasis on rural areas. Given that health is a state subject, state-centric analyses are to be expected.

Process Matters

Even though the term 'social' is part of the concept, the tendency of SDH approaches is to focus on individuals and populations rather than on processes or relationships. All contributors place particular emphasis on processes to both understand and act on social determinants. Yumnam and Dasgupta, for instance, place emphasis on conflict as a process that impinges on health in critical ways—and that is in that sense, a social determinant. Marathe and Shukla talk about creating public accountability as a process integral to action on nutrition and health. Some chapters also seek to highlight institutional roles in these processes. For example, while Ganesan and colleagues mention the role of the MHO, Garg talks about the VHSC. In urban and rural settings, respectively, the roles played by these stakeholders enables the consideration of health and the health system in relation to other factors impinging on it. Mishra's piece underscores the social in SDH as methodology, moving beyond static 'variablizing' markers of identity (gender, caste, etc.) or atomised notions of relationships between them, to understandings that are multilevel and mindful of the operational of power in process(es). Chakravarthi's reflection highlights the more distal, socially embedded processes—like corporate practices—which end up being neglected SDH, even as their social and political implications loom large in the health sector.

It could be said that chapters place emphasis on different dimensions of process. On the one hand, there is emphasis on who is to be monitoring or acting on SDH (i.e., the office of the MHO in urban areas, the VHSC in rural areas, and the community monitoring nutrition). Another thread across chapters is the emphasis on what is to be monitored; while some try to frame health and its determinants in a general sense [i.e. the MHO and Village Health, Sanitation and Nutrition Committees (VHSNC)], others seek to inclusively monitor health issues using an SDH lens (i.e. maternal health, and menstrual hygiene management), others seek inclusion of ignored determinants (i.e. corporate influence, and conflict) or populations (i.e. informal women workers).

Another note on process alludes to differences in scale and geographies in the implementation of methodologies and indicators across chapters. Five of the eight chapters located their application of methodologies and/or indicators in rural India; three of these focused on a specific state (Garg, Marathe and Shukla, Goswami) and two garnered and analyzed data from across the country (Desai, Khanna and Subha Sri B). Of the remaining three, two directed attention to the urban context across different types of cities in the country (Bhan, Ganesan et al.), two discussed a national application irrespective of an urban or rural setting (Desai, Muralidharan), and the last positioned itself in a particular state (Yumnam and Dasgupta). This in part reflects the recent history of health system strengthening in India, which has placed a greater emphasis on rural areas. Furthermore, given that health is a state subject, state-centric analyses are to be expected. We can see in this way that even analyses are determined by societal processes and their undergirding logics. It is therefore important to situate ourselves and recognize the positionality of our work, in such macroprocesses.

Exclusions

Just as important as it is to reflect on the contributions of those in this volume and their linkages to broader discourses, we must also note critical exclusions. We were unable to get feedback from those directly working in government departments as they were simply not able to give time to this kind of thinking and writing. This is an important admission to acknowledge. Bureaucrats and decision-makers active in the public sector simply tend not have the flexibility in their terms of work to take a step back and write about equity and SDH. This is not to suggest that they do not do this, of course, but that the requirement of writing automatically precludes the involvement of certain key stakeholders in such an endeavour. Furthermore, for many of those who were able to give us the time to write, this entailed the sacrifice of time spent on implementation and action—it was perhaps most 'natural' or 'feasible' for those in academia, or those who were already engaged in processes of documentation, to make contributions to this volume.

And Now?

We are happy to conclude, through this exercise, that the richness of India's understandings and action on SDH have no automatic or mandatory linkage to the actual use of the concept. This is a rich and evolved domain, one that demands a more vibrant atmosphere or culture of reflexivity, documentation and evaluation. Whether related to conceptualization, operationalization or oversight, we see that local frameworks exist, that convergence as a concept has to be further unpacked, that processes matter, and that there are always exclusions to consider. To reckon with all these elements in their complexity and political weight, requires nothing short of transdisciplinary might, which is more an art than a science, demanding the collaboration and creativity of policymakers, academics, and civil society practitioners alike. In so doing, we heed the advice of Dr. V. Ramalingaswami who quoted Bismarck, saying that if politics is the art of the possible, 'to secure better health for the developing world in the shortest time is largely the art of the possible, by the closest approximation of knowledge and action' [5]. Onward!

References

1. Commission on Social Determinants of Health. Closing the gap in a generation: health equity through action on the social determinants of health. Final Report of the Commission on Social Determinants of Health; 2008.
2. Nambiar D, Muralidharan A, Garg S, Daruwalla N, Ganesan P. Analysing implementer narratives on addressing health inequity through convergent action on the social determinants of health in India. Int J Equity Health. 2015;14:133. doi:10.1186/s12939-015-0267-7.
3. Visvanathan S. Sum and substance of a real opposition. The Hindu. 4 June 2015. http://www.thehindu.com/opinion/lead/creating-a-viable-left-opposition-against-the-bjp-and-rss/article7268435.ece. Accessed 10 Sept 2015.
4. Gaitonde R. Research on inequities and inequalities in health in India: a mapping of the field. 2015.
5. Ramalingaswami V. The art of the possible. Soc Sci Med. 1986;22(11):1097–103.

Annexures: Indicator Registry

Annexure I
Promoting Intersectoral Action on Menstrual Health and Hygiene Management: Arriving at a Framework and Indicators to Inform Policy and Programs

Indicators for Menstrual Health and Hygiene Management

Knowledge, attitudes, and behaviors related to menstruation

Knowledge	• Proportion of girls who have correct information about: – Pubertal changes in girls and boys – Reproductive system – Menstruation and the menstrual cycle – Nutritious food to be eaten during adolescence, and during menstruation • Proportion of girls who report menstruation as a normal and healthy physiological phenomenon that occurs in women of reproductive age • Proportion of girls who report that the source of information on menstruation is: – Mother – Sister – Other female family member – Friend – Teacher – Other (specify)

(continued)

D. Nambiar and A. Muralidharan (eds.), *The Social Determinants of Health in India*, https://doi.org/10.1007/978-981-10-5999-5

(continued)

	• Proportion of girls who report menstrual problems (specify menstrual problem: infrequent/scanty period, painful period, heavy bleeding etc.) • Proportion of girls who report seeking health care for menstrual problems • Proportion of girls reporting that they seek health care for menstrual problems from: – Mother – Sister – Other family member – Health care facility – Teacher – Others (specify)
Attitudes and menstrual norms	• Proportion of girls who believe that menstruation is normal and healthy, not unclean/polluting/impure/a curse • Proportion of girls who believe that girls/women can pray during menstruation/visit places of religious worship during menstruation • Proportion of girls who believe that girls/women can freely interact with others during menstruation • Proportion of girls who believe that girls can be active/engage in sports during menstruation • Proportion of girls who believe that girls/women can cook for and eat with the family during the menstruation • Proportion of girls who believe that girls/women should not be segregated during menstruation • Proportion of girls who believe that girls/women should eat normal, healthy food during menstruation • Proportion of girls who believe that menstrual norms and taboos can be questioned/challenged • Proportion of girls who believe that they can negotiate norms related to MHHM • Proportion of girls reporting that they received favorable/supportive responses from mothers, teachers, health care providers when they attained menarche or during menstruation • Sources of information of these menstrual norms and taboos
Personal hygiene behaviors	• Proportion of girls who wash their genitals when changing menstrual absorbent/as often as required on a daily basis during menstruation • Proportion of girls who bathe daily during menstruation
Use of menstrual absorbents	• Proportion of girls who use – Reusable homemade cotton cloth pads – Reusable homemade cloth pads made of materials others than cotton – Reusable cotton cloth pads sold by NGOs, entrepreneurs, self-help groups etc. – Disposable sanitary pads (commercially available, manufactured by entrepreneurs, self-help groups) – Other materials (specify) – A combination of homemade/reusable cotton pads and disposable pads

(continued)

(continued)

	• Proportion of girls who change menstrual absorbents regularly every day (specify number of changes in the case of cloth pads and commercially available sanitary pads) • For girls who use homemade reusable cloth pads, proportion who: – Thoroughly wash used cloth with soap and water – Dry washed menstrual cloth in sun – Store washed menstrual cloth in dry, clean place – Dispose of used menstrual cloth every few months – Dispose of menstrual cloth in dustbin – Reasons for preferring cloth over sanitary pads • For girls who use disposable sanitary pads, proportion who: – Dispose of sanitary pad in dustbin (probe for segregation of biodegradable and non-biodegradable components of menstrual pads) – Have knowledge of where to buy sanitary pads – Have knowledge of whom to ask for sanitary pads (e.g., ASHAs in rural areas) – Reasons for preferring sanitary pads over cloth – Affordability or ability to pay for sanitary pads
Health outcomes	
Reproductive tract infections	• Proportion of girls who report RTI symptoms (self-reported symptoms): – Abnormal (thick, curd-like) vaginal discharge – Itching/soreness of the vulva and vaginal area • Proportion of girls who have been clinically diagnosed with bacterial vaginosis or vulvovaginal candidiasis by a health care provider[a] • Proportion of girls who are aware that poor MHM can cause abnormal vaginal discharge and/or itching/soreness of vaginal area • Proportion of girls who report seeking help/health care/treatment for RTI symptoms: – Whom does the girl/woman tell/confide in about symptoms? – From whom does she seek treatment for RTI symptoms?
Menstrual problems/disorders	• Proportion of girls who report having a normal menstrual cycle (i.e., 21–35 days) • Proportion of girls who report the following symptoms: – Painful menstruation (specify time period) – Absence of menstruation (specify time period) – Excessive heavy bleeding (specify time period) – Scanty bleeding (specify time period) – Infrequent menstruation (specify time period) – Premenstrual symptoms – Combination of symptoms • Proportion of girls who have been clinically diagnosed with a menstrual disorder by a health care provider[a] • Proportion of girls who report seeking help/health care/treatment for menstrual problems: – Whom does the girl/woman tell/confide in about symptoms? – From whom does she seek treatment for menstrual problems?

(continued)

(continued)

Nutrition	• Proportion of girls who have correct knowledge of a balanced, nutritious diet • Proportion of girls who have correct knowledge about the importance of nutrition during adolescence and menstruation • Proportion of girls who are aware of the link between poor nutrition and anaemia • Proportion of girls who report following food taboos related to menstruation • Proportion of girls who have misconceptions regarding food intake during menstruation • Proportion of girls who restrict food and liquid intake during menstruation due to poor access to WASH facilities • Proportion of girls who report intake of nutritious food in general, and during menstruation in particular (self-report) • Proportion of girls who are anaemic[a]

[a]Only when clinical diagnosis is acceptable and possible

Social outcomes

Education	• Proportion of adolescent girls enrolled in: – Primary school – Secondary school • Proportion of adolescent girls discontinuing education after attaining menarche (either at primary school level or secondary school level) • Reasons for discontinuing schooling on attaining menarche • Proportion of school-going adolescent girls who miss school days on a monthly basis • Duration of absence from school during the month, on average • Proportion of girls who cite menstruation, menstrual problems, or the inability to manage menstruation as a reason for remaining absent from school on a monthly basis
Gender	• Gender equitable attitudes (includes items on promoting equity for girls) • Empowerment (includes items on mobility, economic security) • Decision making (includes items on decision making related to purchases and to visiting friends and relatives) • Self-confidence/self-determination/self-efficacy (includes items on communication with mothers, teachers and other stakeholders to seek information and health care)

WASH infrastructure

Availability	• Percentage of households, schools, health facilities/Anganwadi with WASH facilities: – Clean water for washing – Clean water for bathing – Handwashing station/space with water – Handwashing station/space with soap – Improved, functional toilets – Toilets with facilities such as latch, water, hook/shelves for storing personal items, dustbins – Dustbins or incinerators for the safe disposal of menstrual absorbents – Considerations:

(continued)

(continued)

	Toilet facilities should be broken down by type of toilet (individual household latrine and toilet blocks, improved and unimproved toilets) In certain settings such as schools, indicators for gender-specific toilets should be included (e.g., proportion of schools which have separate toilets for girls) • Percentage of girls practicing open defecation • Ratio of WASH facilities to people who need to use them in various settings • Proportion of bathing facilities that also have other amenities such as hooks/shelves for clothes and personal items, a place to wash and dry cloths, and disposal facilities
Accessibility	• Proportion of households, schools, health facilities with easily accessible WASH facilities as perceived by girls • Other considerations include: – Location of WASH facility/service – Time taken to reach WASH facility/service
Affordability	• Cost of constructing sanitation/WASH facilities (particularly in the case of households constructing toilets) • Proportion availing subsidy or scheme to construct or install sanitation/WASH facility – Government scheme/subsidy (specify) – NGO scheme/subsidy (specify) • Cost of operations and maintenance of sanitation/WASH facility (particularly in the case of institutional setting with such facilities) • Cost of using public WASH facility/service – Pay per use – Payment by other mode (e.g., monthly charges)
Quality and utilization	• Proportion reporting that WASH facilities are clean (includes visible signs and odour) • Proportion reporting that WASH facilities are functional/in working condition • Proportion who state that toilet facilities are well maintained/regularly maintained • Proportion reporting that WASH facilities are safe or have safety provisions (e.g., door, door with lock, curtain, guard) • Proportion that report that WASH facilities have other related amenities (e.g., toilets have handwashing facilities, hooks or shelves, dustbins) • Proportion who use: – Clean water for washing – Clean water for bathing – Handwashing station/space with water – Handwashing station/space with soap – Improved toilets – Toilets with facilities such as latch, running water, hook/shelves for storing personal items, dustbins – Dustbins, incinerators for disposing of menstrual absorbents

Annexure II
Chhattisgarh Swasth Panchayat Yojana: Convergent Decision Making for Health and its Determinants in Rural India

Indicators for Social Determinants of Health

All indicators are monitored each month by VHSNC.

Health status

Mortality (using death registers)	• No. of infant deaths • No. of deaths due to fever/malaria • No. of deaths due to diarrhoea • No. of deaths due to TB • No. of maternal deaths
Morbidity	• No. of cases of diarrhoea • No. of cases of fever/malaria
Malnutrition	• No. of malnourished children in 0–3 year age group
Violence	• No. of cases of domestic violence against women

Access to local health services

• Whether monthly immunization session conducted by ANM
• Whether BP measurement done in ANC by ANM
• Whether drugs provided free of cost by ANM
• Whether anti-malarial drugs available with Mitanin
• Whether referral transport available

Access to food security, water, sanitation, education

• No. of non-functional hand pumps in village
• No. of schools without functional toilet
• No. of girls (6–18 years) out of school
• Whether teachers in government schools taught regularly
• Whether subsidised food-grain entitlements given by Public Distribution System (PDS)
• Whether NREGA wages paid in time
• No. of children not accessing ICDS
• Whether ICDS provided both pulses and vegetables on all days for 3–6 year olds
• Did ICDS provide weekly rations for under-3 year olds each week
• Did midday school meal provide both pulses and vegetables on all days for 3–6 year olds

Annexure III
Social Determinants of Maternal Health: Dead Women Talking

Indicators for Maternal Health from a Social Determinants Perspective

Individual attributes
• Age at marriage
• Nutritional status—anaemia—HB levels as well as weight
• Occupation—migration (both the woman's as well as her husband's)
• Parity
• Previous medical history as well as obstetric history
• Knowledge of services and entitlements
Family characteristics
• Socioeconomic status—caste/social group/religion, access to resources, below poverty line card and/or score
• Support from natal family
• Violence within the family
• RSBY card, MA card (hospitalization and surgery/procedures cover)
Community characteristics
• Rural/urban/tribal
• Social capital and social cohesion—presence of a people's organization e.g. trade union, dairy cooperative, women's collective etc.
• Distance to facilities/geographical location/access factors
Health services
• Village level health and nutrition facilities in place or not—access to Anganwadi centre, presence of trained and motivated ASHA, whether Village Health and Nutrition days are being conducted or not, the quality of ANC provided in these VHNDs
• Whether the 24/7 PHC is functional or not?
• Whether the CHC is equipped to provide Comprehensive Emergency Obstetric Care?
• Availability of blood—blood storage unit in CHC? Blood bank in the district?
• Availability of emergency transport—ambulance for referral from facilities, satisfactory 108 service
• Sickle cell anaemia services, iron sucrose services

(continued)

(continued)

• Malaria prophylaxis for pregnant women
• TB prevention and control programme
• Postnatal care services
• Monitoring of the quality of all health services
• Grievance redressal mechanism—existence as well as monitoring

Printed by Printforce, the Netherlands